THE LAPTOP
MILLIONAIRE

THE LAPTOP MILLIONAIRE

HOW ANYONE CAN ESCAPE THE 9 TO 5 AND MAKE MONEY ONLINE

MARK ANASTASI

WILEY

John Wiley & Sons, Inc.

Published by John Wiley & Sons, Inc., Hoboken, New Jersey.
Published simultaneously in Canada.

For general information on our other products and services or for technical support, please contact our Customer Care Department within the United States at (800) 762-2974, outside the United States at (317) 572-3993 or fax (317) 572-4002.

Wiley publishes in a variety of print and electronic formats and by print-on-demand. Some material included with standard print versions of this book may not be included in e-books or in print-on-demand. If this book refers to media such as a CD or DVD that is not included in the version you purchased, you may download this material at http://booksupport.wiley.com. For more information about Wiley products, visit www.wiley.com.

ISBN 978-1-118-27179-7 (cloth); ISBN 978-1-118-28245-8 (ebk); ISBN 978-1-118-28412-4 (ebk); ISBN 978-1-118-28557-2 (ebk)

Printed in the United States of America

10 9 8 7 6 5 4 3

I dedicate this book to our intrepid students from around the world, who have become—or are on their way to becoming—the next generation of Laptop Millionaires. By your example, you are lighting a path to freedom for millions to follow.

Contents

Acknowledgments

I would like to thank my mentor, the Laptop Millionaire, as well as the other wonderful teachers who have helped me along the way: Francis G. Taylor, Warren Borsje, Guy Cohen, Ron G. Holland, Dr. Robert O. Young, Marcus de Maria, Anthony Robbins, Robert G. Allen, T. Harv Eker, Mark Victor Hansen, Wayne Dyer, Robert Kiyosaki, Matt Bacak, Ted Nicholas, Mark Vurnum, Andrew Reynolds, Daniel Priestley, Joanna Martin, Brett McFall, Ryan Deiss, Frank Kern, Eben Pagan, and Stewart Swerdlow.

You are inspirational leaders at a time of great change in this world. I am grateful for all you have taught me.

Finally, I would like to thank my beautiful Mira, without whose support this book would have never become a reality. I am grateful every day for all the love you bring into my life.

Introduction

The Laptop Entrepreneur Revolution

Since the late 1990s, a *revolution* has taken place in the way people do business. Thanks to the Internet and new technologies such as e-mail, search engines, affiliate programs, Voice over Internet Protocol, online auctions, video streaming, webinars, and social media, you can now do business all over the world *without ever leaving your house.*

Millions of people are now making a full-time living working from home. After all, if somebody created a *billion-dollar infrastructure* that you could leverage for *free* to connect with 1 billion people around the world, wouldn't *you* want to take advantage of this once-in-a-lifetime opportunity?

This revolution is gathering pace. Over 1 *trillion* dollars a year is being spent online. One in every four advertising dollars is now being spent on online advertising. And people are spending, on average, 40 minutes a day on social media websites such as Facebook, YouTube, and Twitter. And yet, most people are completely unaware of the incredible opportunities this has created for them.

In this book and the related blog I have brought together the success stories of 100 of my seminar attendees and students. You will find out . . .

- How single mom Mili Ponce went from zero to making $2,500 a month thanks to Twitter, in less than 90 days.
- How George J. went from working in a supermarket to making $6,000 a month thanks to YouTube, in less than eight weeks.
- How Tom Chambers went from zero to making $20,000 a month thanks to Facebook, in less than five months.
- How Georgina Lany went from zero to making $8,000 a month in passive income thanks to outsourcing, in less than six weeks!
- How Kevin Taylor makes over $8,000 a month thanks to Fiverr.com!

- How Ciaran Doyle makes $7,000 a month thanks to SEO, and moved to a beach in Cambodia!!
- How Tiziano G. went from zero to making $11,000 a month thanks to list-building, in less than 90 days! (And moved to Thailand!)
- How Laura Wilson makes $12,000 a month thanks to local business marketing, working just eight hours a week!
- How Rory K. went from zero to making $15,000 a month thanks to his e-book, in just nine weeks!
- How Corinna X. went from getting fired for the fifth time and being unemployed for over a year to making $16,000 in 90 minutes, thanks to webinars!
- How Lucy Johnson went from personal trainer to making over $40,000 a month thanks to membership sites, in less than four months!
- How Jonathan N. went from massive debt to making over $30,000 a month thanks to SEO, in six months!

These laptop entrepreneurs are using simple Internet business strategies, revealed in this book.

In this book I also share with you how I met my mentor—*the Laptop Millionaire*—and how his advice helped me go from being completely broke in my early 20s to making over 7 million dollars in online sales. You will discover in these pages . . .

- How I went from zero to making $10,000 a month thanks to e-books, in just 28 days.
- How I made $50,000 in three days, thanks to a direct-mail letter.
- How I turned $952 into $36,000 in seven days, thanks to Facebook Ads.
- How I made $90,000 in a day, thanks to a licensing deal.
- How I made $380,000 in 30 days, thanks to an online product launch.
- How I made $200,000 in 90 minutes, thanks to a live webinar.
- And many more strategies that I've never revealed before.

I do not mention these numbers to impress you, but simply to illustrate the fact that these strategies really work! Laptop entrepreneurs are quietly making a fortune from the comfort of their own homes—*and indeed, from anywhere around the world where they can connect to the Internet!*

You can now earn a full-time living thanks to Twitter, Facebook, Facebook Ads, Facebook pages, local business marketing, mobile marketing, YouTube,

Google AdWords, search engine optimization, webinars, joint ventures, joint venture webinars, affiliate marketing, cost-per-action marketing, Fiverr.com, e-books, eBay, outsourcing, media buying, pay-per-click advertising, list-building, lead generation, membership sites, and hundreds more strategies!

If you are stuck in a job that you hate, or worse, you are currently without a job, this book will show you how you can make a full-time living from home, thanks to the Internet. If you *have* a business, even better! This book will show you how you can *leverage* the Internet to dominate your market, get more clients, and turbocharge your sales and profits.

My intention is to inspire you to take advantage of the most incredible opportunity of the twenty-first century and help you achieve the freedom and success you desire.

If I could, I would reach out and grab you, shake you, and scream at the top of my lungs: *"Wake up! You don't have to spend the next 30 years in a job that is crushing your soul, just to make a living! There are so many fantastic opportunities for you to take advantage of! Just do it!"*

The Laptop Entrepreneur Lifestyle

Today, thanks to the Internet, entrepreneurs still in their 20s or 30s are setting up home-based Internet businesses that they run in their spare time, bringing in $5,000 to $30,000 a month. They can travel anytime they want, and they have the freedom to run their business from anywhere in the world. And best of all, their websites are making money *for* them, *while they sleep!*

In his book, *Rich Dad, Poor Dad,* author Robert Kiyosaki explains that to escape the rat race you need to spend less than you earn and invest the difference in buying *income-producing assets* (for example, shares or rental properties). The goal is to eventually have the income from your assets *replace* your earnings from your job. That's how you achieve financial freedom, he explains.

When I was starting out with my business I was $12,000 in debt, I had zero income, no job, and I was homeless. Buying income-producing assets wasn't an option. Instead, I decided to *build* income-producing assets. Eventually, these web businesses would grow to generate thousands of dollars a day.

By the time I reached my late 20s, I had 64,000 clients in 116 countries worldwide, and 16 different income streams. I could work from home . . . or while travelling around the world . . . or from the luxury cabin of a cruise ship in the Caribbean. In fact, I could do this from anyplace on the planet where I could get an Internet connection!

Furthermore, my first Internet business only cost $400 to set up and yet was bringing in more than $10,000 a month in income! When you compare the costs of running a normal bricks-and-mortar business to those of an Internet business, the differences are striking!

Costs of Running a Simple Home-Based Internet Business

Internet connection	$20/month
GetResponse autoresponder service	$60/month
GoToWebinar webinar service	$99/month
Hosting	$15/month
Two outsourcers (web design and customer service)	$500/month
Total	**$694/month**

Imagine having a business that . . .

- Costs practically nothing to set up.
- You don't need staff to run.
- Doesn't need offices.
- You can run from home or anywhere in the world.
- Other people are selling your products for you, for *free*! (e.g., affiliates)
- Runs on autopilot (people buy your products from your websites automatically).
- Allows you to leverage incredible technologies such as e-mail, search engines, affiliate programs, Voice over Internet Protocol, online auctions, video streaming, webinars, and social media!
- And all you need . . . *is your laptop!*

Other benefits of the laptop entrepreneur lifestyle include:

- Total flexibility! You can work when you feel like it. You can get up as early or as late as you want—no more alarm clocks. You can take days off whenever you feel like it.

- You don't have a boss! No more taking orders from a nincompoop! You can even experience the satisfaction of firing your boss! (Laptop entrepreneurs often start their businesses in their spare time, while still working at a job. Eventually when the income from their laptop business exceeds that of their salary, they fire their boss!)
- You don't have to deal with annoying coworkers any more! No more bickering, no more office politics, no more endless, pointless boring meetings.
- You can be a stay-at-home dad or a stay-at-home mom! No need for nurseries, or a nanny. You get to see your children grow up.
- You can spend more time with your loved ones, your family, your friends. You can visit them and stay with them in different countries around the world.
- No more commuting . . . getting stuck in traffic every day . . . wasting hours every day . . . spending a fortune on gas.
- You can travel any time you want, visiting different countries.
- You can go to seminars, take a course, learn new things, expand your horizons.
- You can live by the beach. You can retire to the sun—*now*—rather than wait until you're 65!
- You can live in a low-tax or zero-tax jurisdiction—no more spending a fortune and weeks of your time on accountants every year!
- You can give yourself a pay raise every month! (You can increase your earnings every month, simply by growing your mailing list!)

My typical day looks something like this. I wake up, take a shower, and step outside to take in the fresh sea air, admire the view, and play with my golden retriever, Leo.

I then have a breakfast of fresh "green juice" (cucumber, celery, apples, spinach, avocado) with my partner, while relaxing on the loungers by our swimming pool.

I then sit at my laptop, answering some e-mails in which I arrange a joint venture or a webinar or product launch or give assignments to my team of outsourcers.

I then take a break and go cycling through the mountain trails next to our house, taking Leo for a run. In the summer we usually end up on the beach in front of our house, where we love to swim.

In the afternoon I'll usually write, creating products, blog posts, content for my membership sites or my books and e-mails to send to my mailing list. Or sometimes I'll study a new course to learn about new business strategies.

In the afternoon my partner and I go play tennis, or we go out with our friends for a meal, or for some relaxation at the spa at our resort. In the evening, we like to just relax by the fireplace, have a nice meal, and watch a DVD.

Once a week, on average, I do a 90-minute webinar for my clients.

We go on six to seven trips a year, around Europe or to more exotic locations such as Thailand, the Maldives, Bermuda, the Caribbean, Senegal, Egypt, Australia—you get the picture.

If you like the sound of this, welcome to the world of the laptop entrepreneur!

Living Free—Why You Must Become a Laptop Entrepreneur

More and more Internet entrepreneurs are choosing to live in Thailand, the Philippines, South America, Cyprus, or other countries where the cost of living is as little as $10 to $30 a day.

They can experience an amazing lifestyle, while saving thousands of dollars, pounds, or euros and building their wealth (often tax-free), every single month.

There are certain places—Tanzania, Thailand, Cambodia, Ecuador—that are so incredibly cheap that it seems unreal. Or Chile, in South America, a stable and safe country where the cost of living is about 40 percent less than in Europe.

Quite a few of my fellow laptop entrepreneurs, like David Cavanagh, Mitch Sanders, Greg Jacobs, Jim Graham, and Aaron Darko, have moved to Thailand where —according to one of them—*"You can live like a king, for just $1,500 a month!"*

I believe most people could experience a *dramatic* increase in their enjoyment of life, quality of life, and standard of living by making just a few smart lifestyle decisions.

Furthermore, in today's world, to ensure that you preserve your wealth and your standard of living, you need to take active steps to minimize your tax and protect your assets. This can mean choosing to live in a country with a high standard of living, as well as fantastic weather and very low taxes!

The world is changing. Governments are broke. They're selling off their assets to pay off their massive debts (the wonderful euphemism for that is "privatization"), they are devaluing their currencies (through inflation), and increasing taxes.

By printing a *lot* more money—more money than there are products or services for—central banks are essentially devaluing their currency and making everything much, much more expensive for you, the consumer!

As a result, the average worker is now on a relentless mouse wheel, where they have to keep running faster and faster just to stand still (the aforementioned rat race).

In many Western countries, workers' purchasing power keeps falling, and the prices of goods and services keep rising while taxes keep eating away at your income more and more. You might find that soon, having an Internet-based business, far from being some fancy idea, becomes an absolute must! Many Internet marketers today set up their businesses in Singapore, and get a Singapore or Hong Kong bank account. In certain circumstances—*and please get the advice of a professional international tax lawyer before taking any action on this*—they can pay as little as zero tax!

Did you know that in the Seychelles, the personal tax rate is zero, the corporate tax is zero, the capital gains tax is zero, there is no VAT or GST tax, and you do not need to file accounts?

Did you know that if you don't live in a specific country for more than four months of the year (the perpetual tourist or PT lifestyle) you could, in certain circumstances, not have to pay taxes in *any* country?

Laptop entrepreneurs' Internet businesses allow them to take advantage of great lifestyle opportunities and make the most of cost-of-living and lifestyle arbitrage opportunities between countries.

Imagine earning British pounds, Swiss francs, or Australian dollars . . . and spending just a few Thai baht, Philippines pesos, or Indian rupees!

On the other hand, if you own a traditional bricks-and-mortar business, you are pretty much tied to the country your business is based in, and forced to pay tax to the government of that country.

Not 1 in 100 entrepreneurs understand their true options. Less than 5 percent of entrepreneurs truly understand how they can leverage these offshore opportunities, but as Simon Black, the editor of the "Sovereign

Man" newsletter, points out, investors and business owners are becoming more and more fed up with the situation at home and are increasingly considering a move overseas:

> We live in a world where geography and borders are becoming less relevant . . . no longer the ball and chain that they used to be. Technology is making it easier to live where you want, and work where you want, without the two necessarily being the same.
>
> This isn't just for online businesses and bloggers, though those two business models clearly work in a borderless world. There are literally hundreds of options—self-employed professionals who have infrequent client meetings, traders, designers, programmers, media workers, telesalespeople, analysts, customer service workers, and so on.
>
> Over the next several years, I predict a massive demographic shift as more and more people begin to push beyond their home country and explore these kinds of opportunities to live overseas while earning a living back home.
>
> This is a consequence of all the various debt, economic, and resource crises around the world; fed up with the situation at home, whether it be rising crime, higher costs, lack of job prospects, or the growing police state, many people will start considering a move overseas, where in many cases, the grass actually is greener.
>
> —Simon Black, www.sovereignman.com

How I Met the Laptop Millionaire

From Zero to $10,000 in 28 Days

I left Greece when I was 18 years old to come to England with the hope of a better life. Somehow things didn't quite turn out that way.

I ended up working as a security guard for two years, earning just $5 an hour, barely scraping by. During that time, banks were practically *throwing* credit cards at me, and—not surprisingly—I was getting more in debt each month.

I worked for a while at a telesales job that paid a paltry $6 an hour, in the hope that I would earn commissions and pay off my debts. I made just one sale in 14 months, and I was so awful at my job that I got fired.

By November 2003, in my early 20s, I was $12,000 in debt, I had no money, no job, and no prospects.

To top it all off I got kicked out of my apartment; I hadn't paid the rent in two months. I felt so embarrassed and ashamed about my situation that I didn't tell anyone what was happening. In any case, my family back home— with whom I wasn't really on speaking terms—was in no position to help me, anyway.

With no money and no place to stay, I ended up taking shelter in a derelict building in London, with a handful of other homeless people. Those were scary times. You would try to get some sleep, not knowing if you were going to get mugged or beaten up. I lived with the constant fear of getting thrown out, or—more routinely—not being able to buy food.

I remember going into a supermarket and trying to decide whether to buy a cucumber or some broccoli, then breaking down in tears because I couldn't afford either. "I'm $12,000 in debt! It will take me years to pay that debt off! I can't even afford 37 cents to buy broccoli! I should use that 37 cents to pay off a bit of my debt!"

I remember trying to get $30 out of an ATM, on one of my last remaining credit cards, and the ATM screen said "Insufficient Funds"! *"That's it!"* I thought to myself. *"I have nothing left!"*

And yet somehow, almost miraculously, week after week the banks would top up the credit limit on one of my credit cards. I was getting even more in debt, but at least I could buy some food and survive a few more days.

Every day I would look at the classified ads and job postings. But nobody wanted to hire me. Some days I was so depressed that I couldn't even muster enough energy to get out of bed (I was sleeping on a damp, dirty mattress on the floor).

The whole time I kept telling myself over and over again what a no-good loser I was. Negative thoughts kept dragging me further into depression.

"Enough!" I yelled out one day, crying. I just *had* to get out of my head. Those thoughts were driving me crazy. I ran out of that building, down that street, and I just kept running in the freezing rain, crying the whole way. My lungs were burning and I could feel the cold air through my rain-soaked clothes.

I ended up hiding in the Old Brompton Road Cemetery in Earls Court, to get away from the rain and the crowded streets. I didn't want anyone looking at me.

There was nobody there, and, after running to the end of the cemetery, I collapsed amongst some seventeenth-century tombstones. After a while I sat up, looked around, and noticed one of the tombstones. I forget the name, but this young man had lived from 1654 to 1674. "Almost my age," I mused. It made me think about what would happen if I died right there and then.

"I wonder what it would say on my tombstone, if I died today. Maybe all it could say would be Mark Anastasi, worked as a security guard, never hurt anybody, never did anything important. Dead."

As despair and depression started to take grip of me again, and tears started welling up, suddenly a question popped into my head: *"What did you give?"*

"What did I give? What do you mean, what did I give? I'm broke! I don't have anything to give! Let me have something first, then I'll give!" I said out loud, exasperated.

Again, this voice asked:

"What did you GIVE?"

In that moment, a realization struck me. I realized that I had been focused on *taking* and *getting* my whole life. I had never stopped to think about whether I was really contributing to others. Was I helping people? Was I adding value? Was I making a difference?

I got up, looked at those tombstones, and I made a vow:

"I am going to turn this around. This is *not* the end. This is just the beginning. I *am* going to figure out how to turn my life around and I *will* devote my life to helping others do the same!"

I decided to view this as a test—a test that I absolutely was going to triumph over. I was going to break through this challenge. They say that problems are the gym on which we sculpt our souls. Well, let's start a-sculpting!

My resolve was total. I had made an incontrovertible decision and had cut off all other possibilities. I was going to make it, *no matter what!*

I walked out of that cemetery the freest I had ever felt.

I didn't know this yet, but 28 days later I would launch my first Internet business, bringing in more than $10,000 a month.

The Seminar that Changed My Life

Not far from where I was staying, a personal development seminar was taking place for free that weekend. It promised to reveal the "success strategies of millionaires." I was skeptical at first, but since I had absolutely nothing left to lose, I decided to go.

"Who knows? I might meet somebody there who could give me a job!" I thought to myself.

The things I learned at that seminar would end up changing my life. The content was phenomenal, and as it happens, at that seminar I got to meet the man who would later become my mentor.

He was sitting next to me, and during the first break I introduced myself, asking what he thought of the seminar and what he did for a living. Little did I know that this attempt at making small talk with a stranger would change the course of my life.

"Hmm . . . what I do . . ." he said. "Well . . . I make money, thanks to my laptop," he said with a smile.

I laughed at the bizarre answer this affable 40-year-old stranger had come up with, not understanding what he meant.

After much prodding, he proceeded to tell me that he had many websites, selling many different products, such as e-books, for example, for which he was paid commissions. He could run his entire million-dollar-a-year business from his *laptop*, from anywhere around the world as long as he had an Internet connection.

Now, my father had been sitting at his computer for 30 years, as a journalist, getting paid very little money. We were always broke. How on earth could this gentleman sitting next to me make a million dollars a year *thanks to his laptop?*

"You know, since the late 1990s the way business is done has been completely revolutionized, thanks to the Internet. Whole new industries have mushroomed. Old industries and millions of jobs have disappeared. And most people have no idea that this revolution has taken place. And they have no idea of their options," he said, as way of an explanation.

This completely flew over my head. I was still thinking, "Could this guy give me a job? All this sounds great, but I need a job . . . ."

We got along well during that weekend, and at the end we exchanged contact details. By that point I had started calling him "Mr. Laptop Millionaire" —L.M. for short.

The next day I did some of the exercises that were recommended to us at the seminar, including writing down my goals, writing down 20 things I loved about myself, 20 things I was grateful for in my life, 100 reasons *why* I had to make more money, and brainstorming 100 ways *how* to make more money.

When I did that final exercise, I remembered something that the Laptop Millionaire told me—a simple strategy he used for making a couple thousand dollars a month online.

I called him up from a payphone.

"Hi, L.M. Listen . . . I need your help."

"What's going on, Mark?"

"Well . . . for starters . . . I'm calling you from a payphone outside an abandoned building that me and some homeless guys are squatting in. I'm broke. I've been trying to get a job for months, but no luck. I got kicked out of my apartment last January. I've been pretty much homeless the past four months . . ."

"Let me guess . . . you need some money."

"No . . . no . . . I'm not calling to ask for money. I read somewhere that you should work to *learn*, not just work to *earn*. Basically, try to work for someone who can teach you valuable things. Anyway, that's not important . . . remember how you told me at the seminar that you were making money by selling an e-book on the Internet? Are you still making $1,800 a month from that e-book?"

"Well, actually, I'm now making $2,400 a month from that specific e-book."

"REALLY?! That's fantastic! Listen, I'm willing to work for you for *free!* I'll help you with anything you need in your business! All I ask is that you please teach me your strategy!"

The Laptop Millionaire chuckled and said I didn't need to do that. I think he realized that I would not stop pestering him until I got him to share his secret!

"Come over to my house, and I'll show you what I do."

Mentored by the Laptop Millionaire

Later that week I visited him at his place in London. He had some work to finish off, so I just sat on the couch in his home office.

He was sitting a few feet away, with his back to me.

"He he he . . ." he sniggered, as he watched his computer screen. "Making money is *sooooo* easy!" he said out loud. He sat back smugly, not taking his eyes away from the screen. He had just made $15,734 in less than five minutes at the touch of a few buttons on his laptop.

As I sat there, seething with anger at that insensitive comment—I was broke, unemployed, and in a lot of debt—"*What do you mean, 'making money is easy'?!! Everyone knows that making money is hard! That's why my family has always been broke!"* I thought to myself, as I glared at him. But I didn't say anything. I was angry, but I still wanted to learn his strategy!

As I looked around his office I saw dozens of personal development books and courses lying around. From the titles of these courses, I realized that he had invested a lot of time and money into learning about marketing, business, and investing.

I would later find out that he had attended over a hundred personal development, wealth creation, business, and investment seminars, where he had learned dozens of marketing and trading strategies. He had also paid mentors and coaches for step-by-step guidance. He had spent more than $70,000 on this continuing education, and thanks to this investment, making $10,000 in five minutes thanks to his laptop was now easy for him. In fact, he seemed to have Midas-like abilities—everything he touched turned to gold, so to speak.

As I surveyed his impressive library, a mental picture came to me, a bit like a daydream. In my mind, I saw him piling up all his notes from seminars he had attended, piling up all the books he had read, all the CD and DVD home study courses he'd learned from, and climbing atop of them. From up there, he had a different perspective on things. He could see over this big grey wall. Below him lay a vast expanse of wealth and opportunities. Down where I stood, all I could see was this grey wall. Most people don't see the opportunities all around them. From that vantage point up there, the Laptop Millionaire could genuinely say, "Wow! Making money is so easy!"

"I need to learn these strategies, too, so that I can make more money, like you do," I said.

"You are right, you do. The more you learn, the more you earn," he said, still not lifting his eyes from his screen.

"In fact, that is what I call a 'Millionaire Secret.'" He still didn't lift his eyes from his screen.

Millionaire Secret 1: The More You Learn, the More You Earn

Eventually he turned around, looked at me, and said:

"It's simple. If you can take a successful person's entire lifetime of experience and knowledge, condense it to a book, and then read it, it's like getting a lifetime of experience and ideas in just a few hours. You don't have to go through an entire lifetime of trial and error. Imagine if you studied 100 successful people this way! This sort of education is the highest form of leverage."

It made me think of my dad, and how he always thought he knew best, he never studied anything about business or marketing, and yet he went on to try more than 30 different money-making schemes, from gambling at casinos, to launching a magazine, to setting up an ice cream parlor. Every time, he *lost* money.

Eventually, over the years, I would spend close to $100,000 on my continuing education in marketing, wealth creation, and personal development (I'd rather pay a little bit of money for the advice of successful people than go through years of trial and error—and thanks to that small investment I've made 100 times more money).

But on that day, I was a complete beginner.

Hence the Laptop Millionaire's next question.

What is Money?

L.M. got up and joined me on the settee.

"So, you want to make more money, eh?" he asked.

"Yes. I have to . . ."

"Well, let's start with the basics. Do you actually know what money is?"

"Umm . . . money is what you pay for stuff with. Right?"

"Sure, but how did it start? Why was money created? What was there before money? What does money actually *represent*?"

Seeing that I was drawing blanks, he continued: "You see, money is simply a means of exchange. In olden times people used to barter goods and services. 'I'll give you a sword in exchange for 10 chickens.' Imagine how inconvenient it was to do your daily shopping, paying for services at your local market in swords and chickens.

"So, money was created to represent the value of those goods and help people exchange goods and services more easily.

"What does this mean? This means that money is nothing but the *measure* of the value that you create and deliver for people.

"This also means, of course, that money flows to the people who are providing the most amount of *value*."

This was definitely a different belief than what I was taught growing up. "Rich people are greedy, exploitative, and mean! You get rich by bribing the government!" my dad would often say.

The Laptop Millionaire explained to me that successful people think very differently from poor and broke people.

For example, successful people believe:

- "Money is nothing but the *measure* of the value I create for other people!"
- "I find out what problems people have and I help them by providing great solutions! That is why I am making more money!"
- "I get paid in direct proportion to the amount of value I deliver according to the marketplace!"
- "My income is in direct proportion to my ability to add massive and measurable levels of value to other human beings!"

The Laptop Millionaire explained to me again that the money one has in the bank is simply a representation of how much value they have created and delivered. Ergo, if you want more money, simply figure out how you can create more value!

He continued, "it is thanks to the efforts of entrepreneurs—who keep adding more value for people—that the economy grows. By organizing the efforts of people, capital, creativity, and time, they create more *value*! The more productive they are and the more *leverage* they use, the more *value* they can create!

All of that value is added up as the gross domestic product (GDP) of a country. The more the GDP grows in a country, the more money is printed, to allow people to exchange all that value. This process raises everyone's wealth and standard of living. This means that the more *value* we, as entrepreneurs create, the more money and *wealth* there is to share."

I had a tough time wrapping my head around this at first and said, "well, this is very different from anything I've been told before. Assuming that you are right, how does this help me make more money, exactly?"

"That's just the thing! If you want to make more money, asking yourself, 'How can I make more money?' is the wrong place to start! Instead, ask yourself, 'How can I create more value?'"

This was a huge aha moment for me. A lot of my old beliefs about money—beliefs that I held since childhood—were being shattered in that moment. I used to think that money was something that other people *have*, that it wasn't fair, and that we needed to *take* it from them!

"Okay, so how can I create more value?" I asked. I wasn't sure where this was going exactly, but I was glad he was sharing with me what he'd learned. This was interesting.

"Great question!" he said, with a giggle. He was enjoying this. "You create value by solving problems for people, and giving people what they want! Start by asking yourself: 'What problems do people have?' 'What do people want?'

"People want more money, more time, more holidays, entertainment, fun, adventure, more sleep, less pain, to eliminate diseases, to be fit, to be sexy and attractive, cars, houses, food, fuel, transport, and on and on. And guess what! *If you can provide some of these solutions for them, they'll pay you money in exchange for that value you have just created for them!*

In fact, no one has ever handed over a single dollar to someone else without expecting to get some value in return! Think about it. Do you ever pay money to someone without expecting to get some value in return?

What is Business?

"A business is simply a connector of people and solutions. The purpose of a business is delivering value to people," the Laptop Millionaire continued.

"A business is an intermediary between a group of people with a common set of problems (a target market or niche market) and a set of solutions that they need (the value that the business provides).

"For example, people who want to lose weight, that's a *target market*. And exercise equipment, gym memberships, a coach, diet recipes, and so on represent the *value* or *solutions* they want to buy. The role of the business is to connect the target market with the solutions that it needs. Simple!"

Figure I.1 depicts the Laptop Millionaire's explanation of how a business connects value with a target market.

The Laptop Millionaire continued my education by explaining the basics of business. He said, "Sometimes, I look at businesses simply as a vehicle that picks up the solutions and goes and delivers them to the appropriate target market. Simple!"

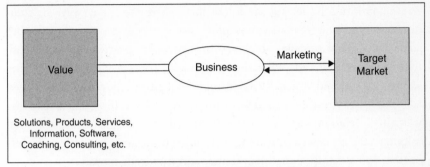

A Business is an **interface** between VALUE and a Target Market.

A Business is a **vehicle** that delivers VALUE to a Target Market.

Marketing is the process of **communicating** the BENEFITS of your offers to your Target Market.

FIGURE I.1 Connecting Value with a Target Market

This was another big aha moment for me. If I wanted to make money, I had to stop acting like the world owed me a living, and instead I had to do three things:

1. Decide what group of people I was going to help.
2. Decide and create the solutions that they needed.
3. Set up a business to connect that target market with my solutions.

What is Marketing?

"Now . . . what is marketing?" the Laptop Millionaire continued.

"Ads on TV?" I ventured. Not a great response, I know, but better than just standing there in silence, with a dumb look on my face.

"Well, that's one kind of marketing, sure. But more simply, marketing is simply the process of communicating the benefits of your product to your target market. It's not something weird or esoteric. Marketing is simply like saying, 'Yoo-hoo! Hello Mr. Prospect! I have the perfect solution for your problem over here! Yoo-hoo!'"

He said that last sentence with a high-pitched, camp voice, which he found very amusing. Ah, the British sense of humor. But I *got* what he meant. "Now that you've decided who you are going to help—what group of people you will be providing solutions and value for—and you've put together this value, now, of course, you need to tell them about it!"

He continued by letting me know that "there are many ways of communicating to a target market nowadays. For example: blogs, online banner advertising, viral e-books, joint ventures, posters, postcards, direct mail, television ads, radio ads, PR campaigns, books, pay-per-click ads, YouTube videos, solo ads, ad swaps, flyers, promotional gifts, Yellow Pages, classified ads, fairs, conferences, and trade shows, free DVD offers, telemarketing, webinars, teleseminars, newspaper advertising, magazine advertising, infomercials, review sites, posting in forums, billboards, bench boards, bus boards, sponsorship, e-mail marketing, and hundreds more!"

I had asked him how I could make more money, and so far he'd shared with me his definitions of money, business, and marketing. It was definitely challenging my way of looking at things, but I wanted to know how I could make money on the *Internet*, like *he* did!

What is Internet Marketing?

"How does this apply to Internet marketing? What is Internet marketing, then?" I asked, eager to learn.

"Great question. Internet marketing is simply marketing . . . that is done on the Internet! Really, it's that simple. It boils down to two simple things: traffic and conversions. We drive *traffic* to websites, where people are *converted* to a buyer or a subscriber."

The Laptop Millionaire then drew this simple diagram, to explain how he makes over $1,000,000 a year thanks to his laptop (see Figure I.2).

FIGURE I.2 The Laptop Millionaire's Diagram

The Laptop Millionaire then explained his business to me, with a simple metaphor I could understand. He said that what he did was like getting customers into a bakery.

"Imagine a bakery on a busy street. If 100 people walk into that bakery, that's 'traffic.' If 10 of these 100 potential customers buy something, this means they were converted from a prospect to a customer. That's 'conversion.' Ten people buying, out of 100 visitors, represents a 10 percent conversion rate.

"If these 10 customers spent $15 each on average, the baker makes $150 in sales from these 100 visitors. That's $1.50 'earnings per visitor.'

"It's exactly the same in the online world. The three main things we look at are the traffic, the conversion rate, and our earnings per click.

"The three important numbers I needed to always look at in my Internet business are:

1. How many people clicked on my link and became *visitors* of my website? (traffic)
2. How many visitors *converted* to a sale? (conversion rate)
3. And how much did I earn per visitor? (earnings per click or EPC)

"For example, every visitor you get to a website might be worth 10 cents to you or they might be worth $1 to you or they might be worth $10 to you, on average. It depends on what you are selling, who you are selling it to, and how you are selling it.

"The great thing is that if you understand these three numbers, every day you can increase your income. Increasing your income is now in your control! How? It's simple:

- You can increase your traffic.
- You can improve your conversion rate.
- You can improve your earnings per click.
- You can offer more products to your customers.

"Going back to the bakery example:

- A baker needs a constant stream of people visiting his shop.
- He needs a percentage of them to buy the products on display in his store (his *conversion rate*).
- The baker adds value by creating and delivering exactly what his prospects want: bread and baked goods!

- The nicer the store and the more compelling his products are, the larger the percentage of visitors that actually spend money in his store!"

"Simple!" as the Laptop Millionaire liked to say.

Financial Independence Begins at 400 Clicks per Day

"I believe that financial independence begins at 400 clicks per day," the Laptop Millionaire continued.

"If you earn $0.25 to $0.50 per click, and you get 400 visitors per day to click on your links online, that represents $100 to $200 a day in earned commissions or sales. That's $3,000 to $6,000 a month.

"Heck, even at $0.15 per click on average, you would make $60 a day!

"For most people around the world, earning $60-$100 a day on the Internet ($1,800 to $3,000 a month) means they can pay their rent or mortgage, their bills, food, gas for their car, and so on. That's their basic needs covered, for themselves and their family."

He added that "for laptop entrepreneurs, traffic is the lifeblood of their business."

"Traffic = money" he often repeated. "And by this rationale, free traffic = free money!"

"I understand!" I shouted out loud! I was eager. I wanted to make money online.

"Great," he continued. "Now that I've explained a bit about the mindset of successful laptop entrepreneurs, you're ready to learn your first Internet business strategy."

MILLIONAIRE SECRETS

What is Money?

Money is simply a means of exchange, used to *represent* tangible value. Money is nothing but the measure of the *value* you create for other people. Find out what problems people have and help them by providing great solutions. You get paid in direct proportion to the value you deliver.

What is Business?

A business is simply an intermediary between a group of people with a common set of problems (a "target market" or "niche market") and a set of solutions that they need (the value that the business provides).

What is Marketing?

Marketing is simply the process of communicating the benefits of your product to your target market.

What is Internet Marketing?

Internet marketing is simply marketing done over the Internet.

The three main things in Internet marketing are how much traffic you are getting, your conversion rate, and your "earnings per click" (EPC).

Financial Independence Begins at 400 Clicks per Day

If you earn $0.25 to $0.50 per click, and you get 400 visitors per day to click on your links, that represents an income of $100 to $200 a day.

1 E-Books

As I sat there listening attentively to the Laptop Millionaire, I was beginning to see the bigger picture. But I still had that burning question in my mind: How could I *actually* make money on the Internet, like he does? How can I make $2,400 a month from an e-book, like he does?

Finally, I asked him: "What is the first thing I need to do so that I can begin selling on the Internet? What do you recommend I do?"

The Basics of Selling E-books

"The first thing you should do is create your very own e-book. There are many reasons why selling e-books online is a great idea," he said.

He proceeded to enumerate a whole litany of reasons why selling these e-books was a good idea. (Frankly, I was sold on the idea from the start!) One of the key Millionaire Secrets he taught me that day, and often repeated over the years, was this: "Sell products rather than exchanging your time for money!"

His words of wisdom still resonate today. Think about it this way: Most people sell their time, a finite resource, and then wonder why they are not getting rich. Their time is limited, and, therefore, if all they sell is their time, then of course their earning potential is limited, as well!

But when you are selling products, your earning potential becomes virtually endless. Why? Because there is no limit to how many products you can sell and how many people you can sell them to! Every new product can be a new income stream for you.

14 REASONS WHY YOU SHOULD CREATE AND SELL E-BOOKS

1. Selling *products* means no more exchanging time for money. Your earning potential becomes unlimited.
2. You can create multiple streams of income; every new product is a new income stream.
3. E-books have 100 percent profit margins; because they are a digital product, whether you sell 1 or 10,000 your costs remain the same: zero.
4. They provide instant gratification.
5. You can access a huge global market.
6. You add more value to people's lives—give them great solutions and highly valuable information.
7. Massive leverage. You leverage the Internet, affiliates, ads, and so forth. You can enlist an army of affiliates to sell an e-book for you. And you get to leverage your knowledge, and sell it to people all around the world.
8. It costs practically nothing to set up. My business cost me $400 to set up. E-books have very low start-up costs, which means it's a very low-risk business.
9. You can work from home.
10. You can automate your business.
11. No need for expensive inventory and no packing, shipping, and postage fees.
12. An e-book can establish you as an expert in your niche.
13. It's fast! You can create and start selling an e-book in less than eight hours.
14. Minimum skill is required. And you can start part-time if you wish.

That was another huge aha moment for me. Why hadn't I been taught this at school?! The Laptop Millionaire kept talking passionately about this idea.

"Also, when you are selling products you can automate your business, and you can access a global market and scale your business up rapidly!"

"And, of course, selling products is what gives your business the opportunity for leverage. For example you can leverage affiliates, joint venture partners, websites, blogs, advertising, e-mail marketing, autoresponder messages, Google AdWords and so on—all selling your products for you . . . even while you sleep!"

This made sense to me. It made me wonder why millions of people went to work each day, selling their time. From a young age, I'd watched people get up early in the morning and go off to jobs they didn't like. I always asked myself why on earth do they do that?!

The Laptop Millionaire proceeded to share with me one of his simplest Internet marketing strategies, which has just four simple steps. It was the $2,400-a-month strategy he'd mentioned to me during the seminar: *selling e-books*.

I couldn't have even dreamed that 28 days later I would be making $10,000 a month in passive income! But there, sitting on that couch, listening to every word the Laptop Millionaire uttered, I took notes furiously.

The four-step strategy that the Laptop Millionaire taught me was very simple:

1. Find a niche market with a problem that needs solving, research some great solutions, and create a Word document with that information in it. This can be a simple 30-page Word document, with one really good idea in it!
2. Pay $50 to join ClickBank.com as a vendor. You will then be able to sell your digital products (not *physical* products) through its marketplace.
3. Have someone create a website for you. You will need just two pages: a sales page where people can find out more about the product and buy it, and a thank-you page where your customers download the product.
4. And finally, you need to drive traffic to your sales page.

"Thank you so much! This is great! I can *do* this!"

The Laptop Millionaire smiled. I guess he found my enthusiasm refreshing. I did have one question though. "What should I write my e-book about? How do I find a good niche market?"

"That is a great question, Mark. Because that, of course, is the starting point. So let me ask you this question: What group of people do you want to serve? If you truly want to become wealthy, you must first decide who you want to serve."

"If You Truly Want to Become Wealthy, You Must First Decide Who You Want to Serve"

The Laptop Millionaire explained to me that entrepreneurs' business success is virtually assured if they discover a "pain point" in the market and simply cater to it. Find out what people want; find out what they are interested in buying now, and give it to them!

What most first-time entrepreneurs do, apparently, is come up with a business idea, launch it . . . and only *then* look to see if there's a market for it.

"So who do you want to serve? Investors? Traders? Business owners? Reflexologists? Advertising executives? People who want to lose weight? People who suffer from a health problem? Men who need dating advice? People looking to buy cheaper jewelry? People looking to buy plasma screen TVs? There are literally thousands of possible target markets."

He then told me that once I'd chosen a target market of customers, I needed to decide a specific way that I was going to add value for them—a specific type of *solution* that I would provide. I could:

- Help them make more money.
- Help them get more clients, improve sales, and grow their businesses.
- Help them learn how to use webinars.
- Help them get better return on investment.
- Help them with dating advice.
- Help them with relationship advice.
- Help them overcome illness and get healthy.
- Help them lose weight.
- Help them get fit.
- Help them look great.
- Help them have more fun.
- Help them relax and enjoy great holidays.
- Help them save time.
- Help them save money.
- Help them enjoy their hobbies more.
- Help them with their children.
- Help them with their careers.
- Help them quit an addiction.

The Laptop Millionaire then told me his five simple criteria for choosing a target market. He said these criteria ensured he made money on a new project 9 times out of 10. To find a *great* target market, ask yourself:

1. **Is there a large enough market for your product?**
   Are there at least 30,000 to 100,000 searches on Google a month for your main keywords (for example, "arthritis natural remedy")? You can find out by using the Google Keyword Tool at www .googlekeywordtool.com.
2. **Is there a lot of pain in this market?**
   Are people irrationally passionate about this topic or about finding a solution? Are they actively looking for solutions?
3. **Are they already spending money on the type of solutions you want to offer?**
   Do they have high disposable income?
4. **Is there good back-end potential?**
   This means that once they make the initial purchase, are there more products and services you can sell them, at higher price points, for months and years to come? This leads to a high lifetime customer value, which dramatically reduces your advertising expenses and dramatically increases your profits. It is seven times easier to sell to an existing client who knows you, likes you, and trusts you, than to try and get a new, cold prospect to buy from you.
5. **Are they easy to reach?**
   The group of people that you want to help are easy to reach if they type certain specific keywords in Google, visit a number of specific websites, read specific magazines and newsletters, are on specific mailing lists, or attend specific events or conferences. This means that you can advertise at specific locations to get your product in front of them.

"If your target market idea satisfies these five criteria, you're probably onto a winner!" concluded the Laptop Millionaire. "And if you can help people make more money, lose weight, or look great, then you'll always make money. You can never be too rich, too thin, or too beautiful."

The Laptop Millionaire gave me another important tip. People are making a fortune now, by "micro-niching" themselves. Thanks to the Internet, you can now become an expert and publish information cheaply, for smaller and smaller segments of a target market. You can become *the* number one expert in a tiny niche, almost from day one!

People's attention spans are so short in our modern world that you must position yourself in a way that is very easy for them to remember. Make sure your brand fits into a tiny nook or cranny of their brain. Be so specific in what you offer—and who you offer it to—that they can't help but remember you! Make it super clear in their minds.

I didn't understand what he meant, so he gave me the following examples of some of his friends and clients:

- The marketing consultant for printing companies.
- The property coach for U.S. physicians.
- The relationship coach for single career women.
- The life coach for advertising executives.
- The business coach for massage therapists.
- The expert for landlords with HMOs (Houses in Multiple Occupation).
- The wealth coach for black women.
- The marketing expert for fitness instructors.
- The marketing coach for musicians.
- The copywriter for Neuro-Linguistic Programmers (NLP) and coaches.
- The search engine optimization expert for U.K. tradesmen (carpenters, plumbers, and so on).
- The director of a golf camp for women.
- The quit-smoking-in-one-session NLP therapist.
- The Twitter queen who helps people make money using Twitter.
- The webinar expert who shows people how to grow their businesses using webinars.
- The blogging expert who helps people make money by blogging.
- The mobile home guru.
- The chiropractor who changed his branding to become the back-pain expert for U.S. executives.
- The reflexologist who changed her branding to become an "arthritis natural remedy expert" in Montreal, Canada.
- The personal trainer who changed his branding message to "The 10-Week Total Body Transformation Expert for Executives Who Are Outstanding in the Boardroom and Only Average in the Bedroom!"

One of the products the Laptop Millionaire was selling online was an e-book about bronchitis. He had suffered from bronchitis for 20 years, and he had tried many home remedies over the years. Eventually, he found that by combining some of the different methods, he was able to completely clear up his bronchitis.

He wrote a short e-book about it (a 50-page Word document) and started selling it for $37. His target market was people who suffer from bronchitis. He suggested I follow in his footsteps and do some research into alternative treatments. He even recommended five or six different niche markets I could go for.

"Okay, I think I've decided on my target market. Now what do I do?"

"Now is when the real fun begins. You've got to create your product. Don't worry. It's one of the easiest things to do in the world. I will show you 12 simple ways for you to create as many e-books and information products as you want!"

The 12 Easiest and Fastest Ways to Create an E-book!

As the Laptop Millionaire explained the 12 steps he used to create information products, I kept writing down these ideas as fast as I could. The first tactic he mentioned was the "flycatcher page" strategy.

Set Up a Flycatcher Page

Step 1: Set up a flycatcher page.

A flycatcher page is a website page where you ask your prospects and clients what they want the e-book to be about, what topics should be covered, what questions should be answered. They fill in their answers in the box provided, and when they click submit, you receive their questions in your e-mail inbox.

Step 2: Research and write down the answers to those questions.

For example, if you get 12 major questions, you then create 12 chapters in your e-book, and you answer each question in a chapter. There you go, your e-book is ready!

Some entrepreneurs go to Elance.com, ContentDivas.com, vWorker.com, or Guru.com and hire someone to write the e-book *for* them.

Figures 1.1 and 1.2 show examples of flycatcher pages.

Les Brown

"As a public speaker, what's your most important question about delivering MORE memorable and MORE effective platform presentations?"

Directions: Type-in your question below, and then click "Submit My Question"

Submit My Question!

FIGURE 1.1   Flycatcher Sample: Les Brown

Listen To Brian Tracy

"If you had one chance to ask Brian Tracy ANY Question about his selling strategies what would that question be?"

(Please be specific as possible)

Directions: Just type-in your most important selling strategy question below, and then click "Here's My Question Brian!"

Your First Name:

Your Primary E-Mail:

Here's My Question, Brian!

FIGURE 1.2   Flycatcher Sample: Brian Tracy

Brett McFall, a former copywriter for an Australian advertising agency, used this strategy to great effect in 2004, when he was starting out with his own Internet-based business.

He was watching television one morning, when a news item came on about how scrapbooking had become the number one new hobby of people in Australia that year. This gave him a fantastic idea. He would create an e-book about scrapbooking!

He set up a flycatcher page with this text:

"This e-book, priced at $27, can be yours for FREE for a limited time only IF you send me your number one question about making money with scrapbooking."

He hadn't created the e-book yet, but he was promising to send it for free, once it was ready, to anyone who would leave a question on his page.

He started driving a bit of traffic to the page, thanks to Google AdWords. Within a few days, 33 people had submitted a question, and Brett created a list of the 12 most common questions about scrapbooking and how to profit thanks to scrapbooking.

He then posted on the outsourcing site Elance.com that he was looking for a writer to research and answer these 12 questions.

Fourteen days later he had his e-book ready. It had only cost him $800 to get it written, and yet in his first year made over $33,000 in profit by selling it on ClickBank.com!

Flycatcher pages are a fantastic way to ask your target market—your clients, your prospects, or your subscribers—*exactly* what they are looking for.

Interview Experts, Record the Interviews, and Transcribe them

My favorite product creation strategy involves interviewing experts. You don't need to be an expert yourself. You can create products by simply being a reporter.

Decide what product you want to create, and then research experts in your niche to interview. You can find experts to interview, by going to:

- Amazon.com (authors of books).
- ClickBank.com (authors of e-books).
- Ezinearticles.com (authors of articles).
- Technorati.com (bloggers).

- RTIR.com (radio and television interview report; it is a database of authors and experts that want to be interviewed).
- Facebook fan pages.
- Google.

Over the years I have recorded more than 100 interviews by simply using Skype, the CallBurner Skype application, and a headset. And I did this all from my laptop, of course! You can also record interviews by organizing a teleconference through www.freeconferencecall.com and then download the call as an MP3 file.

A very important point: You don't need to do the work yourself! You can hire someone to transcribe the interviews (iDictate.com or Elance.com) and you can hire someone to write a 12-chapter e-book or course based on the information gleaned from the interviews. You can outsource this work to people on Elance.com, vWorker.com, Content Divas.com, Guru.com, and other similar sites.

I know of people who make a fortune from interviewing experts.

- Matt Bacak made his first million dollars by interviewing people and creating products this way. He built a mailing list, and then went and got the content from experts.
- David DeAngelo has a CD-of-the-month club, where he interviews one new dating-advice-for-men expert every month, and then ships the CD to his clients. His business is generating more than *10 million* dollars a year!
- Randy Charach also interviewed experts and created CD home study courses that he sold via direct mail. At one point, he was making as much as $1,000,000 a month.

"Experts are a dime a dozen," I often heard the Laptop Millionaire say. "What there is a lack of . . . is good marketers!"

"Why would an expert agree to do an interview with me? I'm nobody!" I often hear my students ask when they're starting out.

You will be amazed at how many experts say yes to you just because you've asked. For most of them, it will be the first time anybody has asked them for an interview. They'll be flattered; it will make them feel important, significant, and it will make them feel like their opinions matter. And most experts are grateful for any additional exposure they can get, because usually they are completely ignorant about how to market themselves.

Here's how I usually ask for an interview. *"Hi, my name is Mark Anastasi, and I would love to interview you for my upcoming e-book/book/blogpost/ membership site. This interview will go out to my 10,000 subscribers, who would love to hear about you and your work."*

If appealing to their egos doesn't work, I try to entice them with the offer of one of my products, tickets to my seminars, tickets to my workshop, a speaking slot at a seminar, a promotional e-mail to my list, a DVD product license, a Twitter account and Facebook page set up for them, or whatever other incentive I can think of.

If all else fails, I offer to *pay* them for their time. You would be amazed at how cheaply you can buy one hour of an expert's time.

For example, if you wanted to interview eight chiropractors about how they get clients and how they grow their business, you could pay them $100 each for their time, and you would wind up with an amazing product for just $800! That could become an eight-CD home study course.

Set Up a Teleseminar, Record it, and Transcribe it

You can, of course, set up a flycatcher page, find out the top 10 questions that your prospects are interested in, and run a teleseminar through FreeConferenceCall.com, for example.

A teleseminar is like a conference call, where hundreds of people from around the world can dial in to listen to what you are saying. During the teleseminar, you answer participants' questions one by one. You record your teleseminar and then download it as an MP3 file. Then get your recording transcribed (iDictate.com, or Elance.com), and voilà! You have an e-book ready to sell. If you print the e-book and you burn the MP3 onto a CD, you have a CD home study course package ready.

You could also combine strategies and invite a few experts onto your teleseminar and have *them* answer the questions for your prospects.

You could pay them a fee for their time—say, $100 for 60 minutes—or offer to give them the product to sell, as well!

Set Up a Webinar, Invite Two to Three Experts, Record it, and Transcribe it

Same as the strategy above, but you answer the questions on a webinar. A webinar is an online seminar, usually 60 or 90 minutes long, where attendees from all around the world get to see your computer screen and hear your voice at the same time. You will need an account with GoToWebinar.com ($99 a month) to do this (for more information, check out Chapter 11).

Just as in the previous strategy, you can record your webinar and then download it as an MP4 video file. You can get your recording transcribed (iDictate.com or Elance.com), and you've got yourself an e-book! If you print the e-book and you burn the MP4 onto a DVD, you have a DVD home study course package ready. (Check out www.kunaki.com for CD and DVD duplication and fulfillment.)

Of course, you could just record the webinar and sell the MP4 file as a product.

A really cool feature on GoToWebinar is that when you set up a webinar registration page, you can ask registrants a question. For example, "What is your number one question about making money with Twitter?"

We got over 300 questions submitted in 24 hours, including:

- How can I increase my number of Twitter followers?
- How can I convert my Twitter followers into buyers?
- How many hours a week does it take to make $700/week?
- How soon can you expect to have a return on the investment?
- How do I do it without looking like a spammer?
- How can I use Twitter without getting my accounts suspended?
- How many tweets need to be sent per hour?
- What should I say in my tweets?
- How do you find a targeted audience in Twitter?
- How can you find out what they really need?
- Is it smart to hire an outsourcer to do direct messaging?
- Do I really need software to grow my list of Twitter followers?
- Is it free?
- Is it easy?

This market research is invaluable in helping us create an e-book or an information product. Based on what our target market is asking us, some of the products, courses, or features we could include in this product might be:

- "How to Get 100,000 Twitter Followers in 30 Days!"
- "How to Convert Your Twitter Followers into Buyers!"
- "How to Make a Full-Time Living on Twitter in Just Two Hours a Day!"

- "How To Profit from Twitter *without* Looking Like a Spammer!"
- "How Many Tweets to Send per Day, and How to Write Your Tweets!"
- "How to Use Outsourcers to Automate Your Twitter Business!"
- "How to Start Your Twitter Business in the Next 90 Minutes!"
- "Eight Mistakes that Newbies Make that Get Their Twitter Accounts Banned, and How to Avoid Them!"

Create an MP3 or Audio Course

Once you have a list of 8 to 12 questions or topics that your prospects are interested in, you could, of course, just record the answers and create MP3 files or an audio course or audio book this way.

I use the free software Audacity to do this. You can download it at no charge at http://audacity.sourceforge.net. You plug in your headset, open up Audacity on your laptop, and then press "record." Then you simply say or read out loud the answers to each question. When you're done, you click on "stop," and then click on "file," and "export as MP3." There you go. You've just saved that MP3 onto your desktop.

You can sell that MP3 file as a product, you can have it transcribed and turned into an e-book, or you can burn it onto a CD and ship it to your buyers. (I recommend www.kunaki.com for CD and DVD fulfillment.)

The average typist will type about 50 words per minute. The average person speaks at about 160 words per minute. So the fastest way to write is: dictate!

Make a list of 10 chapter titles (your prospects' top 10 questions.) Then make a short, bulleted list (maybe just a word or two) under each title. Now, record yourself simply expanding on the ideas in your simple outline. Just explain it as if you were talking to a friend or colleague. If you dictate for six hours on one day, you will dictate over 57,000 words in a single day.

This reminds me of one of my coaching clients, Suzy Dior. Suzy was a stock market trader and an international property investor. For a couple of years she had been trying to write her first e-book about how to invest in property in Morocco, but she was never able to get going with it. Finally, she asked me to coach her one-on-one.

When I asked her why she hadn't completed her e-book in the past two years, she told me, "I don't know how to write an e-book!"

"Okay," I said, "but tell me, what are the top 10 questions that your customers and prospects ask you regarding investing in Moroccan real estate?"

"Well, that's easy!" she said. "They ask me where they should invest, why they should invest there, how can they get financing, what are the risks, what return on investment they can expect, and how they can convert currency."

I interrupted her, "Wait! Grab a pen, grab a piece of paper, and write down these 10 questions. Those 10 questions are the 10 chapters of your book. Simply write down the questions and fill in the blanks!"

Within four days her e-book was ready, and I received the following note:

Incredible! My *Morocco Property* e-book is generating 500 leads a month for my business! This will save me over $47,200 a year in marketing costs! Thank you, Mark, for showing me how to get it written and launched FAST!

Buy PLR Products and Revamp them

Another product-creation idea involves buying private label rights (PLR) e-books and using them to create new information products.

PLR e-books or courses are products that give you the right to:

- Change the title.
- Change the contents.
- Put your name on them as the author.
- Sell them and keep 100 percent of the money.

Some websites that sell PLR products include:

- www.master-resale-rights.com
- www.plrebooks.co.uk
- www.sallys-ebooks.co.uk
- www.floodle.net
- www.plrwholesaler.com

For example, Internet marketer Roy Carter found a PLR e-book about boat safety. He changed the title, put his name and picture on it, changed the sales letter slightly and started selling this e-book as *The Boat Owner's Safety Bible* at www.boatownerssafetybible.com.

Not only was he able to make a few thousand dollars a month from selling the e-book, but he also was able to profit from selling the *leads* his website was generating to boat maintenance, yachting, and marina-related businesses for top dollar!

Other ideas include creating a new product by putting together four to five different PLR e-books on a topic or recording a PLR e-book and turning it into an MP3 audio course or creating an audio book!

License Products

One of my favorite product-creation strategies actually *doesn't* involve *creating* a product. Instead, I simply *license* one!

If I come across an interesting course or e-book, I'll often contact the creator of that product and offer $500 or $1,000 to license it. This means that I'll have the right to sell it and keep 100 percent of the money.

Depending on the terms of the licensing agreement (usually a single sheet of paper—see the licensing agreement sidebar), I might be able to change the title and contents of the product or even put my own name to it.

I then put the product on my website, I e-mail my list, and usually make a few thousand dollars in sales straightaway! Even better, I now have a brand-new income stream from the ongoing sales of this new product!

I have licensed courses on copywriting, article marketing, YouTube marketing, Twitter marketing, Facebook marketing, solo ads marketing, and many, many more. Over the years I've also licensed products such as the 28 Day Rockstar course for guitarists, some YouTube marketing software, and the Speed Money Seminar concept. A friend of mine licensed the Lamborghini Energy Drink for the Cypriot and Scandinavian markets. Licensing has often been the fastest way for me to make some extra money.

Buying licenses can be great. But selling them is fantastic, too. I've licensed my Clickbank Millionaire Summit and Ultimate Facebook Marketing Seminar concepts to other seminar promoters in the United States and Australia.

Recently, a publishing entrepreneur wanted to sell my DVDs to his mailing list of clients. I sold him a single sheet of paper (a resell license for nine of my DVD home study courses) for $90,000. It took me just 10 minutes to put together the offer and agree to the deal. I could have sold the master resale rights for much, much more!

If you want to license products, check out trade magazines or trade shows. If you want to license e-books and courses, check out ClickBank. com, or the Warrior Forum, and get on different people's mailing lists. If you see a product that is interesting, contact the author and make an offer!

How to Make $90,000 in 10 Minutes Thanks to a Single Sheet of Paper! (Licensing Agreement Example)

Certificate of Reprint and Duplication Rights Full, Lifetime, Reproduction, and Reseller's Authorization

Is Hereby Granted to:

Mr. John Smith

This authorization grants the named holder of this certificate full authority to duplicate and distribute at retail level, the following Product:

"XXXXXXXXX" course and assorted bonus materials

1. These rights include the right to change the price or title of those products, in whole or in part, and the right to sell those products individually, or combined with other products.
2. They do not include the right to resell or grant rights to others.
3. The copyright notices on the products may not be changed.
4. These products may not be given away free.
5. This course may not be sold for less than $47.00.
6. The products may never be sold in any format on any online auction site (e.g., eBay.com) nor as part of any multilevel marketing program.
7. The product may not be altered in any way—the name of the author and links contained within the course must not be removed.
8. These products may not be marketed using spam (unsolicited e-mail).
9. This license may not be transferred or resold.

Signed _____ the Licensee

Signed _____ for XYZ Ltd.

Date _____

Create or License Software Applications

What if I told you that you can create as many software tools as you want, for very little money. Would you be interested?

I got a suite of software applications created by going to www.vWorker .com and hiring programmers to design software for us. I was astonished! They could create software products for as little as $500 to $1,500 per product.

A friend of mine had created some powerful YouTube-related marketing software. This software allowed users to find popular YouTube videos that weren't promoting any affiliate links or website links and contact the owners to offer to buy their YouTube accounts from them.

I licensed it for $2,000, and we charged a $37-a-month fee to use the software. At one point we had as many as 1,187 clients on this membership program!

In another example of licensing software, let me tell you about "TX," a young entrepreneur from Australia in his mid-20s. He attended my Speed Cash Seminar and started making money online pretty quickly. A few months later I introduced him to a friend of mine who is a software developer.

TX ended up licensing the software from this programmer, packaging it, and selling it for $2,000.

Once a day, he would run a webinar with a different joint venture partner (someone who would promote the webinar to their mailing list). By marketing this powerful social media automation software tool, TX did $2.5 million dollars in sales in just four months, thanks to joint venture webinars.

Adapt Successful E-books into Other Languages

Gunnar Kessler is an Internet marketer from Germany, and he flies over to the United Kingdom regularly to attend my seminars. Gunnar now makes over $14,000 a month thanks to his e-books!

His e-books are about mundane topics such as "How to Overcome Your Cat Allergy," "How to Fix Your Car Yourself," and so forth. But the twist here is that his e-books are in German.

That's right. He simply saw what type of e-books sell well in the United States and created similar products for the German-speaking market. He now sells 18 different e-books, and he is releasing one new e-book per month.

Watch this space! More and more people are telling me that they are going to start selling e-books to the Chinese market soon.

Collate Free Articles from EzineArticles.com and Videos from YouTube.com

This is probably the easiest way to create a quick e-book. Simply collate free articles from EzineArticles.com and videos from YouTube.com!

Your e-book can be a simple collection of other people's articles and videos on a specific topic.

Here is the eight-step process:

1. Pick your subject (for example, knitting).
2. Go to www.ezinearticles.com and find articles on your subject (note: you can use these articles for free as long as you keep the author's "resource box" at the bottom of the article).
3. Collect 50 to 70 articles.
4. Highlight, copy, and paste.
5. You could also add some links to interesting and relevant blog posts.
6. Go to YouTube and find links to videos about your subject. Select a dozen interesting videos. Highlight, copy, and paste.
7. Turn the Word document into a PDF document (I use the free PDFCreator software from http://sourceforge.net/projects/pdfcreator. com).
8. Done.

Create Screen Capture Videos

One of my favorite product-creation strategies involves using Camtasia software ($400, www.techsmith.com) to create screen capture videos. You just need your laptop, a headset, and your screen capture software.

Screen capture software such as Camtasia, or the free software tools such as Jing (www.techsmith.com/jing), or Camstudio (www.camstudio.org), allow you to record your computer screen while also recording your voice. You then produce that recording as an AVI or MP4 video file, for example.

This allows you to create a product in as little as a day, simply by filming your screen while describing what you are doing on your computer.

For example, Internet marketer Jani G. recently put a new e-course on ClickBank.com about how to use Facebook ads. He did $300,000 in sales in just seven days. His e-course consisted of eight Camtasia videos of him logging into his Facebook advertising account and showing how he creates a new Facebook ad!

Film a Seminar

Now, this is my personal all-time favorite strategy for creating an information product, but it takes *a lot* of time and money.

I organize a seminar, I invite experts to speak, I get the seminar filmed, and then we produce the DVDs of the event. The whole process can cost over $40,000, but typically, the sales made at the event cover these costs.

The best part? I do it once, and then I can sell the DVDs and the licenses forever!

Recently I organized a seminar about Facebook marketing, and I had 16 experts on the topic come and speak, including many of my students who were now making a full-time living thanks to Facebook.

We filmed the event, created the DVDs, and I also created a 110-page e-book containing the strategies these experts shared from the stage. I launched the e-book on ClickBank.com, and we did $380,000 in sales.

How I Generated $380,000 in Sales in 30 Days Thanks to an E-book

This e-book product launch sold over 5,000 copies of my e-book in 30 days and brought in $380,000 in sales. This process had three steps:

1. I collected the information from the experts and created the e-book.
2. I set up the website to sell the e-book.
3. And finally I had to get my joint venture partners to promote the e-book to their subscribers on the same day.

I was amazed to see over 2,447 affiliates from ClickBank.com sign up for their affiliate link to promote the e-book on launch day! (Affiliates on Clickbank.com typically earn 50 to 75 percent commission for each product they sell for you. All they need to do is drive traffic to your website, where the product is being sold.) That's one of the benefits of selling your e-books through ClickBank.com. There are over 120,000 affiliates there just *waiting* for new products to promote!

How to Take your $27 E-book and Turn it into a Sizzling $4,000 Product!   Brett McFall, author of *How to Make Money While You Sleep* and co-founder of the World Internet Summit, shared this fascinating idea on how you can take a $27 e-book and turn it into a higher value offer. Here is the nine-step process he suggests:

1. Create an MP3 (audio) version of your e-book by recording it with the free Audacity software. You can double the price, while your costs remain the same because it's just a digital file.
2. Add Camtasia video tutorials. You can add $500 to the price.
3. Add interviews with experts in your industry, recorded through Skype. You can add another $500 to the price.
4. Offer personal coaching. You can add another $1,000 to the price.
5. Record the coaching sessions and add those into the product, too.
6. Turn your product into a live seminar with a ticket price of $2,000.
7. Record the seminar and add all the DVDs/CDs into the product.
8. Sell the whole package for $4,000.
9. Sell the product license for the whole thing for $10,000.

Selling My First Product Online

After the Laptop Millionaire had shared his 12 ways for creating an e-book, he told me to go ahead and create my first info-product and to let him know how I got on with this project. And with that the meeting was over and I left his home.

I used an old computer at a local Internet café to do some research and create my e-book, and I found a web designer who lived locally and who was just starting out. He agreed to help me set up my website with the promise that I would pay him once I started earning money.

My e-book was a simple 70-page Word document with interesting how-to information about alternative health solutions I'd found out about regarding Diabetes. I was simply a reporter, reporting on these natural health discoveries. I didn't need to be an expert. The e-book took just two-and-a-half weeks to put together.

I then needed to write the sales page—this is the text that goes on your website that explains the benefits of buying your product. The Laptop Millionaire told me to copy another website's sales page and simply change the words. (Today, I would go to www.Elance.com and hire a copywriter for $1,000 to $3,000 to write the sales copy for me.)

Twenty-eight days later my first-ever website was live!

By driving a bit of traffic to it, thanks to Google AdWords (a couple hundred visitors a day), I started selling five e-books a day, on average. At $67 per e-book, I was making more than $300 a day in passive income.

I went from being broke to making $10,000 a month in less than a month. And even better . . . most of these sales were happening while I was sleeping!

I was over the moon! The business had cost less than $400 to set up, and I was now selling to people all around the world.

By modeling the Laptop Millionaire's simple strategy, I made $10,000 in sales *in my first month online!*

I launched another five e-books later that year, and after a short while ClickBank affiliates started promoting them for me, in exchange for a 50 percent commission. They have earned me hundreds of dollars a day in passive income for the best part of eight years (Figure 1.3).

Weekly Sales Snapshot

Week Ending	Gross Sales
2011-05-25 (current week)	$1,814.46
2011-05-18	$5,661.97
2011-05-11	$3,123.00
2011-05-04	$2,690.85
2011-04-27	$2,813.70

Daily Sales Snapshot

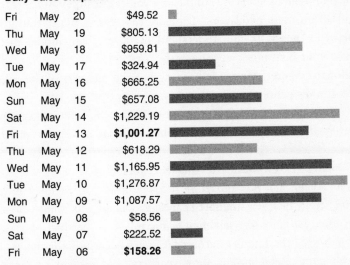

Fri	May	20	$49.52
Thu	May	19	$805.13
Wed	May	18	$959.81
Tue	May	17	$324.94
Mon	May	16	$665.25
Sun	May	15	$657.08
Sat	May	14	$1,229.19
Fri	May	13	**$1,001.27**
Thu	May	12	$618.29
Wed	May	11	$1,165.95
Tue	May	10	$1,276.87
Mon	May	09	$1,087.57
Sun	May	08	$58.56
Sat	May	07	$222.52
Fri	May	06	**$158.26**

FIGURE 1.3 Imagine waking up every morning and you've already made money . . . while you were sleeping!

Over the years I've made close to $2 million in sales thanks to e-books, and I now have more than 64,000 clients in 116 countries worldwide. I owe this to this simple business model that the Laptop Millionaire shared with me on a crisp winter morning all those years ago.

Millionaire Secrets

A few weeks after our meeting, I went back to see the Laptop Millionaire. I was excited and I couldn't wait to tell him how well his strategy had worked and how my life had changed in the space of a few short weeks!

The Laptop Millionaire was very happy for me. To the news that I was able to pay off my debts, regain my confidence, and improve my life, he responded, "That's great! You're welcome! And of course it worked! I knew it would work because you were applying five millionaire secrets all rolled into one simple strategy!"

I wasn't sure what the five millionaire secrets were but was anxious to find out. I felt like I was about to experience a new aha moment . . . only this time, I was excited! I had realized in a very real way that this information was *priceless!*

"The millionaire secrets are simple and you can seamlessly apply them to any and all business endeavors. They are the secrets that wealthy people have used for years. If you understand them, you can model them and benefit in your own life."

Millionaire Secret: Money is nothing but the measure of the *value* you create for other people.

"By creating and distributing your e-book, you are delivering more value every day than you did when you worked as a security guard or in telesales.

Millionaire Secret: Money = Value × Leverage.

If your e-book had just stayed on a floppy disk, you wouldn't have been delivering value, and you wouldn't be making money. But, what you actually did was use a lot more leverage than before.

You leveraged the Internet, technology, sales pages, web designers, advertising, affiliates, social media, autoresponders, and systems to reach more people and deliver more value.

Millionaire Secret: Work for passive income, not earned income.

You stopped exchanging your time for money. You stopped working for earned income in a job. Instead, you worked for passive income, which helped free up your time so that you could grow your business.

Millionaire Secret: Sell products; don't sell your time.

If you want to become financially free, you must start selling products.

Instead of selling your time, you started selling products. The link between how much time you spend and how much money you earn was broken.

Selling products = no more exchanging time for money. Your earning potential becomes uncapped.

Millionaire Secret: Get a mentor and copy a proven success formula.

Instead of going for the trial-and-error approach, you modeled a successful business formula. It is crazy in today's world to be going for the trial-and-error approach to business. Just get a mentor and follow a proven success formula.

You see, it was only natural for you to suddenly make a lot more money! By selling e-books online, you were actually applying five millionaire secrets.

I had to admit, what he was saying was making perfect sense. I was hoping he would teach me something else that day, and he did not disappoint. As we were wrapping up lunch, he looked up from his seafood linguini and asked, with a cheeky grin: "Would you like me to share with you a sixth millionaire secret?"

Case Study–Alex Brennan

"I make thousands of dollars a month in passive income thanks to ClickBank!"

Alex Brennan is a former management consultant from the United Kingdom. He attended some of my seminars and decided to join my mentoring program.

As one of my clients, I helped him find a niche and create his first few information products.

Check out how selling products—rather than exchanging his time for money—has changed his life.

In 2008, Mark offered a six-month mentoring program to a handful of his clients, and I didn't hesitate. I signed up straightaway.

It turns out that this was one of the best decisions I've ever made.

Within four months and having no clue of a niche or a product, I had written and published *The pH Diet*, an alkaline diet e-book based on my personal story of having lost 50 pounds or 22 kilograms in six months.

When I sold the first few copies of *The pH Diet* at $47 while I was on the ski slopes in Val d'Isere—my first passive income ever—I couldn't believe it! I was making money *while I slept!* I was hooked!

Mark then promoted and organized a weight loss seminar in London for me, where I got to present my program for the first time, and I got the DVDs of the event as well—this product is still selling today from my website.

I then also launched a weight loss e-book for new mothers, based on the experiences of my partner who lost 30 pounds using my weight-loss principles, and then I launched a weight loss e-book for mid-life men.

I then relaunched these products as 12-week *audio* home study courses, I created a membership site, and also offered a 6-week webinar series where I coached participants live to alkaline diet success.

These eight information products, built on the knowledge and skills I learned directly from Mark, earn me thousands of dollars a month in passive income via ClickBank!

One-on-one coaching, group coaching, teleseminars, and webinars provide additional income, too.

I get traffic to my sites thanks to YouTube videos and online articles.

I have been working full-time on my Internet business since October 2008 and I love what I do.

I now get to live part-time in sunny Cyprus, and I have the freedom to do what I want *when* I want!

Helping others by sharing information feels truly profound and very purposeful.

Persistence and great mentoring have been the critical keys for success—thank you so much Mark for helping me create a successful online business and a life of joy and passion!

Case Study–Kalpesh K.

"Over $1 million a year thanks to ClickBank!"

Kalpesh worked at a bank, and although he earned good money, he didn't feel this job satisfied him—and he wanted to have more *freedom*.

He launched his first Internet business, selling e-books and courses on "How to Ace Your Investment Banking Job Interviews."

He kept launching one product after another, understanding that each new product he launched was like having *a brand new income stream* direct to his pocket!

By selling the leads his e-book sales were generating to "coaching floors"—teams of salespeople that call your prospects to upsell them other offers—he started generating additional revenues.

Apparently he now generates over $1,000,000 a year thanks to ClickBank and his Internet businesses!

Case Study–Rory K.

"I make $15,000 a month thanks to my e-book on ClickBank.com!"

The week before running my first-ever seminar, I delivered a one-day trial seminar at my friend Rory's house.

In front of Rory and two of his friends, I shared the story of how I had gone from zero to making $10,000 a month. I explained how to create and promote e-books and how to increase your profits from upselling other relevant products and offers to your customers.

At the time, Rory had been unemployed for a couple of years, and he really wanted to turn his financial situation around as he had a baby daughter to provide for.

One of the last things I had these three "attendees" do before we wrapped things up that day was to brainstorm 100 business ideas and niche markets (the "100 Ways to Make Money" exercise).

That night, at 2 A.M., Rory burst into my room, all excited, and shouted: *"Mark! I've got it! I know what I will write my e-book about!"*

Six months later he'd put his *Urinary Tract Infection* e-book on ClickBank.com and quickly started making over $15,000 a month!

Summary

- Selling products is what gives your business the opportunity for leverage. For example, you can leverage affiliates, joint venture partners, websites, blogs, advertising, e-mail marketing, autoresponder messages, and pay-per-click advertising to sell your products for you even while you sleep!
- Information products allow you to add more value to more people's lives by giving them great solutions and highly valuable information. Selling products means you are no longer tied to exchanging your time for money, your earning potential becomes uncapped, and you can access a global market.
- You can create multiple streams of income. Every new product is a new income stream, and selling e-books and digital information products is

a very lucrative business to be in because the production and delivery costs are practically zero and yet you can sell them at $47 to $997.

- An information marketing business costs practically nothing to set up, it's very fast to set up, and you can work from home or from anywhere you want in the world.
- The four-step strategy for selling e-books online:
  1. Find a niche market with a problem that needs to be solved, and create a Word document with that information in it.
  2. Pay $50 to join ClickBank.com as a vendor. You will then be able to sell your digital products (not physical products) through its marketplace.
  3. Get a website created for you. You will need a sales page and a thank-you page.
  4. Drive traffic to your sales page.
- The five key criteria in choosing a good target market:
  1. Is there a large enough market for your product?
  2. Is there a lot of pain in this market?
  3. Are people already spending money on solutions?
  4. Is there good back-end potential?
  5. Are they easy to reach?
- Twelve ways to create a lucrative e-book or digital product for you to sell:
  1. Set up a flycatcher page and find out your prospects' top 10 questions.
  2. Interview experts, record the interviews, and transcribe them.
  3. Set up a teleseminar, record it, and transcribe it.
  4. Set up a webinar, invite two to three experts, record it, and transcribe it.
  5. Create an MP3 or audio course.
  6. Buy PLR products and revamp them.
  7. License products, e-books, and online courses.
  8. Create or license software applications.
  9. Adapt successful e-books into other languages.
  10. Collate free articles from EzineArticles.com and videos from YouTube.com.
  11. Create screen capture (Camtasia) videos.
  12. Film a seminar.
- You can take a $27 e-book and turn it into a $4,000 product by adding Camtasia video tutorials, adding interviews with experts, offering

personal coaching, turning it into a live seminar, filming it and creating DVDs, and adding the product license to your offer.

- The five millionaire secrets that make selling e-books so lucrative:
  1. Money is nothing but the measure of the value you create for other people (e-books allow you to deliver a lot of value to a lot of people easily).
  2. Money = Value × Leverage (e-books allow you to use a lot more leverage).
  3. Work for passive income, not earned income (e-books sell while you sleep).
  4. Sell products; don't sell your time.
  5. Get a mentor and copy a proven success formula (this formula *works*).
  6. To find out more about how you can profit from selling e-books and affiliate marketing, check out The ClickBank Millionaire Masterclass on DVD at www.laptopmillionaire.tv/dvd. (Twelve successful marketers show you how they earn over a million dollars a year each thanks to ClickBank, selling their own or other people's e-books).

2

List-building and E-mail Marketing

Sending an e-mail can be a direct way to communicate a message to an audience. Building a list simply means that you give away some *free* information or product (for example, an e-book, a video, an interview, a PDF report, etc.) in exchange for someone's name and e-mail address.

Millionaire Secret: The Money is in the List

"If you're ready for the sixth millionaire secret, I am going to share with you the business strategy that will take your business from six figures a year to seven figures a year," the Laptop Millionaire continued. His secret? The money is in the list.

On that day, the Laptop Millionaire taught me the power of millionaire list-building. Implementing that lesson and building my mailing list was one of the smartest things I ever did.

I now have hundreds of thousands of subscribers, in different markets, whom I can reach via e-mail at the touch of a button.

By the way, list-building is simple.

You build your list by driving traffic to your opt-in pages (visit www.markanastasi.com/21secrets to see what an opt-in page looks like). The more traffic you get and the more opt-in pages you have, the faster you grow your mailing list. (More on how to set up an opt-in page later.)

As was now my custom when meeting with the Laptop Millionaire, I had my journal with me. I knew that when he had that look and assumed that tone, it meant I was in for a marathon note-taking session!

The Laptop Millionaire began by explaining to me the seven reasons why business owners *must* build their lists.

"Before I explain to you *how* you build your mailing list, you need to understand the very important reasons *why* you must do this," he said. He continued, "Just this morning, for example, I sent out an e-mail to my 16,000 opt-in subscribers—people who opted to be on my mailing list in order to receive information from me regularly. I was e-mailing them to let them know that my new product is available on my website.

"Within a few hours I got 870 clicks on the links in my e-mail—which means I got 870 of my subscribers clicking on the link and visiting my website—and 120 of them bought my $50 product straightaway.

"You know what that means? That means I made $6,000 before breakfast, at the touch of a button. So my question to you is this: How would you like to be able to make money at will, at the touch of a button?"

Seven Reasons Why You *Must* Build Your Mailing List

If you want to make a lot of money online, building your mailing list can be one of the best decisions you ever make. There are seven very important reasons why having a mailing list is incredibly powerful and highly *lucrative*.

Reason 1: Having a Mailing List of Subscribers Means You Control the Traffic
When you have a mailing list you can get free traffic just by sending out an e-mail! Which means *you* control the traffic.

Thanks to my mailing list, I can get 60,000 to 90,000 clicks a month.

Web traffic is the lifeblood of any Internet business. Essentially, in twenty-first century business, traffic equals money. And *free* traffic equals *free* money!

In other words, having a mailing list allows you to make free money.

When you pay nothing—zero, zilch—and make $1,000 in profit just by sending out an e-mail, well, that is quite simply an incredibly lucrative business model.

Reason 2: Having a Mailing List Means You Benefit from Mass Leverage
Think about this for a second. If you have 10,000 subscribers on your mailing list, it means that you can communicate directly with 10,000 prospects anytime you want, at zero cost!

Think about the power of that! It is almost like having access to the earning power—or wallets—of 10,000 people.

With such incredible leverage can come incredible profits!

Reason 3: Having a Mailing List Means You Can Make Money *on Demand*!

Imagine making $1,000 to $2,000 just by sending out *one e-mail*.

A while back I remember sending out four e-mails to my mailing list in a one-week period while I was on holiday. It took me less than 45 minutes to prepare and send out these short e-mails, and I made $5,708 in free money!

I didn't even have to do any of the work, because I was promoting four affiliate offers, which meant I collected 50 percent simply for sending out an e-mail.

Having a mailing list can be like having your very own ATM machine in your living room.

Reed Floren, who has 200,000 subscribers on his mailing list (he's only 25 years old), says he has three ATMs—pointing to the three laptops on his office desk, whirring away as they send out e-mails to his list. (He makes close to $100,000 a month thanks to his list!)

In fact, it is not unusual for Internet marketers to send out direct-mail letters to their customers (their *client* database) and make $50,000 to $100,000 or more in just three days.

Build your list once . . . and make money forever!

The money is in the list!

Reason 4: Having a Mailing List Means You Can Make Money from Anywhere in the World

I believe that having a list is key to escaping the rat race and achieving financial independence. And best of all, you can work from home, or, indeed, from anywhere around the world.

Whether I'm staying in Thailand, Greece, France, England, Ireland, Australia, New Zealand, the United States, Canada, Bermuda, Egypt, the Maldives, Germany, the Czech Republic, Malaysia, Singapore, Hong Kong, or skiing in the Alps or enjoying a cruise in the Mediterranean, I can open up my laptop, connect to the Internet, send out an e-mail to my list with a great offer and make thousands of dollars!

Having a list means that you can make money from *anywhere* in the world.

Having a list equals *freedom*!

Below is an article by Craig Ballantyne, editor of the *Early to Rise* Publication, on how he was able to quit his job thanks to list-building.

Finding Prosperity Through the "Great Equalizer"

The world wide web is the great equalizer in today's economy. It's the business equivalent of having a second passport, foreign bank account, and second residence, all rolled into one.

You see, the Internet allows you to play the role of David in the battle against Goliath. It allowed Penny Halgren [. . .] to create cheap websites where she sells hundreds of thousands of dollars of quilting books and information each year. Oh, and her cat helps, too, by being the "voice" of her emails sometimes. (And no, her cat is not named Simon Black.)

But you don't even need to create your own product to generate a second income or full-time income on the Internet. One of the affiliates for my fitness product, Rusty Moore, started generating thousands of dollars per month through his website by selling other people's fitness products.

And he did all of this while working full-time as a sales manager at a men's clothing store in Seattle. Eventually Rusty was able to quit his job and now makes three times his old salary with his website business.

[. . .] Simply put, if you have an Internet connection, you can start and operate a number of very successful businesses for minimal cost. I still remember the feeling I had when it first really hit me that I could make money anywhere in the world as long as I had the Internet.

I was sitting on a plane in Dubai in 2006 ready to return home after visiting a few friends who had moved from Canada to the UAE for work. Back in those days I was still working part-timer as a personal trainer while building my online fitness business.

> Being in Dubai, I obviously had to give up my training income for the week, however, by writing a few emails to my fitness list, I was able to make over $1500 that week in online sales, including $300 the morning I checked my sales on my Black-berry while sitting on that plane ready to go home.
>
> That's when I knew I had beat the system.
>
> The Internet remains the greatest opportunity for the average person to control their economic future.
>
> Craig Ballantyne, editor of *Early to Rise*

Reason 5: Having a List Means You Can Give Yourself a Pay Raise Every Month   As an Internet marketer, you should be making, on average, $1 per subscriber per month. This means that, on average, having 1,000 subscribers equals $1,000 a month, 5,000 subscribers equals $5,000 a month, 10,000 subscribers equals $10,000 a month, and so on.

This means you can give yourself a monthly pay raise simply by growing your list. You want to make an extra $1,000 this month? Great! Simply add another 1,000 subscribers. This is why list-building allows you to grow your business fast.

The faster you grow your list (i.e., generate leads for your business), the faster you grow your business.

Well-known British direct marketer Andrew Reynolds says that "for every 1,000 customers on your list, you should make $157,335 a year in sales to them."

John Alanis, from the United States, qualifies this further: "For every 1,000 customers you have (someone that gives you $300 or more), you can make $1,000,000 a year in sales to them."

In my own experience, I have to say that this is absolutely true!

The money is in the list!

Reason 6: The Majority of the Profit in Any Business is in the Back End   In any kind of business that you are in, in any market, and in any industry, it is vital that you build your mailing list of prospects and your mailing list of customers. Why? Because if you don't have a mailing list, you are not able to generate repeat business from existing customers.

And—as cliché as this may sound—it truly *is* seven times easier to sell to an existing customer than to try to get a new customer. And furthermore, you can better inform your prospects and clients about the *value* of your offers, solutions, products, and services (it takes seven exposures to a message, on average, before a prospect takes action).

By having your prospects and clients on your mailing list, you don't just get one bite of the apple, you get the opportunity to sell to them over and over again and propose better and better solutions! Figure 2.1 illustrates the importance of driving customers from your opt-in page to sales pages to make additional revenue.

Finally, having a mailing list is vital, because by staying in touch with your clients and prospects, you show that you *care*. That's right. People need to feel significant and important, and they need to feel that you care.

A study was done years ago that showed that the number one reason people stopped using a business's services or stopped frequenting an establishment was perceived indifference. One of the single biggest killers of revenue is perceived indifference, meaning customers' perception that a business doesn't care about them or their business.

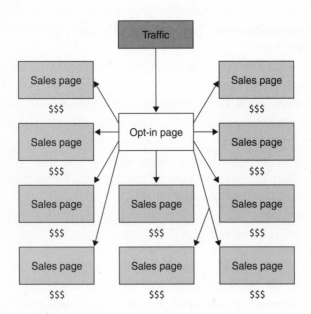

FIGURE 2.1   Drive traffic to your opt-in pages, so that your prospects get added to your mailing list, and then you can direct them to any page you want, for years and years.

Stay in touch with your prospects and clients, send them e-mails twice a week, send them a letter or newsletter every month, send them a catalog every quarter; stay in touch regularly!

It has been proven that *consistency* of contact with your clients and prospects generates trust, which ultimately means many more sales.

How can you stay in touch with them if they're not on your mailing list?

Reason 7: You Earn a Lot More Per Click if Your Traffic is from Your Subscribers Rather than from Cold Traffic Matt Bacak, an Internet marketer and entrepreneur, has calculated that he earns $0.70 per click that he generates by sending e-mails out to his subscribers. I know from our own statistics that we only earn $0.14 per click from Twitter, for example (cold traffic or people that we don't yet have a relationship with).

Ultimately that's the difference right there.

You will make *five times more money* from traffic from your mailing list than from other sources.

Plus, you can get this traffic over and over again, whereas other traffic sources would require you to keep spending money (or time) to generate visitors.

Four *more* reasons why you should build a list:

1. Having a list means you can survey your customers and find out what they want to buy.
2. You can leverage your list to attract joint ventures.
3. Having a large list almost *guarantees* the profitability of nearly any new business venture and recession-proofs your income.
4. Your list of customers is a sellable *asset*.

How to Build Your Mailing List

Now that you understand the importance of e-mail marketing and the benefits of building a list, the next step is actually doing it. As long as you're willing to think strategically, building a list is a simple process. To start building your mailing list, you need to do just four things:

1. **Choose your target market**. Who do you want to serve? You can focus on people interested in, for example, weight loss, foreign exchange, dating advice, making money, acne, arthritis, you name it.

**"How YOU Can Copy The Exact Formula's
They Use To Capture Hordes Of Highly Targeted Subscribers
And Build Massively Responsive Lists Fast..."**

**Allowing You To Generate Insane Profits
Every Time You Send An Email!**

Even if you haven't got a product of your own...

29th – 31st January 2010, London, UK

To Get On The High-Priority Notification List For The
Ultimate Listbuilding Masterclass simply type in your name and email address in the
box below and click 'YES, Tell Me More!'

Enter Your First Name :
Enter Your E-Mail Address:

Yes! Tell Me More!

FIGURE 2.2 Regarding the design of your opt-in page (how it looks), I recommend visiting various Internet marketers' opt-in pages and modelling the design.

2. **Create a free offer.** This can be a free e-book, PDF report, an interview, a video, a course, and so on. (See Chapter 1 for product-creation ideas.)

3. **Get a GetResponse.com account and set up an opt-in page.** GetResponse is an autoresponder service provider. It allows you to automatically send out a series of e-mails to your new subscribers, and it also allows you to send an e-mail broadcast to all your subscribers whenever you need to. I recommend hiring a web designer at Elance.com or vWorker.com to help you set up your opt-in page on the Internet. (See Figure 2.2.)

4. **Drive traffic to your page.** There are hundreds of ways to drive traffic to your opt-in page, including Twitter, YouTube, Fiverr.com, eBay, Amazon, ClickBank affiliates, Facebook groups, Facebook pages, Facebook profiles, pay-per-click advertising, SEO, cost-per-action leads, solo ads, banner advertising (media buying), joint ventures/ad swaps, outsourcers, and so on.

How to Get 5,000 Subscribers in 30 Days or Less

At times, my mailing list grows by 400 or more subscribers per day.

Growing your mailing list to 5,000 subscribers in 30 days or less is very, very easy. You just need to be willing to spend the up-front money to do it.

Here are four simple strategies for building your mailing list up to 5,000 subscribers in 30 days or less:

1. **Buy gigs on Fiverr.com**. This is one of my favorite strategies of all time: You can quickly get up to 5,000 subscribers by buying 200 to 400 gigs on Fiverr.com (cost: $1,000 to $2,000) and have them promote your free offer (see Chapter 7 on Fiverr.com).

Fiverr.com is a website for people to share things they're willing to do for five dollars. People can request things they need or post services they can perform. Check out how my coaching client Laila Anderson went from zero to 1,076 subscribers in 30 days thanks to social media sites like Facebook, Twitter, and Fiverr.com, and then made $4,000 from her first webinar promoted to her new mailing list, at www.laptopmillionaire.tv/laila.

2. **Pay-per-click advertising**. Purchase traffic via Google AdWords, Yahoo! search marketing, and other pay-per-click (PPC) advertising services. (Cost: $2,000 to $10,000, depending on the target market and the source of traffic.) Pay-per-click involves a website owner paying an advertiser each time an ad is clicked. As an advertiser, you choose the words that will trigger your ad. When a user searches for one of those words on a search engine, ads appear as sponsored links.

I was in Georgia recently and got to spend some time with my friend Keith W., a fellow Internet marketer. He told me he spends $1,200 a day on banner ads on the Google Content Network, and he gets 4,000 new subscribers per day (yes, that's right—4,000 new subscribers per day). This costs him just $0.30 per subscriber because he has a very high opt-in rate (40 percent, apparently).

He is able to break even on the front-end sales, and then make money on the back end. This means that every day he spends $1,200 in Google Content Network advertising, and he *makes* approximately $1,200 every day thanks to that traffic, selling his front-end offers.

He then profits from upselling other products, services, offers, and so on, to these customers and subscribers.

My student Tom Limb recently told me he spent $700 buying traffic on the Google Content Network and built a mailing list of 8,000 people interested in weight loss . . . in just five weeks!

One of my seminar attendees, Ciaran Doyle, was getting subscribers for just $0.74 per subscriber, thanks to the Google Content Network. He built a list of 5,000 subscribers in less than two months for approximately $3,700.

You can advertise on the Google Content Network by setting up an account at www.google.com/adwords/displaynetwork and you can get banner ads created for you for just $20 at www.20dollarbanners.com.

A word of warning: When it comes to pay-per-click advertising, you'd better know what you're doing before you get started. You can lose a lot of money very fast if you're not careful. The first time I used Yahoo! Search Marketing PPC advertising I ended up spending $7 per opt-in, and I lost thousands of dollars!

3. **Do 10 to 20 ad swaps in 30 days**. This was my favorite list-building strategy when I got started, and for my first three to four years in the business, actually. I grew my mailing list from 6,000 subscribers in 2006 to 20,000 subscribers in late 2009 without spending a dime.

I simply did two or three joint ventures or ad swaps every month. In other words, I would e-mail my list for Marketer X, in exchange for Marketer X reciprocating and mailing his or her list for *me* (driving traffic to my opt-in pages).

The cost is zero—but you must have an existing mailing list of a couple of thousand subscribers in order to be able to reciprocate the ad swap.

Jit Uppal recently built up his list of 30,000 subscribers in nine months, purely thanks to ad swaps. He would arrange one joint venture ad swap per day. I bumped into him in Atlanta in December. He told me he made $20,000 that month, from the comfort of his home, just from e-mailing his list! Mark Lyford told me recently he did an ad swap through http://safe-swaps.com. He got over 1,200 clicks and picked up more than 400 opt-ins from one swap.

With 10 to 20 ad swaps, you can easily grow your list to 5,000 subscribers fast—at *zero* cost!

Check out also http://safe-swaps.com, www.imadswaps.com, and http://adswapfinder.com.

4. **Pay for 10 to 15 solo ads in 30 days**. A solo ad is when you *pay* someone to send out an e-mail to their mailing list on your behalf. For example, a couple of years ago, a client told me about the solo ad provider Webstars2K: http://webstars2k.com/ezine7. He spent $75 for Webstars2K to e-mail its list of 75,000 subscribers, and he got 500 subscribers in a couple of days (cost: $0.15 per subscriber).

I paid $125 for them to mail to their entire list of 125,000 subscribers — with a different offer, of course—and I also got approximately 500 new subscribers (cost: $0.25 per subscriber).

My friend Gary McGeown recently e-mailed me this message: "Hey Mark, I know you were testing solo ads. Did you find anyone that's good? I used SelfGrowth.com a few weeks ago, and I'm booked in again. I got about 400 opt-ins for $400 (cost: $1 per subscriber). Their list size is 82,000 subscribers."

Make sure you are tracking your results, and make sure you are getting clicks and subscribers once you've paid for a solo ad.

Also, be sure your offer is irresistible and that your opt-in page converts very, very well, or you'll lose money. Typically, to build up your list to 5,000 subscribers using purely solo ads will cost you $5,000 to $10,000.

You can always approach an Internet marketer directly, and offer cash in exchange for them mailing their list. I did this recently—I paid two Internet marketers $1,000 each, for them to mail their 300,000- and 50,000-person lists, respectively. It cost me $2,000, but it generated an additional $140,000.

By the way, you can find more than 60,000 mailing lists that you can rent at http://lists.nextmark.com, dubbed "the Google of Mailing Lists" by National Public Radio.

Use solo ads, Fiverr.com, pay-per-click advertising, Facebook, Twitter, and any other strategy necessary to quickly build your initial list of 2,000 to 3,000 subscribers, then *leverage* that list to attract joint ventures and ad swaps.

List-building Tips

The context of how the subscribers find you is very important in how your relationship starts. Be sure that you're providing information in a format that people want and in a way they respect. There are a few things to consider as you build your list:

1. When you use press releases and blogs, potential subscribers see you as an expert . . . it's a very different relationship.
2. There is a *big* difference in value-per-lead depending on whether it comes from online or offline sources.

   According to John Alanis, the lifetime customer value of a lead generated online is $112 for his business, but one that is generated offline (for example, through direct mail or classified ads) is $484. When you are starting out, do whatever it takes to build your 5,000-person mailing list. A mailing list of 5,000 subscribers equals $3,000 to $5,000 a month.
3. Carl Galletti says, "If you're *just* an Internet marketer . . . you're leaving 80 percent of the money on the table." Because the majority of people still only buy and get their information offline, he recommends supplementing your online advertising with offline marketing (direct mail, advertising in trade magazines, using telesales agents,

seminars, and so on). By doing so, he says, you could see a three-fold to 12-fold increase in your income. Also, he advises that a direct-mail campaign followed by a phone call increases your sales six-fold. (Pay per-click advertising expert Glenn Livingston says, "Call your clients when they opt in or when they buy. A 1.5 percent conversion rate can jump to 20 percent.")

4. If you have higher price points in your marketing funnel ($3,000 to $15,000 offers for your clients and your subscribers) you should see considerably higher lifetime customer value and your income could increase very rapidly.

E-mail Marketing Tips

First impressions can go a long way. E-mail marketing is no exception. When you're sending an e-mail or offering content to your list, always be aware of what you say and how you say it. Always keep these tips in mind when working on an e-mail campaign:

- The first paragraph needs to be a single sentence. That first sentence needs to make the whole point. The body must clearly state a benefit for clicking the link.
- People buy from people they know, like, and trust. Demonstrate credibility, expertise, and value to your subscribers by sending them interesting and valuable content (free reports, videos, interviews, webinars, articles) that you have created. Provide exceptional value.
- The worst sin in marketing is being boring! Write your e-mails as if you are the star of your own reality TV show; give glimpses into your personal life. Inject your personality into your marketing. There's only one of you—so that's an instant unique selling point.
- Make it entertaining, educational, and inspirational. Educate while taking your prospects through your sales process.
- Online video is a very powerful tool to connect emotionally with your subscribers. Send them screenshots of your YouTube videos and direct them to those videos in your e-mail.
- To get more clicks per e-mail, always include three links: in the introduction, in the body of your e-mail, and in the close or postscript. Having three links will *double* your response compared to having just one link (this means twice as many clicks, and twice as much traffic!).

- To make more money, send more e-mails. E-mail your list every single day . . . as long as you can give them value and something interesting.

Ryan Deiss, a self-made millionaire and Internet marketer, tells a story in which every single multimillion-dollar marketer who is part of his mastermind says their income went up significantly when they started mailing their list every day.

At the very minimum, send an e-mail once per week.

■ ■ ■

The case studies for this chapter show how some of my clients have built their lists from nothing.

Case Study–Jit Uppal

"I make $20,000 a month thanks to my list!"

Jit Uppal is from Ontario, Canada, and we got in touch a few years ago when he replied to one of the e-mails I sent to my list.

Jit went from 2,000 subscribers to having 30,000 subscribers on his list in just nine months without spending a dime. He built up his initial 2,000 subscribers thanks to joint venture 'giveaway' events, but then quickly ramped things up by doing one joint venture per day.

This meant that every day he would arrange to send out one e-mail to his list *promoting someone else's website* in exchange for that person reciprocating by mailing to *their* list for *him*.

This cost nothing for him to do, and it cost his joint venture partners nothing, either. By using this strategy, Jit was able to quickly grow his list to 30,000 subscribers in just nine months!

When I finally met him at a seminar in Atlanta, he told me the previous month he had made approximately $20,000 thanks to his list of 30,000 subscribers.

Case Study–Riesling D.

"I make close to $18,000 a month thanks to my mailing list!"

Riesling D. is a 27-year-old entrepreneur from France.

Within 90 days of attending my seminar and implementing what he'd learned, he built up a mailing list of 2,000 subscribers.

Thanks to this list he started making $2,000 a month by promoting affiliate products from ClickBank to his subscribers.

As he kept building up his mailing list, he told me he hit the $8,000-a-month point within six months of starting. Then, shortly thereafter, he reached $11,000 a month, still just thanks to e-mailing his list.

He now regularly makes close to $18,000 a month, thanks to his "Lifestyle & Success" e-newsletter for men, in which he provides dating and lifestyle advice.

One of his monetization strategies involves building his mailing list by giving away a free report and then having an affiliate offer on the thank-you page where customers download the report.

"I recommend putting a banner for an affiliate product that pays $100 commission on the thank-you page where people go to download the free report," he said. "Just this alone added $4,000 in revenue this month!"

Riesling e-mailed me recently with this message:

Mark, since attending your seminar and starting my Internet business, I don't have to slave at a job and work with negative coworkers anymore!! (This is priceless!) Overall, I enjoy the freedom and being the master of my life. Also I travel more and life is much more fun. On a side note, I have a *real* sense of financial security because of the marketing skills I developed. Man this is *huge*. It's like I have super powers! Back in 2009, I was broke and jobless in one of the worst recessions in our history. I decided to attend your seminar and it has been life changing. Using some of the concepts you taught, I was able to build a six-figure online business from scratch in less than 18 months.

I now enjoy the freedom to be my own boss and life is much more fun!

Case Study–David Blair

"I made $5,000 last month and $6,300 this month thanks to my list!"

David Blair, an affable 67-year-old entrepreneur from England, uses Twitter to drive traffic to his opt-in pages, and he built a mailing list of 4,500 subscribers in the process.

Thanks to this mailing list he has made $5,000 and $6,300 in the last couple of months.

> Hi Mark, I thought I would just give you a heads up. I was doing between $1,000 and $3,000 per month in commissions mainly through ClickBank. I changed my strategy two months ago and focused on selling to my small list, mainly very low value items from the Warrior Forum. Last month I netted $5,000 for the first time and this month my gross sales exceeded $10,500 giving me commissions of $6,300! More than 80 percent is from WSO [Warrior Special Offers] commissions. All from a small list of only around 4,500 subscribers!

Case Study–Audrey Belle

"We make $3,000 a month thanks to our raw food blog and our mailing list!"

Audrey Belle is a former investment banker from France. About 18 month ago she decided to quit her high-paying job and follow her passion, becoming a nutritionist and setting up her blog (www.raw-foodrecipesonline.com) and her website (www.sosweightloss.com) along the way. After attending a few of my seminars, where she and her partner joined my coaching program, Audrey sent me this update:

> My partner and I went to a raw food class about 3-4 years ago and became addicted to this way of preparing food which is

super healthy and tastes amazing. In order to store all of our raw food recipes, we started a blog and kept posting recipes there.

Our database of recipes kept growing and I got into Internet marketing to discover ways to monitor how much traffic our site was getting.

I found it was fascinating, so I started doing a bit of SEO and I created a free ebook titled '50 Raw Food Recipes' that I give away for free on my blog, to build my list.

Nothing really happened until I found out about doing 'adswaps.' I asked my network of 'raw food' contacts if anyone would be interested in doing an adswap with me, and thanks to our first one we got about 250 people on the list overnight.

The list started growing from that moment on, and in the past 10 months we have reached 6,000 subscribers!

We only started monetising the list 6 months ago with affiliate products and we made $200 with our first email that we sent while we were having our breakfast on holidays in Santa Monica, in California! Earning money from the Internet became a reality but it wasn't consistent until we got the best tips ever from one of Mark's seminar on how to better monetise our list of subscribers.

We applied those tips and since then, we are consistently making around $3,000 in sales per month with affiliate marketing only. All this from a few tips that we heard in a seminar. Thank you so much Mark! We wouldn't be here if you hadn't come our way!

Case Study–Tiziano G.

"I live in Thailand and I make $30,000 a month thanks to my mailing list of 25,000 subscribers interested in the Forex market!"

Tiziano G. is a former investment banker from Italy who attended my Social Media Summit and quickly built up a mailing list of 8,000 subscribers in the "Forex trading" niche. By marketing Forex-related tips and information, he started making $8,000 a month thanks to e-mail marketing!

Hi Mark, I went to my very first IM seminar exactly a year ago and it was one of yours. Now I'm making more than a full time income in IM...thanks to you!! (Thank you!)It's been mostly through building a list (I have 25,000 subscribers now) and promoting affiliate products in the forex niche. Getting some good side-revenue through selling banner space on my site, but that wasn't the original plan. *I made $8,000 in June, $11,000 in July, and it's kept growing where now I've made $25,000 in December!* It's crazy how fast numbers can grow with an Internet business!!

I get my traffic from media buying, SEO, article marketing, solo ads but to be fair 90% of it came from JVs and adswaps.

2011 has been a complete blast for me and this was in great part thanks to your teachings and the inspirations of our conversations . . . and 2012 will be even better! As I read your message I am sitting by an idyllic beach in Koh Pangan, Thailand home to the world's most breathtaking beach, running a $30k a month business not even from a laptop . . . from a flimsy netbook!

I'm building more and more agreements with forex companies and have even been purchasing businesses with mailing lists :)

And none of this would have been possible without your help and inspiration. I now have 2 outsourcers working for me part time from the Philippines and Pakistan . . . still very much centered around email marketing but even than is largely systemized and outstourced.

Listen to my interview with Tiziano at www.laptopmillionaire .tv/tiziano.

Summary

- The money is in the list. As a laptop entrepreneur you should be making $1 per subscriber per month.
- Seven reasons why you must build your mailing list:
  1. You get to control the traffic (send an e-mail and get clicks, at will).

2. You benefit from mass leverage (communicate with 10,000-plus people).
3. You can make money on demand.
4. You can make money from anywhere in the world.
5. You can give yourself a pay raise every month.
6. The majority of the profit in any business is in the back end (repeat sales to existing customers). This is why you need them on your mailing list.
7. You earn a lot more per click if your traffic is from your subscribers (people who know you, like you, and trust you) than if it is cold traffic.

- Building a list simply means that you give away some free information (e.g., an e-book, a video, an interview, or a PDF report) in exchange for someone's name and e-mail address.
- You build your list by driving traffic to your opt-in pages. Generally speaking, the more traffic you get and the more opt-in pages you have, the faster you grow your mailing list.
- How to build your mailing list:
  - Choose your target market (weight loss, foreign exchange, dating advice, etc.).
  - Create a freebie offer (this can be a free e-book, interview, video, etc.).
  - Get a GetResponse.com account and set up an opt-in page.
  - Drive traffic to your page.
- The context of how subscribers find you is very important in establishing your relationship. Press releases, blogs, and books establish you as an expert in their eyes.
- Supplement your e-mail marketing to your list with offline marketing to your list (use direct mail, have telesales agents call them, organize a live seminar), and you could see a three-fold to 12-fold increase in your income.
- If you have higher price points in your marketing funnel (e.g., $3,000-plus offers for your clients and your subscribers) you should see considerably higher lifetime customer value, your profits should increase dramatically, and you will be able to afford to buy a lot more advertising and build your list faster.
- People buy from people they know, like, and trust. Demonstrate credibility, expertise, and value to your subscribers by sending them interesting and valuable content (free reports, videos, interviews, webinars, and articles).

- The worst sin in marketing is being boring. Inject some personality into your marketing. Make it entertaining and educational.
- Online video is a very powerful way to connect emotionally with your subscribers. Send them screenshots of your YouTube videos via e-mail and direct them to go watch your videos on your YouTube channel (see Chapter 4 for more on YouTube).
- To double the number of clicks per e-mail you send, include three links in your e-mail: in the introduction, in the body, and in the close or postscript.
- At the very minimum send an e-mail to your list once per week.
- To find out more about how you can profit from e-mail marketing, list-building, and online lead generation, check out The Ultimate Listbuilding Masterclass on DVD at www.laptopmillionaire.tv/dvd.

Millionaire Secret: Your Invisible World Creates Your Visible World

I had just started implementing the Laptop Millionaire's list-building strategy when he called me up and told me to come over to his place.

"I want to show you the most powerful piece of equipment I have ever seen!" he said with enthusiasm.

I made my way to his apartment immediately. As soon as I walked through the door he said: "Let me show you a tool that will change your life. It's a tool to program your mind."

"Program my mind?!" I asked, incredulously.

"Yes. Advertisers, governments, the media . . . they all program your mind from a young age, subconsciously, through repetition, to do what suits them. Well, now you can program your mind to achieve your goals and create the life you want!"

He continued: "You see, people think that changing their actions will change their life. That is not true. We always revert back to our psychological blueprint. The truth is, that to change your life you need to first change your thinking."

Most people, the Laptop Millionaire explained, have negative beliefs about money and success. These negative beliefs cascade into poor decisions and choices (he called these thoughts, beliefs, choices, and

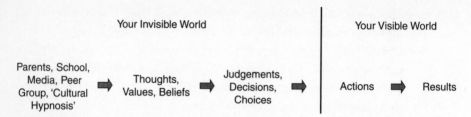

FIGURE 2.3 Your Invisible World Creates Your Visible World

decisions "a person's invisible world"), which ultimately lead to self-sabotaging actions and disappointing results in the visible, physical realm. (See Figure 2.3.)

"Most people try different 'actions' to change their life. For example they'll go on another course, they'll change relationship, they'll change jobs, they'll change where they live . . . but they always end up in exactly the same situation. The solution is to actually change your *beliefs* first, and then your actions and your circumstances will improve automatically. Let me show you how I 'change my beliefs' without lifting a finger."

The Laptop Millionaire showed me his laptop screen, which was a blank, white page. "Do you see anything?"

"No," I replied. "It's just a blank screen."

"Look closer." That's when I saw it. I noticed that from time to time something was flashing on his computer screen. But I couldn't tell what it was. He said this was the most powerful bit of equipment he had in his house.

"What is?" I said.

"This subliminal mind-programming software flashes my goal—for example, 'I want to earn $100,000 a month'—every five seconds on my computer screen, too fast for you to see it, but your subconscious mind does. You can program your subconscious mind with any goal you want to achieve."

I didn't understand exactly how it worked, but if the Lifetime Millionaire recommended it, I wasn't going to say no. So, I gave that software tool a spin, programming myself for "I earn $40,000 a month." I was subconsciously seeing that message pop up randomly on my computer screen approximately 7,000 times a day!

After using the software just over four months, I made $43,000 in sales, but the final $3,000 sale didn't go through in the end, so I ended the month with exactly $40,000 in sales. It was incredible! And eerily *exact!*

I thought to myself, "Surely it can't be because of this software. That would be crazy. Well, let's put this to the test. Let's program in a crazy goal: 'I earn $100,000 a month'!"

Sure enough, the following month I did $150,000 in sales, and I ended that year with $1,160,000 in sales—*an average of almost exactly $100,000 a month!*

I highly recommend you use this incredibly powerful tool in your own life and in your own business. It can help you achieve success much faster than you can even imagine. Why not program yourself with the sentences: "I love my life," and "I effortlessly make $5,000 a month in profit from my Internet business."

(To watch a short video on how to set up and use Subliminal Power software go to www.laptopmillionaire.tv/subliminalpower.)

Over the years I've shared this tool with my seminar attendees and coaching clients, and they've experienced incredible results.

Samantha Nicholas e-mailed me recently: "Hi Mark, I invested in the Sublimal Power software that you recommended (better late than never!!). I cannot begin to say what a difference it has made. In 48 hours I have virtually turned my life around financially. I cannot thank you enough for your advice, help, and inspiration."

Riad H. said to me recently: "I have used Subliminal Power since attending your seminar, and I programmed myself to make $4,000 a month online. I'm now making $4,000 a month in passive income, online!"

Many more clients of mine have used this tool to lose weight, find a relationship, and so on, often with simply incredible results.

3

Search Engine Optimization

Thanks to the Laptop Millionaire, by early 2007 I had launched 28 e-books, I had a mailing list of 20,000 subscribers, and I had generated close to $2.5 million in sales. I did this from home, and while traveling around the world. All I needed was my laptop and an Internet connection.

Just three years after starting my business in rainy old England, I retired to the sunny island of Cyprus in the Mediterranean where I bought an 11-bedroom property in the Troodos mountains, complete with tennis court and swimming pool.

I was only 27 years old.

The island has a wonderful climate, with 330 days of sunshine a year, and I spent most of my time at the beach, windsurfing, going scuba-diving, or playing basketball. In the evenings I would hang out with my friends, go to parties, barbecues, go out for a nice meal, or simply watch a movie at the local cinema.

My entire business was run from my laptop, which meant that when I moved to the island I just needed to plug into an Internet connection and I was in business again! I was earning $300,000 to $400,000 a year from my websites and from simply sending a couple of e-mails a week to my list of subscribers. I worked just two hours a day, making sure everything was ticking along nicely.

The Laptop Millionaire also had a holiday home in Cyprus, overlooking the sea, just a few miles away from where I lived, and we got to meet from time to time whenever he was in the country.

One day, I received an e-mail from him in which he told me that he had more than 100 sites ranked in Google and Yahoo! in less than a month.

He told me that by using search engine optimization (SEO), I could get my sites ranked higher without the help of article writers.

I was excited. Getting your website on page one of Google means that people can find it simply by typing a keyword into Google. (This means you can get *lots* of traffic for free . . . and free traffic equals free money!)

SEO is a process for improving the visibility of online content via the natural search results. SEO looks at how search engines work and what people search for to organically improve the rank of a website. The higher a site's search results ranking, the more people that see it.

For example, there are over 4,000,000 searches a month for the keyword "arthritis." If your arthritis-related website is listed on the first page of results whenever people type the word "arthritis" in the Google search engine, you can expect to get hundreds of thousands of visitors to your website every month *for free!*

Imagine getting 100,000 visitors a month to your website and earning $0.20 per visitor on average. That would mean $100,000 \times \$0.20 = \$20,000$ a month in free, passive income. And if you earned $0.40 per visitor, that would mean $40,000 a month in passive income.

Getting ranked on page one of Google usually takes six months or longer to accomplish, but the Laptop Millionaire had found a way to do it in less than 30 days. I just *had* to find out more.

I called him up straightaway and said: "I'm coming now! I'm already in my car!"

I arrived at his stunning villa overlooking the Mediterranean Sea an hour later. He welcomed me with a beaming smile and gave me a big hug. "I did it!" he said.

"I've finally cracked it! I can now get as much free traffic from Google as I want! This is going to double my business! And this is going to take your business to a whole other level! But first . . . let's eat! We have a lot to catch up on."

As we sat by his pool, enjoying a feast of Greek and Cypriot "meze," I thanked him once again for his help in turning my life around.

"I wouldn't be where I am today if it wasn't for you," I said.

"Nonsense. You had it in you the whole time. I'm just glad you listened to my advice and took action!"

It was truly wonderful seeing him again. I wondered if I could ever thank him enough for his generosity in sharing with me his strategy all those years ago.

After a couple of hours, he had the table cleared and proceeded to explain his "search engine domination" strategy by scribbling and drawing on a piece of paper in front of him.

When it comes to making money using SEO, every keyword typed into a search engine—and there are over 1 billion different keywords typed into Google every single day—is a market to target, dominate, and profit from.

Google, Yahoo!, MSN, and the other top search engines get over 2 billion visitors a *month* (so that's pretty much every Internet user out there!). By getting ranked on their pages for keywords relevant to your business, you can get a constant stream of traffic to your websites for free.

My strategy involves going after long-tail keywords—for example, keywords like "Kingston Jamaica one-bedroom apartment," or "holiday villa Latchi Cyprus," rather than simply "apartment" or "holiday villa." By going after long-tail keywords—where the competition is very low or nonexistent—it is very easy for me to dominate the search engines.

Every time someone types "holiday villa Latchi Cyprus" into Google, chances are they're going to find my website listed there, and they're going to click on the link and visit my website. Bingo! I get free traffic from the search engines.

These suggestions were invaluable to me and you can use them as you build a site. Google uses over 200 different indicators in its search algorithm to determine how relevant your website may be for a specific search query. These indicators include the content on your site, the number of sites linking back to you (backlinks), the name and relevancy of your URL (for example, www.holidayvillalatchicyprus.com), how long your website has been up, how fresh your content is and how often it gets updated, and so on. The two main criteria that matter the most are: *content* that is relevant to the keyword, and *backlinks* (i.e., having relevant websites linking back to your site). But if the competition is really low or nonexistent, even that is not essential.

Before search engines were popular, backlinks were the main tool for web navigation. Now, backlinks are a popular indication of the number of sites interested in a web page. There are two important points to consider when increasing backlinks for your site:

1. Anchor text
2. Authority and relevance of the site

Keeping these things in mind can ensure the value of your backlinks and help to increase your SEO.

RECOMMENDED TOOLS FOR GETTING BACKLINKS

- BruteForceSEO link-building tool ($150/month).
- SerpAssist automated backlinks tool ($97 per month).
- Press releases are good for getting you backlinks (*check out* PRweb.com).
- To get backlinks, use www.buildmyrank.com. (For up to five domains it costs $59/month; up to 20 domains is $99/month; 50 domains is $159/month.)
- Also use http://3waylinks.net ($7 and then $47/month).
- Buy backlinks on Fiverr.com ($5).
- Get eight relevant articles (150 words) written on Fiverr.com, and get them uploaded onto www.buildmyrank.com, for just $5!
- Mass Article Submitter http://massarticlesubmitter.net.
- Onlywire lets you auto-submit your online content and social status to the top social media sites with one click: www.onlywire.com.
- Post videos on YouTube with backlinks to your sites.
- Have a virtual assistant post backlinks and articles on multiple websites, and arrange link exchanges with other websites in your niche.

Using Content and Keywords to Increase your SEO

It can take time, money, and a lot of effort to get ranked high on search engine results, especially for very competitive keywords. But you can make an absolute fortune when you crack their code!

The Laptop Millionaire explained to me his criteria for selecting a specific keyword. By using the Google Keyword Tool (www.googlekeywordtool.com), he looks for keywords that have at least 10,000 searches a month but fewer than than 100,000 competing websites.

He then creates a blog with that keyword in the URL, for example, www .holidayvillalatchicyprus.com.

He found that by targeting these long-tail keywords, where few people were bothering to compete, he could easily get his sites listed on page one of Google.

He planned to monetize his websites by putting Google AdSense ads on them (www.google.com/adsense), as well as give away free reports in order to build his mailing list of real estate investors. His aim was to set up 6,000 real estate-related sites within a year.

In the ensuing 12 months, the Laptop Millionaire used his SEO know-how to set up 6,500 blogs about real estate and he got approximately 20 percent of these sites to the top of Google, Yahoo!, and the other search engines.

Each blog targeted a different long-tail keyword—for example, keywords like Kingston Jamaica one-bedroom apartment or holiday villa Latchi Cyprus.

Thanks to the millions of visitors he got from the search engines, within a couple of years he had built up a mailing list of more than 120,000 property investors.

In 2008, he made $1,200,000 by simply selling the leads he was generating to property developers and real estate companies around the world, and by selling international investment properties directly to his subscribers. By 2011, his sales increased to over $4,500,000 a year!

His 6,500 sites earn him, on average, $0.22 per site per day in Google AdSense revenue (that's $1,430 a day or over $500,000 a year in passive income) and on top of this he is given a house or property for every 7 or 10 that are sold to his leads!

It costs him $10 per site per year to renew the domain registration, so that is $65,000 a year for his 6,500 domains, $12,000 a year for hosting, and another $25,000 a year for his team of outsourcers from the Philippines who update and maintain his network of websites. Still, paying $100,000 a year in order to receive $500,000 a year in passive income is pretty awesome!

Having a site ranked number one in search engine results can be a lucrative accomplishment. Once your site is ranked on page one of Google, you can monetize your well-optimized website by using the following strategies:

- Put Google AdSense ads or Amazon ads on the site.
- Put opt-in boxes on every page of your site, to build your list and/or generate leads that you can sell to other businesses.

- Sell affiliate products.
- Sell advertising space on your sites.
- Rent out your sites monthly to relevant local businesses.

I implemented the Laptop Millionaire's strategy and within a few months I started getting 60,000 to 90,000 visitors a month for *free* thanks to Google, adding an extra $20,000 a month to my business! The key to the Laptop Millionaire strategy is finding sources of passive income. SEO fits perfectly into this strategy. The concepts can be used in websites and businesses you already have or applied as you start a new online endeavor.

■ ■ ■

Case Study–Sotiris Bassarakopoulos

"I make $3,000 a month from my 450 AdSense sites!"

Sotiris Bassarakopoulos is an entrepreneur from Belfast, in Northern Ireland. After attending my seminars he set up 450 websites in six months and worked another six months to get them ranked on Google.

Thanks to this SEO work, he now makes more than $3,000 a month from Google AdSense revenue, ClickBank affiliate products, sales from an autoblogging software tool, Amazon commissions, and other affiliate programs.

That's $6.70 per site per month (or $0.22 per site per day in AdSense revenue, the same as the Laptop Millionaire's websites, interestingly enough).

He currently has the number one position on Google for the keywords "free classified ads London" (www.freeclassifiedadslondon.com), "free ads philippines," "free classified ads Belfast," the number three position for "free classified ads edinburgh," the number six spot for "free classified ads new york," and the number three spot for "subliminal power review."

These are the tools and strategies Sotiris uses to get his sites ranked in Google:

- SEOPressor.com—on-page SEO plugin for Wordpress.
- Mass Article Submitter (http://massarticlesubmitter.net).

- Onlywire—autosubmit your online content and social status to the top social media sites with one click (www.onlywire.com).
- He posts YouTube videos with backlinks to his sites.
- His virtual assistant from the Philippines posts backlinks and articles on multiple websites and does link exchanges with other websites.
- He recently started doing guest blogging on other high-ranking sites.

Case Study–Nick East

"I got to the top of Google in six weeks and I make 3,776 a month thanks to SEO!"

Nick East is another student of mine, and he recently revealed to me in an interview how he easily gets number one rankings in Google:

1. Go to www.amazon.com to find out what items and products are popular in different categories.
2. Select a keyword you want to rank on Google.
3. Check what website is number one at the moment in Google.
4. Type that URL into www.alexa.com, to see if it has fewer than 500 to 1,000 backlinks (websites linking back to that specific site).
5. If it has more than 1,000 backlinks, find another keyword that has fewer than 500 to 1,000 backlinks.
6. Once you've selected your keyword, register a domain name and set a Wordpress blog on that domain.
7. To get backlinks, use www.buildmyrank.com (for up to 5 domains it costs $59/month; up to 20 domains is $99/month; and 50 domains costs $159/month).
8. Also use http://3waylinks.net ($7 and then $47/month).
9. Buy backlinks on Fiverr.com ($5).

Get eight relevant articles (150 words) written on Fiverr.com, and get them uploaded onto www.buildmyrank.com, for just $5!

Time spent: two hours doing research (Amazon, Google, Alexa), and two hours to get everything else done.

This process gets him number one rankings in Google in less than six weeks.

Check out my interview with Nick East at www.laptopmillionaire.tv/nickeast.

Case Study–Matt and Alex Santoro-Emerson

"We get 22,000 visitors a month, we make thousands of dollars a month in passive income, and we've now moved the family to sunny Italy!"

Matt and Alex Santoro-Emerson lived in England until recently, but have now moved to Sicily in Italy—a dream of theirs for many years!

They get more than 22,000 visitors a month to their websites thanks to Google and YouTube, and make thousands of dollars a month in passive income.

Hi Mark. We are really excited about moving from rainy England to sunny Sicily! This has been possible because we have Internet businesses bringing us income even while we sleep.

I got started because I bought one of your how-to-make-money-on-the-Internet products. I can't remember what it was called but it told me everything I needed to know to get started (CPC, SEO, etc.) so I made a product about keeping chickens (www.chickenkit.com) and I've been working on it ever since.

I get most of my traffic from Google (150 visits per day), YouTube videos ranked in Google (400 visits per day) and affiliates (200 visits per day).

Also, my wife, Alex, launched her website www.thelovelife-coach.co.uk. Thanks to free traffic from Google, she gets speaking engagements and coaching clients, as well as selling her $97 Love and Passion DVD product!

Case Study–Ciaran Doyle

"I make $7,080 a month thanks to SEO and I live by the beach in Cambodia on just $700 a month!"

Ciaran Doyle attended my workshop in 2006, and we have remained friends since then. Ciaran now lives by the beach in Cambodia, spending just $700 a month, while his mobile-phone-related websites bring him more than $7,080 a month, thanks to free traffic from Google.

What is incredible is that he only needs 100 to 130 clicks (visitors) a day to make $236 a day in passive income!

I make money now mostly from my mobile phone websites. I have websites that sell mobile phones and mobile phone contracts in the United Kingdom. Check out www.badcreditmobilephone.com.

I drive traffic to these sites thanks to SEO.

My site sells mobile phone contracts. I act as an affiliate. But maybe in a while I might think about actually selling contracts myself. I have been talking to the affiliate people and they think they can start getting special deals created for me. I'm an affiliate for the big guys. I just act as a middleman.

You see, people are searching for particular phones, and I have keywords like bad credit, poor credit, and so on in the articles on my website and when people search random keywords associated with them then my website nearly always pops up for them at the top of the search engines.

"Bad credit mobile phone" is a good keyword. But it's more the long-tail keywords that are the money bringers. Longer tail than just four words.

Targeting is very important. I don't use keywords that are really broad.

Go to www.google.co.uk and type in "bad credit nokia c3." Most phones I have are coming up position one or two. I actually have the top three listings for that keyword!

I created an SEO template that allows my outsourcers to get the same results as I do if I was doing it myself. We are creating systems around every part of it, and for now it is going very good.

I spent a few months reading everything I could about what Google wanted and have set up my sites to comply with Google's rules.

My income is doubling month on month. Up to over $7,080 a month. Hopefully it will go up a lot more next month.

I get approximately 3,000 to 4,000 visitors a month at the moment. But traffic is growing every day. This means that my EPC [earnings per click] is a whopping $1.6 per visitor!

It's so cheap here in Cambodia. It costs less than $700 a month to live. A fancy meal costs just $5. I was just down at the beach. It's so nice here. If you ever fancy a visit get on down here. It's cool man; I don't need much. I have nice little place by the beach, with a cooker, hot water . . .

Case Study–Jonathan N.

"I make over $30,000 to $50,000 a month thanks to free traffic from the search engines!"

Jonathan N., a former IT recruitment company owner with a doctorate in electrical engineering, attended my Speed Cash Seminar a couple of years ago. During this event he learned how to quickly get websites ranked on the first page of Google.

He taught himself how to set up a website, and he started creating as many as 10 sites an hour all by himself. Within a year he was making $30,000 to $50,000 a month thanks to free traffic from Google.

When Jonathan realized how little money he was going to make as an engineer, he started looking around for other, more lucrative opportunities, and that is how he ended up working for a recruitment company. One year later, he quit his job and set up his own IT recruitment company.

"By the age of 30, I didn't have to work. I went and did martial arts in China," he said. "My dad had come to the United Kingdom from Hong Kong, with no money. He set up a restaurant, then more restaurants, and retired in his 40s, a very wealthy man."

With the profits from his recruitment company, Jonathan went into the property development business. Unfortunately, due to the recession he ended up overextending himself in some big building projects, and he had to sell everything. At age 36, he ended up with $600,000 in debts, having to start over. That's when he decided to look into Internet marketing and started attending my seminars.

Within 18 months he had built 5,000 websites (without even the help of a web designer or an outsourcer!) and started making over $50,000 a month by selling physical products online as an affiliate.

Jonathan prefers selling physical products, such as designer floor lamps, contact lenses, lawnmowers, baby monitors, fish pond pumps, theater tickets, holiday packages, male enhancement products, flowers, grills, diamond engagement rings, sapphire engagement rings, and many more everyday products like that.

He also sells leads to other companies; for example, he sells mortgage leads to mortgage companies, real estate leads to real estate agencies and property developers, and insurance leads to insurance companies.

He joins affiliate programs from Amazon.com, Made.com, and hundreds of other merchants of physical products. He tells me he sells physical products because the conversions are better than for information products (his conversion rates can be as high as 10 percent or even 14 percent, compared to the usual 1 or 2 percent for a ClickBank e-book).

He targets specific product names (keywords of things people are looking to buy) for example, "Panasonic HMB 100 xoom digital camera," as opposed to simply "digital camera."

For example, he gets paid $450 to $750 per engagement ring he sells, and the conversions are usually 10 percent to 14 percent! This means that at least 1 in 10 people *buy* that engagement ring, because it's so much cheaper to buy online.

There are tens of thousands of products to promote with tens of millions of keywords to target.

"I'm not even touching 1 percent of the potential here!" he says.

Jonathan sometimes targets a specific type of product—baby monitors, for example—and builds 15 to 20 sites in that niche.

Within three to six months these sites will usually be in the top three positions on page one of Google for the main product keywords in that niche, for example, "Tomy SRV400 Video Baby Monitor."

These products sell for $90 to $250 each, and he can make as much as $800 to $1,100 per site per month, thanks to his affiliate commissions.

"I can sell these sites for $5,000 to $7,000 per site," he tells me. But what I prefer to do is sell my bundle of 15 to 20 sites for six figures ($100,000 to $200,000 usually) to the main merchant in that category!

"I'm 10 percent to 20 percent of their sales. The merchants realize they have to increase my commissions per sale or they buy me out for six figures! I then give them the 15 to 20 sites I've built in that niche. They don't want me to start promoting their competitors, you see."

I caught up with him later on Skype. What he revealed to me was quite astonishing.

My personal websites are consistently delivering multiple four figures (U.S. dollars) every single day—and all from natural SEO for physical products as well as e-products.

Recently I helped a FTSE250 and a FTSE100 company with their online business—with just a few simple changes, the results have been staggering.

I am now able to help large businesses dominate their market, ahead of competitors, and even help smaller firms overtake leaders in their field very quickly, for relatively little spend.

It's not simply about backlinks and content. It's actually how you put the ingredients together in the right sequence with the right timing, at the right temperature.

If there's competition, typically within six to eight weeks you get on page one of Google (positions four, five, or six); then it takes a few more months to get to position one.

I now have 5,000 sites up, that I've built myself. I've never had any help nor any outsourcer. I was working 12 to 15 hours per day in my first year! In an hour I can set up 10 websites, including the keyword research. That's just seven minutes per site!

Out of 100 sites that I set up, 30 will go nowhere, 50 will go on positions three to six, and 20 will make serious money ($200 to $300 per site per month or sometimes more). From my 5,000 sites, only 1,000 make me good money. That's why you need to set up a lot of sites.

Most people don't build enough sites to see something happen. And most people give up after a week or two because they don't have the patience to wait for six to eight weeks or even six months before they start seeing results. You must build hundreds of sites to really make this work!

Jonathan's process:

- Find related buying keywords (e.g., Tomy SRV400 Video Baby Monitor).
- Register the domain, then stick some rotating Amazon ads relevant to the keywords on the site.
- Build the site and have a bit of content on it. Put a blog up on the site and then *ping* it (in the blogging world, a ping is a

mechanism by which a blog notifies a server that its content has been updated).
- Get a few backlinks to your site.
- Note: this all has to be done within a certain timeframe. The first 48 hours of your site's existence are very important with Google. It's about putting the right backlinks at the right frequency at the right time, says Jonathan.

Summary

- When it comes to making money using SEO, every keyword typed into a search engine—and there are over 1 billion different keywords typed into Google every single day—is a market to target, dominate, and profit from.
- The Laptop Millionaire's 6,500 sites earn him, on average, $0.22 per site per day in Google AdSense revenue (that's $1,430 a day or more than $500,000 a year in passive income).
- When it comes to SEO, there are two main schools of thought: You can either set up hundreds of websites, each one targeting a long-tail keyword, or you build one site, deep in content and links (this takes longer, but is arguably a better long-term strategy).
- Google uses over 200 different indicators in its search algorithm to determine how relevant your website may be for a specific search query, but it is widely accepted that the key SEO criteria are how relevant and useful the content on your website is, how many websites link back to your site (and how relevant those sites are), the name of your URL (are your keywords in your domain name?), and how long your website has been around.
- Tip: Optimize your pages for keywords that *convert*. For example, have a web page devoted to the product Tomy SRV400 Video Baby Monitor, rather than simply baby monitor. If somebody is typing the keywords "Tomy SRV400 Video Baby Monitor" into Google it is because they are ready to buy that product. They're not just browsing.

- Tip: Update your website or blog regularly with *fresh* content.
- You can use Alexa.com and Compete.com to find out how many backlinks your top-ranked competitors have in Google and simply get more backlinks than them.
- Use shorter domain names. Don't use numbers; don't use hyphens; and always use .com. Pay for multiyear registration, because the longer the domain is in existence, the better.
- You can use www.registrycompass.com to find expired domains that have hundreds or thousands of backlinks already and that still get traffic.

4 YouTube

By 2008, the way people used the Internet was starting to change. Social media websites like YouTube, Facebook, and Twitter were gaining momentum, and increasing numbers of people were spending time away from their normal day-to-day activities to interact online through social media websites.

YouTube.com was launched on February 14, 2005, and as of 2012, it is the third most visited website in the world (after Facebook and Google) with more than 800 million unique visitors a month. The average American watches 150 YouTube videos every month. Google paid a whopping $1.65 billion to acquire the site in November 2006.

Savvy entrepreneurs quickly realized the potential of this site and started using YouTube to get free traffic to their sites and make money online.

I was first alerted to this online video revolution by a young guitar player named Ben, who had seen me speak at a seminar in Bristol. He was teaching guitar lessons at the time, and when I shared my story about how I sell e-books through my websites, he thought to himself, "Hey! I can teach my guitar lessons online!"

He started filming himself teaching the guitar, and four months later he launched www.vguitarlessons.com, where he sold his video lessons for $14.99 each. By uploading 12 free guitar lessons onto YouTube in 2008, he started getting a steady stream of free traffic to his site and he built up a mailing list of 140,000 subscribers for free! The traffic from YouTube and from marketing to his mailing list could bring him up to $20,000 a month in passive income.

Oh, and did I mention that anyone can open a YouTube account and that it's free of charge?

As soon as I heard Ben's story, I went to www.youtube.com and opened an account. I started uploading clips of my seminars and short videos of myself talking straight to the camera onto my new YouTube account, and I immediately started getting traffic to my websites.

Furthermore, my videos on YouTube proved to be a very powerful way to connect with my audience, communicate ideas and information to them, and get them to want to do business with me. Online video gives you the power to communicate with your customers in ways the written word never can.

When I interviewed Ben about his success on YouTube and I made the interview available to my subscribers, one of the people who would end up listening to it was an American supermarket employee by the name of George.

George worked at stocking shelves in a supermarket in Austin, Texas, and he absolutely hated his job.

Eager to learn more about Internet marketing, he subscribed to my newsletter, listened to the interview, and then spent the next three months uploading 500 videos onto YouTube.

He created simple two-minute screen capture videos, using the software Camtasia (available at www.techsmith.com) to film his computer screen and record himself as he described various products from ClickBank.com.

He placed his affiliate link underneath each of his videos, linking to the website where you could buy the product he was describing. This is how he would monetize the traffic his videos would get.

The result? Within 90 days he was making $1,500 a week and within six months he was making close to $9,000 a month in passive income.

He quit his job very quickly, I can tell you!

His videos were bringing in $14 per video per month on average. What was even more interesting was that he hadn't spent a dime to set this business up. No website, no advertising, no list, no product, no customer service, no shipping.

He ended up making close to $300,000 in four years thanks to this traffic generation method.

Another student of mine, Julia S., copied that strategy and uploaded 70 videos on YouTube, with ClickBank.com affiliate links underneath each one.

She made her first sale within three days of attending my seminar, and before long she was making $1,000 a month in passive income from her videos. Interestingly, that's also $14 per video per month on average.

Many more of my students, subscribers, and seminar attendees would end up using this technique to get more traffic to their websites.

Finding the Right Message

The cornerstone of strong marketing is delivering a message that resonates with your audience. This is an important part of using YouTube to make money online. When deciding what's right for you think about what you want say, how you want to offer it, and your goals for loading the material.

Think about what you're good at or information you want to get to your customers. Uploading the videos is simple and once you do, you're on your way to making money online!

There are several results that you can get from YouTube videos. You can use them to gain subscribers for your mailing list, increase traffic on your website, or find customers for your business.

Magnus Huckvale made $100,000 in passive income in four years by selling his $39 e-book, thanks to free traffic from YouTube.

Magnus teaches people how to use the Emotional Freedom Technique (EFT) to eliminate limiting beliefs and overcome emotional problems. By posting 12 free videos about EFT on YouTube he gets a constant stream of traffic to his website Tapping.com. He has had more than 2,000,000 views to his videos so far.

Joe Hayhow went to his gym and filmed his personal trainer for a couple of hours, demonstrating different fitness exercises (push-ups, crunches, and so on).

Joe then uploaded these 50 fitness videos onto YouTube, each one containing a link to his fitness-related opt-in page. Within a year he built up a mailing list of over 10,000 subscribers thanks to YouTube—for free!

Dawn Mendonca quit her nine-to-five job so she could pursue her passion as a dance teacher. She uploaded 90 videos to YouTube.com and grew an international dance studio business that attracts over 1,500 students a week! She now earns $300,000 a year thanks to YouTube. She built her entire dance career thanks to YouTube, networking, and video SEO and never paid a dime in advertising.

Mark H. quit his job as the manager of his mother's bakery, and set up 10 blogs, each blog selling a single product. He then created 20 to 30 videos for each blog. He uploaded videos on YouTube, driving traffic to his 10 different niche blog websites. He makes over $8,000 a month in passive income thanks to free traffic from his videos on YouTube.

Listen to my exclusive interview with Mark H. at www.laptopmillionaire .tv/markh.

YouTube Hijacking

Take a virtual stroll through YouTube and you'll see videos with high views and users that average large numbers of watchers. You can use this to your advantage and make money online.

Sarah Staar, the owner of a video production company in the United Kingdom, started by using a different strategy: Instead of creating videos and uploading them to YouTube, she offered to buy out or rent popular YouTube accounts that get lots of views and places her affiliate links underneath each video. This "YouTube hijacking" strategy involves contacting YouTube video owners who are getting over 30,000 views a month and buying or renting their accounts. She is making more than $3,500 a month in passive income thanks to her efforts. To find out more on how Sarah makes up to $400 a day thanks to YouTube, watch Sarah's short presentation at my Rapid Income Generation workshop: www.laptopmillionaire.tv/sarahstaar.

Shaqir Hussyin attended many of my seminars and also decided to use the YouTube hijacking strategy that Sarah benefited from. He bought and took over some popular YouTube accounts (sometimes paying as little as $20 for an account) and started making $250 to $1,000 a day in passive income. He made $200,000 in his first year online.

Affiliate Links

As we've discussed in previous chapters, promoting affiliate links is a quick and easy way to make money online. You can do the same thing easily with YouTube.

U.S. Internet marketer Jason Moffatt is credited with being the pioneer of the "YouTube video hijacking" strategy, or simply buying YouTube accounts and redirecting the traffic to affiliate offers. He paid $250 for a World of Warcraft video that got 7 million views. By putting his affiliate link for a World of Warcraft–related product underneath the video, Jason started making multiple sales a day thanks to YouTube.

On stage at Frank Kern's "Mass Control" seminar, Jason spoke about a student of his who had bought a very popular guitar video with roughly 27,000,000 views at the time. That $2,000 investment quickly turned into a $300 to $500 a day passive income stream by simply adding a link in the description area to a popular guitar instructional course.

Using YouTube in Your Laptop Millionaire Strategy

The YouTube website is actually quite unique in how it allows you a multitude of ways to get traffic and generate an income. I've listed a few of these tactics below. Please note, any one of the following seven strategies would allow you to make a full-time living as a laptop entrepreneur.

Seven Ways to Make Money from YouTube

There are many ways for you to profit from YouTube traffic:

1. **Sell your own products or services and market yourself on YouTube.**
   This is what I do, for example, when I promote one of my seminars or one of my products. YouTube is a great way to build relationships and trust with your target market, your prospects, and your clients.
2. **Build your opt-in list.**
   Use your YouTube videos to drive traffic to your opt-in pages in order to build your mailing list. This means you will be able to make money at the touch of a button by simply sending an e-mail to your list with a relevant offer.Note: some people use sneaky tactics to grow their mailing list using YouTube. For example, you will find that many laptop entrepreneurs post comments underneath other people's YouTube videos with a link back to their own websites, or they send a message to specific YouTube users directly to say hello and give them a link back to their website, or they post video responses to popular videos and these appear underneath them.

But generally speaking it is good form to subscribe to some other YouTube accounts in your niche, which makes you their friend on YouTube.

3. **Lead generation.**

   Just as you can use YouTube to build traffic for your own business and grow your own mailing list, you can also generate leads for other businesses and companies using your YouTube videos. This can be particularly lucrative, as you can get leads for free thanks to YouTube, and sell them for $8 to $47 each to offline businesses that don't know how to use Internet marketing or social media sites like YouTube.

   My friend Mark V. makes over $700,000 a year selling leads to real estate developers worldwide, and Barry D. makes over $1 million a year selling leads to window glazing companies in the United Kingdom.

4. **YouTube account management for local businesses.**

   You can offer to set up and manage local businesses' YouTube accounts in exchange for a monthly fee. One person I know, a woman in her 20s, makes a comfortable $7,000 a month from home doing just that!

5. **Dominate Google and get free traffic from Google.**

   This strategy involves using YouTube SEO techniques to have your videos listed on page one of the search engines like Google.

6. **Make money promoting ClickBank affiliate offers or CPA offers.** You can create YouTube videos that promote any one of the tens of thousands of affiliate products listed on ClickBank.com, CJ.com, Made.com, or the dozens of CPA affiliate networks that you can find on www.cpaoffers.com.

7. **Google AdSense.** YouTube can place Google advertising on your videos and split part of the revenue with you. However, for this to happen you need to be part of their partnership program.

   If you want to apply for the partnership, you can go to www .youtube.com/partners. However, there are certain criteria you need to be compliant with before you decide to apply: You must own all copyrights to your videos, you must already have thousands of views on your videos, and you must have a fairly large subscriber base.

   If you are accepted into the YouTube partnership program then you can place ads on your YouTube videos and get a share of the revenue generated.

Seven Simple Ways to Create YouTube Videos

There are many ways to create videos for YouTube. My personal favorites include using a Flip camera or recording a PowerPoint presentation using Camtasia screen capture software. But there are many other ways, too.

1. **Create videos with a pocket camcorder.**

   The Flip video camera is a simple digital camcorder, and has been the best-selling camcorder on Amazon.com since the day of its debut, capturing about 13 percent of the camcorder market. It films high-definition video and has a pop-out USB connector that lets you plug it directly into your laptop and upload the video straight onto YouTube. It is extremely easy to use, and you can buy one on eBay or Amazon for around $70.

   The Kodak Zi8 camera offers similar features, but includes the added advantage of having an external microphone jack, for much better sound than the Flip, as well as an HDMI jack that lets you watch your video on your television set. You can buy one for around $130 to $249.

2. **Create a video with your webcam.**

   Most laptops have a built-in webcam and microphone. If you don't have a webcam already installed on your laptop, you can buy one on Amazon.com or eBay.com. Personally, I find videos of people simply sitting in front of their laptops and speaking into their webcams very dull!

3. **Create a video with your cell phone.**

   Nowadays most cell phones have a built-in digital camcorder that can produce videos as good if not better than webcams and Flip camcorders.

   Film a video, transfer it to your laptop, and then upload it to your YouTube account.

4. **Create a video with Animoto.**

   If you don't like using video editing software there is a very simple solution—Animoto (www.animoto.com).

   Animoto produces TV-quality music videos using your photos and video clips that can be ready to upload onto YouTube in just minutes. It's very easy to use. Simply choose a song as the soundtrack to your video, upload your pictures and images, and Animoto will produce a totally unique video each time.

You can use this service for free to create videos up to 30 seconds long, and it costs $30 a year for the Plus version that allows you to create full-length videos.

5. **Hire actors to film videos.**

If you need someone to star in a video, you can hire an out-of-work actor on www.mandy.com to appear in and film the video. There are many out-of-work actors who own Flip cameras or camcorders because they film themselves for auditions and to improve their acting performances.

6. **Create a video with screen capture software.**

This is my favorite way of creating YouTube videos. I use Camtasia Studio software to film my PowerPoint presentation on my computer screen and record my voice at the same time.

Camtasia Studio is a vital weapon in every laptop entrepreneur's arsenal, as it allows you to create videos that you can upload to YouTube to promote your business, create training videos for your outsourcers, and even create dozens of video-based products that you can sell to your clients.

Free alternatives include Jing (www.techsmith.com/download/jing) and CamStudio (www.camstudio.org). For Mac users I recommend the free software ScreenFlow.

7. **Create a video with Windows Movie Maker.**

You can also create videos with Windows Movie Maker software (already installed on most Windows-based laptops). The program will allow you to not only edit the video but also to add effects like titles, credits, transitions, and soundtracks to make your video an exciting multimedia experience.

I have not used Windows Movie Maker for creating videos, but I use it occasionally to edit my videos (when I need to shorten a video, or change its size, or to add my URL across the bottom of the video).

Some people take the MP3 recording of a teleseminar, or an audio interview, and create videos using Windows Movie Maker by adding images to that soundtrack.

■ ■ ■

Within a couple of months of posting videos on YouTube, I was getting an extra 30 to 40 subscribers a day on my mailing list thanks to free traffic from my YouTube videos. Imagine getting an extra 1,000 prospects a month knocking at your door to do business with you. That list was worth at least an extra $1,000 a month to my business, and YouTube was adding an *extra* $1,000 to my bottom line every month.

The case studies for Chapter 4 show you how to make a part-time or full-time income using the YouTube strategies from this chapter.

Case Study–Dawn Mendonca

This single parent quit her 9-5 job so she could pursue her passion as a dance teacher and now earns $300,000 a year thanks to YouTube!

Dawn Mendonca quit her 9-5 job to pursue her passion as a dance teacher and started uploading videos to YouTube in order to attract more students to her dance school.

She now has more than 1,500 students worldwide going through her courses every week and generates over $300,000 a year thanks to YouTube.

Dawn sent me this e-mail explaining how this happened:

I started with a 90-day challenge of making a video every day for 90 days to promote my dance school. I wanted to get comfortable making videos.

Thanks to that exercise, big-name U.K. dancers saw my videos on YouTube and approached me to help them with their own marketing!

Through making the videos I also got to find out what people wanted, because dancers and dance teachers would leave comments under each video.

I found out that what they wanted was mainly help with their dance businesses, so I provided it through mentoring, coaching, and training on "marketing your dance school" through my website www.danceteachertraining.net/blog.

I have a dance school that I franchise out to other dancers and now have a total of 1,500 students per week going through my classes. I also train dancers to become dance teachers. And clients from all over the world fly over to the United Kingdom to attend my dance courses because they have found me on YouTube!

I'm also partnering with some of my international students to launch my dance teacher training courses in California, Toronto, Ireland, and Malta.

I have built my entire dance business brand with the help of YouTube, YouTube networking, and video SEO, and I have never needed to pay a dime in advertising!

Case Study–Shaqir Hussyin

"I make $250 to $1,000 a day thanks to YouTube!"

Shaqir Hussyin has attended many of my seminars over the past couple of years. He recently revealed to me that he is making $250 to $1,000 a day thanks to the YouTube traffic hijacking method.

As I mentioned earlier, the *YouTube traffic hijacking* strategy involves getting your links on *other* people's videos. You contact the owner to offer to rent the "more info" box of their popular video, or you can even contact the owner to buy their YouTube account outright.

Underneath every video on YouTube is a space called "the description box." When you upload your video you can provide some additional information and include a link to your website in this description box. Since most people who upload videos to YouTube are not professionals or business owners or laptop entrepreneurs, they often fail to include any website link in their description box. What a wasted opportunity!

Shaqir was looking for YouTube videos that get up to 1,000 views a day and have at least 300,000 channel views, and where the owners don't have a link in their description box.

This strategy works very well, but it can be time-consuming to trawl through the millions of videos on YouTube to find videos that fit these three criteria.

This is why Shaqir uses a software tool that automates the majority of this process. This software, YouTube Tsunami, finds videos that get up to 1,000 views a day and don't have a link in their description box.

Shaqir showed me how simple it is to type in a keyword related to your niche and watch the software create a list of highly viewed YouTube videos. By simply typing the keyword "weight loss," the software found 44 videos that had no website links in their description boxes and that had more than 1 million views each.

Case Study–Kevin Clarke

"I have made an extra $8,000 so far, thanks to YouTube!"

Kevin Clarke from Nottingham, U.K., attended one of my seminars a few years ago, and it changed his life. Here is his take on YouTube marketing:

"Seven years ago I got tired of being broke. I was invited to an Internet marketing seminar in Earls Court in London, held by none other than Mark Anastasi! That was when I was exposed to Internet marketing for the first time in my life."

"Mark shared a formula with me. I followed the steps, I went home and did what he said and made $261 the next week through ClickBank! My life started to change for the better. Now it's my turn to share my simple YouTube cash formula:

1. I go to ClickBank.com and look for popular products that I can sell. I get my affiliate link, and then I shorten the URL with www.tiny.cc.
2. I then create a Camtasia video where I review the product. Be sure to give an honest and accurate opinion about the service or

product you are promoting. When creating my YouTube video. I will also make sure that I introduce myself on the video and am polite, I let the viewers know what to expect on the video. I place my affiliate link in the video, I thank my viewers for watching and encourage them to contact me if they have any questions.

3. I upload the video to my YouTube account, placing the affiliate link in the YouTube description box and using relevant keywords in the tags section, so that YouTube users and search engine users can easily find my video when they type in those keywords. Also you might find that other people post your videos to other social networks like Facebook!

4. I then drive traffic to my YouTube videos, for example, by tweeting about them or by paying people on Fiverr.com $5 for them to tell all their Facebook friends or Twitter followers about my video!"

Thanks to this strategy, Kevin has made over $8,000 in the past five months, thanks to free traffic from YouTube.

Summary

- YouTube.com was launched on February 14, 2005, and as of 2012 it is the third most visited website in the world (after Facebook and Google) with over 800 million unique visitors a month.
- Videos on YouTube are a very powerful way to connect with your audience, communicate ideas and information to them, and get them to want to do business with you. Online video gives you the power to communicate with your customers in ways the written word never can.
- Seven ways to make money from YouTube: Sell your own products or services and market yourself on YouTube; build your opt-in list; generate leads and sell them to businesses in that niche; offer a YouTube account management service for local businesses; get your YouTube videos ranked on the search engines and get free traffic from Google; promote ClickBank affiliate offers or CPA offers on your

YouTube videos; join the YouTube partner program and earn money from having Google AdSense pop up on your videos.

- The YouTube hijacking strategy involves contacting YouTube video owners that are getting over 30,000 views a month and buying or renting their account. This has proven to be very successful in the past few years.
- Seven simple ways to create YouTube videos: Use a Flip camera or Kodak Zi8, use your webcam, use your mobile phone, create a video through Animoto.com, hire out-of-work actors at www.mandy.com to film videos for you, create a video with Camtasia software, use Windows Movie Maker.

Millionaire Secret: You Become Who You Spend Time With

One day I was on the phone with the Laptop Millionaire, and he asked me the most peculiar question. "What is the average net worth of the six people you spend the most amount of time with?"

"What do you mean?" I replied.

"Well, I don't think I've ever mentioned this to you, but this is another Millionaire Secret: You become who you spend time with."

"I'm telling you this now because I've just decided to cut certain people out of my life and I'm joining a $25,000 a year Mastermind group of Internet marketers. You've got to make more than 1 million dollars a year to be part of this group, and we meet three times a year to discuss how we can take our businesses forward. It's all about having a better peer group—one that challenges you to grow beyond your existing comfort zone."

"And this is how you tell me that you don't want me in your life?" I said, jokingly.

"Ha ha! No! I'm glad to say, you've made the cut! But I do have people in my life who are not happy about seeing me succeed, because of how it makes them feel about themselves and their own situations. I need to remove them from my life."

If you are truly committed to achieving your goals, as harsh as it may sound, you may want to consider who you allow to be in your own peer group. Your life and personal happiness are simply too important to allow any dream stealers in.

You see, ever since we were born, we've learned that we can only survive if the people around us love us and accept us.

Whereas in the rest of the animal kingdom, most offspring are out on their own pretty quickly, the human baby is born *years* prematurely and can't fend for itself. It therefore must rely on its parents' love for survival and protection for many years.

Deep down in the subconscious of every human being, there is this irrational, intense fear that "If the people around me don't like me or love me, I'll die."

The result is that we often sacrifice our own desires and aspirations just to fit in with the people around us or just to make other people comfortable, or just to please people.

This means that if the people around you are broke and miserable you will find a way to be broke and miserable, too. Subconsciously, this is hard-wired into us.

The cool thing about this is that you can use this to your advantage.

How? By hanging out with happy, successful, rich people!

You will be amazed at how fast your subconscious mind will help you succeed and make a lot more money out of fear that your new rich friends won't like you, accept you, or love you if you don't! This little technique is very, very powerful, and not to be underestimated!

I joined a Mastermind of highly successful Internet entrepreneurs and I changed my peer group to surround myself with high-net-worth individuals. I found that spending time with people for whom the minimum expectation was to earn at least a million dollars a year automatically raised my own standards of what I expect of myself. Within a year my annual turnover quadrupled to over 1 million dollars.

Look at the six people you spend the most time with. That's who you will become.

5

Facebook

Facebook is the world's most popular social networking service with more than 800 million active users (if Facebook were a country, it would be the third largest country in the world).

What is truly remarkable is that unlike most websites that people only visit fleetingly, according to the Nielsen ratings agency, the average user visits Facebook four times a day and spends 19.5 minutes a day on the site!

In the war for user attention, Facebook is king.

Facebook was launched to the wider public on September 26, 2006, and in the space of just a few years has skyrocketed to a stock market valuation in excess of $80 billion.

A few more statistics regarding the Facebook phenomenon:

- Facebook is available in more than 70 languages.
- There are more than 350 million active users currently accessing Facebook through their mobile devices.
- The average Facebook user has 130 friends on the site.
- The average user is connected to 80 community pages (Facebook pages), groups, and events.
- On average, more than 250 million photos are uploaded per day. (Source: www.facebook.com/press/info.php?statistics.)

And Facebook is no longer just for kids and students. Thirty-one percent of Facebook users are over the age of 35 (that's over 250 million people) and it's the fastest-growing segment in Facebook.

THREE REASONS WHY FACEBOOK IS FOR MORE THAN STAYING IN TOUCH WITH FRIENDS

1. Facebook Ads are a cost-effective promotional tool.
2. Small businesses can connect with customers.
3. Entrepreneurs and small business owners can connect with one another.

With so many visitors and so much traffic coursing through this site every day, it is no surprise that thousands of laptop entrepreneurs are making a full-time living using Facebook from the comfort of their home.

If you're not on Facebook yet, now is the time to get started. If you're on Facebook already, now is the time to start thinking like a laptop entrepreneur. Facebook is another way to make money online. All you need to do is find the tactics and strategies that work for you.

The Keys to Making Money on Facebook

At around the same time I was exploring YouTube marketing tactics, I got an e-mail from Tom Chambers, a 25-year-old Australian living in London.

Tom had attended my Speed Cash Seminar, and he was letting me know that he had made $2,700 that month promoting ClickBank products on Facebook.

I congratulated him, wished him well, and thought little more of it. That is, until he sent me an e-mail two months later informing me that his Facebook venture had grown to a $20,000-a-month business!

Tom's strategy was simple, though it went against the Facebook terms of use that stipulate that each user can only have a single Facebook account. Tom created hundreds of Facebook profiles (accounts) and Facebook Pages, each one targeting a specific niche market (for example, weight loss, fear of flying, and so on).

The benefit of having Facebook accounts and Facebook pages is that you can broadcast your message to thousands of friends and fans every single day, simply by posting an update on your personal Facebook wall or on your Facebook page wall. You can get a lot of traffic and a lot of exposure this way, for free!

Let me explain. A Facebook page or Facebook fan page is a miniature landing page on Facebook, kind of like a blog, that allows a business or an organization to communicate with other users (check out www.facebook .com/MarkAnastasiSeminars). It is different from a Facebook profile, which represents you as a person.

Having a Facebook page allows you to have tens of thousands of people "like" your page (by clicking on the "Like" button) and becoming a fan.

This means that when you write a status update on your Facebook page, the fans of your page get to see it in their newsfeed on Facebook.

Another great thing about Facebook pages is that they can be incredibly viral, because friends of your fans (or even friends of the friends of your fans) can see that, for example, John Smith likes your page and go and check it out, as well.

Back to our story about Tom . . .

Tom started adding thousands of Facebook friends across his various Facebook profiles every week and then invited them to join his various pages.

Every day he posts information on his wall that would be relevant to their particular interests (for example, articles or YouTube videos about overcoming the fear of flying), and from time to time he promotes relevant affiliate products to them in the same way.

He found that by promoting ClickBank affiliate products, he could make approximately $0.20 per fan, per month. This means that for every 10,000 Facebook fans he got, he could earn as much as $2,000 a month from his laptop!

If every month just 10 people out of every 1,000 fans you have buy a product for $40, and you make a 50 percent commission, this means that you've made 10 $20 × or $200. In other words, if just 1 percent of your Facebook fans buys something you've recommended to them every month, you could be making $0.20 per fan per month.

Tom hired a handful of outsourcers to help him manage all of his different Facebook accounts and Facebook fan pages, and with this added leverage he quickly grew his reach to more than 100,000 Facebook fans. This rapidly grew his income to more than $20,000 a month.

Watch our exclusive video of Tom revealing his strategy step-by-step on stage at the Social Media Millionaire Summit at www.laptopmillionaire.tv/ tomchambers.

When I posted this story on my own Facebook wall and asked my other students if they had made money using Facebook, I immediately started receiving a deluge of responses.

Georgina, a former mortgage broker, didn't know anything about Internet marketing, but one day she stumbled across Facebook, and she quickly found out that for every 1,000 friends she had on Facebook, she could make $100 a week ($400 a month, approximately) through promoting products.

So she decided to get as many Facebook friends as possible, in the shortest time possible. She hired 10 outsourcers from the Philippines, paying them $200 each to grow her various Facebook accounts for her. Within two weeks she had 20,324 new Facebook friends and she started making over $8,000 a month thanks to Facebook!

Georgina now makes $11,000 a month, on autopilot, by having her outsourcers promote ClickBank affiliate products to her Facebook friends and Facebook fans in a dozen different niche markets. Listen to my exclusive interview with Georgina at www.laptopmillionaire.tv/georginalany.

Another response came from Glen, a 25-year-old musician. He was looking for a way to make money so that he could focus on doing what he loved: playing music with his band.

Glen attended my ClickBank Summit and watched my social media webinars online, where I was sharing some of my strategies with my clients. Like Tom Chambers, Glen started building up hundreds of Facebook accounts and Facebook pages, and by promoting relevant offers to them he found that he could make $0.20 to $0.25 per fan per month. Thanks to Facebook, Glen was able to make as much as $3,000 a week.

Watch our exclusive video of Glen on stage at The Ultimate Facebook Marketing Seminar at www.laptopmillionaire.tv/glenkirkham).

I also received this message from Vesna Flo, a coaching client of mine from Slovenia:

"Hi Mark, thank you for your coaching. By the way, I made $1,600 in just seven days, simply by posting a massage therapy offer of mine on my Facebook profile!"

Paul Wakefield sent me a message informing me that he'd made close to $3,000 in eight days thanks to Facebook and $12,000 in nine weeks by promoting his marketing service to his Facebook friends:

"In the past four months I have been on pretty much all your webinars. I implemented what I learned and made $3,010 in eight days and

$12,568 in the following nine weeks, thanks to Facebook! Thank you, Mark, for all your advice. I look forward to following and learning more from you."

Another message came in from Jonathan Pitts, a young entrepreneur who learned about how to use Facebook fan pages and got three businesses as clients:

"I attended your seminar five weeks ago and I'm already making money thanks to Facebook! I set up a professional Facebook fan page and I'm managing the Facebook marketing for one of the top cosmetic dentists in the country.

"I charged $300 for the fan page design, and for every fan I get to their page I earn $0.60, so for every 1,000 fans I get to like their fan page I make $600.

"I also have two more clients lined up who were fascinated at what Facebook could do for them!"

Martin Welch wrote in to let me know he also was profiting thanks to Facebook: "I agreed to a $3,000 deal to do Facebook marketing for a company within four weeks of studying your course. My input is only about 20 minutes a day. Thanks for adding the value Mark."

Many more of my coaching clients wrote in to let me know of their successes with Facebook marketing, including Nadeem Malik, who makes $1,200 a month thanks to his Facebook pages, and Peter Osigbe, who e-mailed me to let me know that he's made $10,000 in three months thanks to Facebook, since joining my coaching program.

Personally, I use Facebook to stay in touch with my fans and my students and to promote my webinars, workshops, and seminars to them through my Facebook fan page at www.facebook.com/markanastasiseminars.

Thanks to Facebook traffic, I regularly get a few thousand visitors a month to my websites. But I prefer to use Facebook to promote specific events, through the Facebook Events application (more on this later).

The first time I ran a Facebook event to promote one of my seminars, it resulted in getting 60 more attendees and $40,000 in extra sales.

Another time, I ran a five-day marketing campaign to promote a webinar exclusively through Facebook, as a test. I promoted this live event to my 14,000 friends and fans on Facebook, and in five days I got 881 registrations for my webinar, at zero cost. The webinar generated $22,000 in sales.

How to Turn $952 into $30,000 in Seven Days Thanks to Facebook Ads

Facebook Ads are a way to advertise to Facebook users, beyond your fans and friends. The ads allow you to reach your target customers by deciding age, location, and interests of the people you want to see the ad. You can also promote your Facebook page or website and have people "like" it to keep building your online community.

I was once asked by my friend Nik Halik to help him promote his one-day seminar in Cyprus. His promoter had let him down, so I stepped in to help him fill the room, and with just seven days to go until the event, I started a Facebook Ads campaign.

Anyone can get a Facebook Ads account (you just need a Facebook account and a credit card). It is a self-service ad platform, which means you don't need to call a number, negotiate with sales reps, or spend time jumping through hoops to qualify for an account.

Facebook Ads allow you to advertise to the 800 million Facebook users.

For a small ad that I created, I paid $0.18 per click (every time someone clicked on my ad and visited the website, I was charged $0.18). By the end of my seven-day advertising campaign, I had spent $952 to get 11.5 million ad impressions, 5,170 clicks on the ad, and 192 registrations for the seminar.

Our $952 investment in Facebook Ads, over seven days of marketing, resulted in $30,000 in sales during the event.

Eight Ways to Get More Facebook Fans

If you want to get a lot of free traffic thanks to Facebook every single day, your best bet is to build some Facebook pages (go to www.facebook.com/pages and click on Create Page).

Once you've created your Facebook page, you need to get thousands of people to "Like" your page and become fans. Through doing research, I've found that people can earn on average $0.05 to $0.25 per fan per month, as long as you promote good, relevant offers to your fans.

In other words, if you want to make, say, $4,000 a month using Facebook pages, ask yourself, "How can I quickly get 40,000 fans to my various Facebook pages?"

Here are eight ways for you to get more fans:

1. Invite your Facebook friends to "Like" your page.
2. Post interesting, relevant, useful updates two to four times a day, to benefit from viral growth. The more your fans comment on and share your posts, the more of their friends see your posts as well and the faster your number of fans grows.
3. Have a link to your fan page on every page on your website and in the signature file at the bottom of every e-mail you send out.
4. Offer a great incentive for people to become a fan (for example, give people access to a free e-book of yours in exchange for liking your page, or give them a chance to win something).
5. Go to Fiverr.com and pay people $5 to promote your Facebook page to all of their Facebook friends, their Facebook fans, or their Twitter followers. (I got 11,300 fans in six weeks by spending $320 buying 64 such gigs on Fiverr.com.)
6. Hire outsourcers to invite relevant Facebook users to become fans of your page (they could contact people who are members of Facebook pages and groups about weight loss to like your Atkins Diet page). Some sites where you can find outsourcers include Elance.com, vWorker.com, oDesk.com, Freelancer.com, Guru.com, ContentDivas .com, 123Employee.com, ScriptLance.com, HireMyMom.com, and PeoplePerHour.com.
7. Contact other Facebook page owners and suggest doing a free-of-charge cross-promotion: "I'll promote your page to my Facebook friends and fans in exchange for you promoting my page to yours."
8. Use Facebook Ads to pay for traffic to your Fan page. Anthony Mink spent over $10,000 to get 100,000 fans to his Pittsburgh Steelers page (www.facebook.com/steelersfever). Within a few months this had grown virally, at no extra cost, to 400,000 fans, and he started making up to $24,000 a month by promoting relevant offers to them!

Six Ways to Make Money Thanks to Facebook

Now that you have Facebook fans, the next step is using those fans to generate revenue.

Drive Traffic to Your Websites and Build Your Mailing List

You can get traffic to your websites by simply posting updates on your Facebook wall and on your Facebook page wall. This is how I like to use Facebook to drive traffic to my websites, my seminar registration pages, and my live webinars. By promoting my websites to my 14,000 Facebook friends and fans, I get thousands of clicks a month for free.

Whether you have a business, website, newsletter, or service to promote, Facebook is a compelling way to drive traffic.

As I mentioned earlier, Vesna Flo made $1,600 in seven days by simply posting an offer for her massage business, and Paul Wakefield made close to $3,000 in eight days and $12,000 in the following nine weeks by promoting his marketing service on his Facebook wall.

My friend Chris Farrell, a former radio DJ, told me he's getting close to 13,000 targeted visitors to his website every month thanks to Facebook, for free.

Dean Hunt, another Briton living in the United States, posted on his Facebook wall that he got 37,000 hits to his website in a single month, just thanks to Facebook!

Affiliate Marketing

In the same way, instead of driving traffic to your own websites or opt-in pages, you can drive traffic to affiliate offers or cost-per-action (CPA) offers.

Tom Chambers, Georgina Lany, and Glen Kirkham started making money online by promoting some of the 12,000 available affiliate offers from Click Bank.com.

For example, Tom built a Facebook page about how to overcome the fear of flying and was making as much as $800 a month by promoting affiliate products that help overcome this phobia.

Georgina Lany set up a Facebook page about dating advice for gay men and started making up to $1,000 a month by promoting affiliate products to that niche market.

Nadeem Malik set up his Facebook page and started making $1,200 a month on average, by promoting affiliate offers to the 4,500 fans of his page.

You can see how by setting up 20 or more Facebook pages in different niche markets, it is no surprise that so many laptop entrepreneurs are making a full-time living just thanks to Facebook.

Facebook Events

A cool feature of Facebook profiles and of Facebook pages is that they allow you to organize a Facebook event. Facebook notifies your friends and fans about your event, and this event is then is displayed in your friends' and fans' calendars on Facebook up until the date of the event.

And best of all, you can invite all your Facebook friends and fans to attend your event and even message them via Facebook (up to 5,000 people at a time). And of course, they can invite all of their friends to register for your event, too.

Setting up a Facebook event could not be simpler and only takes a couple of minutes. Once you've logged into your Facebook account, go to www .facebook.com/events/create and set up your event by typing in the title, the date, the location, a brief description of the event and how someone can sign up. You can also upload a picture.

You can use Facebook events to promote your product launches, your webinars, or your live events, and you can interact with your attendees on the event wall.

As I mentioned earlier, the first time I created a Facebook event to promote one of my seminars, it resulted in 60 more attendees and $40,000 in extra sales. And when I ran a five-day marketing campaign to promote a webinar exclusively to my 14,000 friends and fans on Facebook, I got 881 registrations, and I generated $22,000 in sales during the webinar.

Facebook Management and Social Media Management

There are over 100 million small and medium-sized businesses around the world, and more and more of them are realizing that their traditional approach to marketing—Yellow Pages, classified ads, radio and TV advertising—is simply not working anymore, because the way people live, spend time, and access information has changed.

With 800 million users, Facebook presents a golden opportunity for businesses to find and communicate with their prospects online. Business owners worldwide know that they need to have an online presence and use social media, but most don't know how.

This has created a massive opportunity for savvy marketers to offer Facebook marketing services. They can sell services such as:

- Setting up a Facebook page.
- Managing a Facebook page and updating it daily.
- Getting more fans for a customer's Facebook page.
- Creating a Facebook app for a client's business.
- Generating leads via Facebook and selling them to businesses.

Jonathan Pitts signed up three businesses as clients for his Facebook services within five weeks of attending my seminar. He charges $0.60 per fan that he gets for a client.

Martin Welch agreed to a $3,000 Facebook marketing deal with a company within four weeks of studying my course.

Fifteen-year-old Jelle Kaldenbach made $2,781 in three weeks by selling Facebook apps to local businesses in his area.

This type of service represents a huge growth area! (Find out more in Chapter 9, Local Business Marketing.)

Joint Ventures

Facebook can be a *goldmine* of joint venturing opportunity. Thanks to Facebook's pages, groups, and search functionality you can find hundreds of entrepreneurs in your field with whom to network and do business.

I use this strategy to find speakers for my seminars, marketers to do joint venture webinars with, or simply other Facebook page owners who I can do joint venture cross-promotions with.

My friend Tracy Repchuk recently connected with an entrepreneur via Facebook that resulted in a $250,000-a-year business deal.

Social media expert Robert Grant used Facebook in 2009 to identify and contact potential joint venture partners in his market. As a result, he generated more than $500,000 in sales in his first year in business.

You might find that by using Facebook you only need to connect with a handful of key people to completely change your life (I've seen this described as "the secret to turning your Facebook friends into $100,000 a year").

Go to www.facebook.com/pages and search for entrepreneurs and Facebook pages relevant to your topic or field, contact the owners with a complimentary message about them or their Facebook pages, and propose a joint venture with them.

For example, you might say something like this: "Hello George, I hope you are well. I love your page/website/product, and I would like to help you get more sales/business/traffic. Would you be interested in doing a joint venture? I can promote your website to my 11,000 subscribers for free in exchange for you promoting my website to yours. What do you think? Let me know if this sounds interesting. I would love to do business with you, and I welcome your ideas and suggestions. Warm regards, John."

Facebook Ads

Facebook Ads have proved to be a boon to marketers all around the world, because they allow anyone with a Facebook account and a credit card to advertise to the 800 million or so Facebook users worldwide, even if they're just starting out with $100.

What is revolutionary about Facebook advertising is that Facebook gives you more data than any other advertising medium has ever done. Why? Because people on Facebook tell you what they're interested in! Facebook Ads provide you with seven key targeting options:

1. Geographic location
2. Age
3. Birthday
4. Likes and interests
5. Education
6. Workplace
7. Relationship status

This type of demographic and personal data allows you to laser-target your advertising, which means you can advertise to *only* the people you know are going to be interested in your offer, which in turn means less wasted money and a much higher ROI on your advertising campaigns.

What is fantastic about having these various types of data is that they create numerous possible combinations. You might find that your ad works incredibly well for women, ages 35 to 38, living in Sydney, Australia, or that it appeals to men ages 27 to 32, living in Paris, who are interested in football. The possibilities are endless!

I shared with you earlier how I turned $952 into $30,000 in seven days thanks to Facebook Ads, but as I started doing some research about this advertising medium I realized that a lot of laptop entrepreneurs were making a fortune from this strategy.

- Twenty-four-year-old American student Justin Dupre, living in Thailand, spends $20,000 a month on Facebook Ads, promoting affiliate and CPA offers, getting a 50 percent or more daily ROI for a total profit of approximately $10,000 a month. "Average figures look like anything $300 to $1,000 a day. Good months can bring in $50k plus for me just on Facebook," he says.
- Twenty-six -year-old Jonathan Volk did $3,693 a day, on average, for 10 months, generating over 10 million clicks and raking in $1,107,963 in the process thanks to affiliate marketing through Facebook Ads.
- Adeel Chowdhry, a successful marketer, recently did $144,998 in sales in a single month, thanks to Facebook Ads promoting his webinars.

To create a Facebook Ad, go to www.facebook.com/ads and click on Create an Ad, and then type in a title, some body text, and add an image. Then select your targeting options (for example, men ages 45 to 49, living in London, who are single, and who are interested in marketing).

The key here is to *test* different ads. Create three or four ads, and see which one gets the most clicks at the cheapest cost. That ad becomes your control ad.

Then play "beat the control"—this means deleting the other two or three ads, and creating two or three new ads to try to beat the results of the control ad. Delete the worst-performing ads, and continue trying to beat the control until you are happy with the results.

By doing this, you'll end up with one ad that works very well. Make sense?

Also, be very careful when buying traffic or paying for online ads, as you could lose a fortune if you're not careful and you don't know what you're doing.

Educate yourself about this method and start small.

With mobile marketing, Facebook apps, proximity marketing, and Bluetooth marketing being some major marketing innovations and breakthroughs on the horizon, a lot of entrepreneurs consider Facebook to be the future of online advertising.

Let's jump into a few longer case studies that describe how others have used these strategies.

■ ■ ■

Case Study–Nadeem Malik

"I make $1,200 a month thanks to Facebook pages!"

Nadeem Malik is of Polish and Indian descent and lives in the United Kingdom. He attended many of my live seminars and joined my coaching program. During one of our monthly coaching calls, he mentioned casually that he was making $1,200 a month using Facebook.

"Oh, by the way . . . in the past 30 days I set up a Facebook page, got 4,500 Likes for the page, and made $1,200 in affiliate commissions."

What is even more interesting is that he has continued to average $0.26 per fan per month.

Nadeem set up a Facebook page called Millionaire Club. You can find it at www.facebook.com/millionaireclub.

Typically he will post a daily quote about wealth, success, or how to become a millionaire, and he alternates posting affiliate offers on his Facebook page's wall (some sales earn him as much as $400 in commission!).

Listen to my exclusive interview with Nadeem at www.laptopmillionaire.tv/nadeemmalik.

Case Study–Suraj Sodha

"I make $1,300 to $1,600 a month thanks to Facebook pages!"

Suraj Sodha also lives in the United Kingdom and has attended quite a few of my seminars.

He now makes $1,300 to $1,600 a month using Facebook pages, as he explains below:

My main Facebook profits come from the NLP/personal development niche and also the IM (Internet marketing) niche. I am working on building pages for other niches but those two are the ones I can talk about with confidence.

For the NLP (neuro-linguistic programming) and personal development part I have one page with approximately 200 fans. I also have a group for the same niche with around 420 members. I update the page more regularly than the group because group messages risk being seen as too much like spam if too many are sent. With a page, the message shows up in members' newsfeeds, which is much less obtrusive.

I update the page at least twice a week if there is a relevant product or event to promote. I will mix it up so I won't be putting out the same updates about the same event for two weeks straight. With the group, I will message maybe once a month or twice a month at most.

I usually use that group list for joint ventures with other NLP people or clients who are NLP trainers and coaches. Depending on the product or event, I will make about $400 to $800 a month from that group.

In terms of the strategy for adding members to that group, the way I started doing it was to invite some of the leading speakers and experts in that industry. Then when they joined (and they all did) people who were Facebook friends with them saw on their profile that they had joined this group. Using that power of association, lots of others joined, too, and that became viral.

I also tag photos of industry experts and make a special photo album in the group so people can see who our favorite speakers are. By tagging them, it displays on their walls, too, so others see it and join the group, too.

I also have some private groups that cannot be found unless you are invited. These are made up of clients, people I meet at specific seminars, and other hand-selected individuals. This creates the sense of an exclusive club, and I promote products and events in these groups, too.

In terms of the Internet marketing niche, I focus more on Facebook pages here because they are more visible to the search engines (groups are completely blocked from search engines).

The strategy for adding members to the pages is the same as above. I promote Internet marketing events and products and my own services to these groups and pages. I have about 500 combined members in the Internet marketing niche on Facebook.

From the IM niche pages and groups I make around $600 a month depending on how aggressively I promote offers to them.

I update my IM page about six to eight times a month depending on my blog content frequency. Sometimes, if I have a particularly good product to promote, I'll promote it to the group/page using Facebook Ads, but it's not something I do very often.

I rely on SEO and other people sharing the content from the group/page, which, in turn, attracts others to join, too. I also use Twitter and e-mail signatures to invite people to join my groups and pages.

Listen to our exclusive interview with Suraj Sodha at www.laptop millionaire.tv/surajsodha.

Case Study–Ben H.

"I make $1,000 to $5,000 a month thanks to Facebook!"

Ben H. is another of our seminar attendees who profits from using Facebook. Having attended a few of my seminars, Ben decided to start building up his Facebook groups, and he now makes $1,000 to $5,000 a month by marketing to his group members.

Here's what he has to say about this strategy and his results:

I have a number of Facebook groups, ranging from 200 members to about 1,000. The reason I like to have groups is they are like mini mailing lists that are totally free. Here is how I do it.

First, I create three Facebook accounts, and I add friends to them and build them up. I do this is by joining other groups in the relevant niche. Then I just add everyone and when there are 200 friends or so in a Facebook profile I create a group. I then invite all my friends to join my group. I add them all to the three Facebook profiles. A fair number will join each time; then I just build my account and do the same again. I then message all the people in my group—I *never* just send out a link to an affiliate site or my own website; I always send them to my blog. That way I don't get spam complaints. I send them to a specific post and they will usually click through the link I have in the post, which could be a ClickBank affiliate link or whatever. Just provide valuable information and they will love it.

I now make between $1,000 to $5,000 per month from this technique alone.

It's really a cool way to do it and super easy and best of all—it's *free*! I message the people about once a week, sometimes twice. It's pretty flexible. I personally love this method. It is simple, free, and builds a list you can market to.

Case Study–Vlad Danciu

"I make $3,000 to $4,000 a month from selling Facebook pages!"

Vlad Danciu is a 22-year-old student from Romania, who has been following my seminars online in the past year.

Whereas Tom, Georgina, Glen, Peter, Ben, and others you have heard about, created Facebook groups and pages in order to promote affiliate products or their own offers, Vlad likes to *sell* his groups and pages (complete with approximately 5,000 members or fans) to other entrepreneurs for $650 to $1,000 *each*.

He posts this message on his Facebook account wall from time to time:

Hey guys—I can do 5,000 fans to a fan page or 5,000 members to a group for $650. The package also contains customization of the page design and integration of squeeze page. That's $0.13 per fan or member. Message me if you're interested.

He gets about 10 requests a month from entrepreneurs who want Facebook pages and groups built for them, but he can only fulfill five of these requests per month and has to put his clients on a waiting list.

Vlad makes $3,000 to $4,000 a month this way, and by the way, the average income in Romania is only $300 per month.

Here's a 22-year-old earning 10 times the average monthly income in his country—and he does this from his laptop!

How does he quickly get 5,000 fans or members to his pages and groups?

One shortcut he used involved buying various Facebook accounts and Facebook fan pages from friends of his.

When he takes on a client, he promotes their page or group to all his Facebook friends, across 27 accounts; this helps him quickly get 5,000 members into a Facebook group or page at zero cost to him.

Why do *so many* entrepreneurs want to build Facebook pages and groups with 5,000 members or more?

Answer: because they *know* that each member or fan can be worth at least $0.20 per month, by promoting your website, your business, affiliate offers, CPA offers, and webinars to them.

Listen to our exclusive interview with Vlad Danciu at www.laptop millionaire.tv/vladdanciu.

Summary

- Facebook is one of the most trafficked websites on the Internet. Make sure you have a presence on Facebook. Don't miss out!
- Remember: traffic equals money.
- Facebook users typically log on to the site four times a day and spend an average of 19.5 minutes a day on the site.

- If you want to make more money, build some Facebook pages, grow your list of fans, and interact with and add value for your fans. You could be making $0.05 to $0.25 per fan per month by promoting interesting and relevant offers to them.
- Share valuable content with your Facebook fans. Give them exclusive content from time to time.
- Monetize your Facebook fan pages in multiple ways. (Build a list, promote CPA offers, promote ClickBank offers, promote a "done for you" offer, promote your webinars, etc.)
- There are 100 million small and medium-sized businesses worldwide, and the majority of them need a presence on Facebook.
- You can leverage other people's Facebook networks and their thousands of fans, by arranging joint ventures with them or by buying gigs on Fiverr.com.
- Facebook Ads have proved to be a boon to marketers because they allow them to advertise to Facebook users worldwide, and they provide insight into what these users are interested in.
- To find out more about how you can profit from Facebook marketing check out The Ultimate Facebook Marketing Seminar on DVD at www.laptopmillionaire.tv/dvd.

6 Twitter

Twitter.com is a free microblogging platform. It allows you to post tweets (short messages of 140 characters or less) that can be seen by your followers on Twitter.

When you log in to your Twitter account, you can see the latest tweets from the people you follow. You can follow your friends, people in your industry, or experts in a specific field. For example, perhaps you follow some football-related blogs and online magazines, and you get to see in one place all the latest tweets from the world of football.

Twitter recently announced that it has 100 million users logging in at least once a month and 50 million active users who log in every day (again, just like Facebook, this represents a *lot* of traffic).

Twitter's founder, Jack Dorsey, says, "Our mission is to instantly connect people everywhere to what's most meaningful to them."

Naturally, the more Twitter followers you have and the more often you post tweets, the more exposure and traffic you can get to promote your business, build your mailing list, or promote affiliate offers.

You could have 100,000 Twitter followers or even 1 or 2 million Twitter followers. It's not surprising to get 100,000 Twitter followers in 30 days.

I was first alerted to the fact that laptop entrepreneurs could make money by using Twitter when I spoke to a woman who came to my Internet Millionaire Bootcamp in early 2009. Her name was Mili Ponce.

Mili explained to me that she knew nothing about Internet marketing when she started. She was a single mom working in IT support. And yet, within a month she had built up a few thousand Twitter followers and made $800 online by promoting affiliate products to them.

She told me that she had spent a whole month researching everything she could about Twitter and how to get traffic by using the microblogging site, and she tried many different strategies.

Cheekily, she did this while still working at her IT job, which required her to sit at her laptop all day long but afforded her some free time in between dealing with support inquiries.

In her second month online, Mili made $1,700. Then, in month three, she made $2,500. By month five, she started running Twitter marketing campaigns for speakers, authors, and various small businesses, and made $10,000.

I caught up with Mili recently, and she informed me that she can now get up to 800 clicks in half an hour thanks to her tweets, and she makes over $30,000 a month from promoting affiliate products, her own products, as well as her own webinars, workshops, and social media services through Twitter!

How much did it cost her to set up her business: Nothing! Zero! And the best part of all, is that she can run her business from anywhere around the world . . . *from her phone or laptop!*

To help her growing business, Mili hired five outsourcers in the Philippines who are working every day to increase traffic to her site using Twitter and other social media channels (more on outsourcing in Chapter 9).

Watch Mili Ponce on stage at the Social Media Millionaire Summit at www.laptopmillionaire.tv/miliponce.

Profiting from Twitter Traffic

Many more laptop entrepreneurs have profited from huge traffic flows on Twitter since then.

Paul O'Mahony worked as a manager for a large corporation in Ireland, and after seeing me give a brief talk at an event in Dublin he decided to attend my workshop. Mili Ponce happened to be there as well that weekend, and she shared her Twitter marketing strategies with the rest of the attendees.

Paul took action straightaway. He went home and set up some Twitter accounts and started building up his numbers of followers on the site.

Thanks to Mili's Twitter-related strategies, to his utmost surprise he made his first two sales online *during* the workshop! In fact, they happened while he was asleep before the second day of the workshop! In the ensuing seven months he made $50,000 by using Twitter to promote ClickBank affiliate products to his followers as well as by offering to set up and manage Twitter accounts for businesses.

To listen to an exclusive interview with Paul O'Mahony, go to www .laptopmillionaire.tv/paulomahony.

I shared Mili's strategy with my friend Alexandra. Alexandra decided to try her hand at using Twitter as well, and thanks to software like TweetAdder.com she was able to attract 96,000 new Twitter followers within three weeks and over 200,000 followers within two months!

She now gets close to 400 clicks *per tweet!* She regularly makes $400 to $500 a week from promoting ClickBank affiliate products to her Twitter followers.

Alexandra then shared this strategy with her brother Johny, an out-of-work actor, who was working as a construction worker in Slovakia to make ends meet and take care of his newborn daughter. Before long, he was making up to $700 a week from his laptop. No more grueling construction work for him!

With some help from his sister, Johny started building up his Twitter accounts. Within a couple of months he had over 100,000 Twitter followers, and that's when he started promoting ClickBank affiliate products to them every day.

He made $83 his first week online, then $185 in his second week, $350 his third week, and $433 in his fourth week. That's $951 in his first month online!

Within three months he was able to make $700 a week thanks to affiliate marketing. (His record is $834 in a single week.) As you can imagine, this has completely changed his life.

Alexandra then coached her friend Corinna on how to use Twitter. Corinna was 26 years old and had worked in television production in the United Kingdom for a few years. Although she was very good at what she did and she worked hard at her job, by the time she reached her mid-20s she had been made redundant four times!

This time, she had been unemployed for a year, and she was no longer keen to find another job—she had learned that having a job did not necessarily mean having financial security, and she made up her mind to set up her own business.

Her unemployment benefits were about to run out, and she knew she had to take action quickly. She attended a couple of my seminars in London, and with Alexandra's help she started building up her Twitter accounts.

Thanks to a powerful Twitter-related software tool, Corinna was able to set up 120 Twitter accounts in just minutes, and within five weeks she had more than 110,000 Twitter followers across her various accounts. She was now ready to start monetizing her Twitter business by promoting affiliate offers in her tweets.

She went to ClickBank.com and selected a handful of interesting products that were selling very well from the 12,000 or so products available on the site. By tweeting about two products and including her affiliate link in her tweet, she made $21.10 on her first day.

When she saw that she had made money online she burst out of her room shaking, she says. She was in shock! She simply couldn't believe that something that she had tried *had actually worked!* The excitement and trepidation were such that she said she thought she would faint.

She ended up making $94.35 in her first week, $219.72 her second week, and $250.55 her third week. She then started using Twitter to build her mailing list, and within 90 days she had 3,600 subscribers on her mailing list.

She now makes over $500 a week thanks to Twitter, social media, and her mailing list, and she even made $16,000 in 90 minutes thanks to her first webinar. (Find out more about webinars in Chapter 10!)

Check out my interview with Corinna at www.laptopmillionaire.tv/corinna.

Just this week, I found out that Alexandra coached her friends Raoul and Marika in Slovakia, and now they're making a hundred dollars a week using Twitter!

Six Ways to Make Money Thanks to Twitter

If you want to get more traffic and make money using Twitter, the first thing you need to do is set up your Twitter account at www.twitter.com. The process only takes two minutes and it's free of charge.

I recommend that you use a professional-looking background; you can get these done for free at www.twitbacks.com.

Once you have your Twitter account, you can start looking at ways to monetize your Twitter traffic. There are five main ways to use Twitter to make money:

1. Promote Your Business to Your Followers

You can get free traffic to your website and promote your business by simply sending tweets to your followers. Twitter allows you to stay in touch with your prospects, fans, and clients, and represents another way to communicate news and information about your new products as well as emphasizing the benefits of doing business with you.

And, of course, you can find potential customers on Twitter and get them to become prospects and then customers of your business. One effective way to build your mailing list is by posting tweets letting your followers know that you are giving away a free report, for example.

Mark Curtis-Wood has been a client of mine for a few years now, and he posted this message on my Facebook wall after attending my social media seminar:

> Hi Mark, I launched a whole site through Twitter that generated an opt-in list of over 350 people in just 10 days and *brought in over $9,832 worth of revenue.* by selling a $297 course to 33 of my new subscribers.
>
> I have gone on to use Twitter to build niche lists in specific sectors and continue to make regular online income using Twitter. The ability to reach such a wide Market so quickly makes Twitter such a critical part of my future traffic strategy.

2. Promote Affiliate Products to Your Followers

This is the monetization strategy that Mili, Paul, Alexandra, Johny, Corinna, and Raoul all started with—as did countless other laptop entrepreneurs—and it simply involves posting tweets that promote affiliate products.

For example, you could set up a Twitter account about snowboarding, and then use Twitter's Who to Follow function (see Figure 6.1) or its search function to find people who are interested in snowboarding or who are snowboarding experts, or who are talking about snowboarding. You would then click to follow them, and typically 30 to 40 percent of them will follow you back.

So, for example, if you follow 300 snowboarding enthusiasts a day, you could be growing your Twitter account by 100 or so of them per day, or approximately 3,000 a month.

And of course, from time to time you could promote some snowboarding-related offers and products to those followers.

FIGURE 6.1 Twitter's Who to Follow Function

One of my students, Sotiris Bassarakopoulos from Belfast, in Northern Ireland, attended a few of my seminars and when he saw how many people were profiting from using Twitter, he quickly set up some Twitter accounts and started promoting ClickBank products to his followers. He told me later that he made $3,000 in sales in just one month thanks to Twitter.

Note: Although this strategy has been one of the fastest ways for beginners to make their first few sales online, we have found that because so many Twitter users flag these tweets as spam (because people promote products without considering their relevance to the interests of those users), Twitter is quick to disable their Twitter accounts. It is more sustainable in the long run to use Twitter to build up your mailing list or simply drive traffic to your blog.

3. The Direct Response Approach

You can make money with Twitter even if you don't have a single Twitter follower. How? Simply by using its search function.

Once you've set up a Twitter account, log in, and use the search box to identify people in your target market. For example, you could type: "I must lose weight" or "I need a date," "get back at my ex," "I need a job," "lost my iPhone," "broke my iPhone," "looking for a camera," "feeling depressed," and so on.

You will find hundreds of tweets from people that typed that specific sentence on Twitter, and you can contact them directly by simply replying to their messages. (See Figure 6.2.)

FIGURE 6.2 Twitter's search box

FIGURE 6.3 Finding prospects on Twitter is easy!

For example, my partner teaches the HypnoBirthing technique to pregnant women who want to have a natural, pain-free childbirth (check out www .hypno-birthing.org.uk). The Twitter search function helps us find hundreds of women every single day who need help with childbirth. (See Figure 6.3.)

4. Sell Your Tweets to Advertisers

An alternative way to make money using Twitter is to *sell* your tweets to advertisers.

If your Twitter account has around 10,000 followers, you can expect to get paid approximately $6 to $10 per tweet. Imagine having 10 Twitter accounts with 10,000 followers or more in each—you could make $50 to $100 a day.

If you are interested in getting paid to tweet, register with these sites:

- www.twtmob.com
- www.sponsoredtweets.com
- www.twittad.com

You can also get paid $5 to send tweets to your followers on the micro-outsourcing site Fiverr.com. The site gets 2 million visitors a day, and the most popular $5 gigs they sell are Twitter-related ones like this one:

Fiverr.com is not the only microsourcing site out there. You could also sell your tweets here:

- www.tenbux.com
- www.zeerk.com
- www.gigbucks.com
- www.mturk.com
- www.dealerr.com
- www.sevenstew.com
- www.jobsfor10.com
- www.gigswood.com
- www.gighour.com
- www.taskarmy.com

You can also charge money for retweeting other people's tweets to your own Twitter followers. Check out the following sites:

- www.retweet.it
- www.twithawk.com
- www.adretweet.com

5. Buy Twitter Traffic

This is the reverse of strategy number four above. Just as some people choose to sell their tweets to advertisers and marketers, you could also buy these services and drive traffic to your website this way.

For example, a student of mine sent me this e-mail:

You can find people with 100,000 followers that can get you mass clicks. Last month I had a $10,000 sale come in from Twitter using this method. I paid $5 to have someone promote my offer to their Twitter list . . . I made $10,000!

At www.retweet.it or www.twithawk.com you can pay as little as 5 cents for people to retweet your messages to their Twitter followers!

One of the biggest secrets I learned with Twitter, Facebook and YouTube is that 99 percent of people think because they're *free* sites, they will market for free. The smart 1 percent know it's still a business and any cost is an investment, hence it makes sense to invest in Fiverr.com, Facebook Ads, or Twitter PPC (pay-per-click), which most people have never heard of.

The "Twitter Autopilot Joint Venture Cash" Strategy

The laptop entrepreneur Vivek Narayan shares an intriguing "Twitter Autopilot Joint Venture Cash" strategy on his website.

He explains that because Twitter is mostly used by individuals who are passionate about a subject and have tens of thousands of followers but do not necessarily know how to monetize that huge list of followers, this creates a very interesting win-win opportunity for savvy laptop entrepreneurs.

To start, find potential joint venture partners with large follower bases on Twitter. Specifically, you are looking for people who are fans or experts on a topic but who never promote any income-generating affiliate links or cost-per-action (CPA) offers or simply do not seem to know how to monetize their Twitter accounts (if you don't see any blue clickable links in their tweets, it's a sure bet that they are not monetizing their traffic).

To find these people, go to www.twitter.com/who_to_follow and type in some keywords that relate to your niche; for example, "weight loss," or keywords such as the names of celebrities, sports stars, famous people, or experts.

For example, I found this Twitter user (see Figure 6.4).

This Lady Gaga–related Twitter account belongs to a fan (not to Lady Gaga herself), it has 139,798 followers, and is very active with over 15,000 tweets. What is amazing is that nothing is being promoted to these 140,000 followers! There are no links whatsoever!

You could find relevant CPA offers, ClickBank offers, or other affiliate offers (e.g., Lady Gaga ringtones, Lady Gaga merchandise and CDs, Lady Gaga

PropaGaga

@PropaGaga view full profile →
Worldwide

*The official Twitter account for the largest Lady
Gaga fan site. Providing fans with news since
2008. (Previously Lady-Gaga.net).*
http://www.propagaga.com

15,209	**1,055**	**139,798**	**1,301**
Tweets	Following	Followers	Listed

FIGURE 6.4   Fan of Lady Gaga has 140,000 Twitter followers

concert tickets, etc.) or simply have regular CPA offers such as "Win a free
Xbox" and post a message that says "Find out how Lady Gaga fans can win a
free Xbox! Click here."

And whereas *you* know how to find interesting affiliate offers, they don't.
Hence, the opportunity. You can message that Twitter account user with a
message like this: "(Firstname), would you like to make $1,000 in PayPal
cash today? I have a free offer for your followers. Please reply to this
message if you are interested."

Once the person replies, there is a 90 percent chance the deal is done.
Simply get them on Skype and describe the deal like this: "I have got a
perfect offer for your followers—it's free and I am sure that your followers
will love it. Plus, it can easily make you $500 to $1,000 and more.

"The best thing is that you don't have to do any hard work—all you'll
have to do is tweet my ready-made message.

"Whatever we make out of this promotion, we'll divide it 50–50 and I'll
send your share via PayPal. You'll be able to see all the statistics in real time.
Just let me know if you are ready and I'll provide you the message right away."

Once they accept the deal, provide them with the message (which
includes your CPA or affiliate link), have them tweet it to their followers a
few times, and watch the cash fill your CPA account.

Send your Twitter partner his 50 percent share as soon as possible to
cement the relationship and trust between you. In fact, Vivek recommends
sending an extra $100 to $200 as a thank-you bonus. This has resulted in
300 percent more joint venture income, he says, as people appreciate the

gesture so much that some of them keep blasting that message out to their Twitter followers regularly for weeks and even months.

Over time, you could have a couple hundred Twitter users (or more) making money for you day in and day out. I'm sure you wouldn't mind splitting the sales 50–50 with 200 people if they're doing all the work for you!

The 'Blog JV' Strategy

You can also apply the same joint venturing strategy to blogs.

Simply find blogs in your niche market, and offer a 50-50 joint venture deal, where you provide them your advertising banner (check out www.20dollar-banners.com) and they post it on their blog, or you provide them with a website link or affiliate link and they review the product on their blog!

Here is a list of "Paid Review" brokering sites–these are sites where you can pay bloggers and website owners to review your product.

http://PayPerPost.com
http://Smorty.com
http://Blogsvertise.com
http://SponsoredReviews.com
http://BuyBlogReviews.com
http://LoudLaunch.com
http://Linkworth.com
http://TextLinkAds.com
http://SocialSpark.com

How to Get 100,000 Twitter Followers

When it comes to promoting your business or affiliate offers, or selling your tweets to advertisers, the starting point is that you need to build up a substantial list of Twitter followers in a specific niche.

Here are a few suggestions on what you can do to get more followers on Twitter:

1. Have a Link to Your Twitter Account in Your E-mail Signature and on Your Website

You can simply have a link to your Twitter account in your e-mail signature at the bottom of each e-mail you send out and at the bottom of the home page on your website, so that people interested in your work can follow your updates on Twitter. This is the simplest approach, but it takes years to build up a large following this way.

Send Valuable Content to Your Twitter Followers on a Regular Basis

Tweet good information as often as possible. Every two hours is good. That will encourage people to check you out more often, and they can retweet your message to their friends on Twitter, which can help you grow your Twitter account virally.

Look into automating your tweeting with services such as socialoomph. com, twuffer.com, feedmytweeterpro.com, and twitterfeed.com.

This might seem counterintuitive at first, but there is strong evidence to suggest that the more often you tweet—even to levels that might seem excessive, for example, every 20 minutes—the larger and more engaged your audience becomes on Twitter.

The automation tools I just listed can help you schedule the release of content via Twitter throughout the day for weeks and months ahead.

Add Them Manually

As I mentioned earlier, you can use Twitter's Who to Follow function or its search function, or even its Browse Interests function, to find and follow people who are interested in a specific topic.

Typically 30 to 40 percent of them will follow you back, either automatically because they have this as a setting on their Twitter account or out of curiosity or reciprocity.

So, for example, if you follow 1,000 people a day from a specific target market across multiple Twitter accounts, you could be adding 300 or more new followers a day.

Note: Due to Twitter's built-in rules and limitations, you can only follow up to 2,000 people more than you have followers (so, for instance, if you have 35,000 followers in an account you can only be following as many as 37,000 people). This means that from time to time you will have to stop following the people who haven't followed you back in order to stay within that required range and be able to follow new people.

Buy Gigs on Fiverr.com

An alternative is to pay for some gigs on Fiverr.com. My suggestion is to go on Fiverr and search for Twitter. You'll find gigs such as:

- I will get you 1,000 new Twitter followers in 5 days max for $5.
- I will add more than 600 targeted Twitter followers to your account for $5.
- I will add over 200 followers to your Twitter account in 24 hours for $5.

If you buy 100 gigs like these, you would pay $500 to get thousands of Twitter followers. A word of caution, these followers may not be as closely targeted as you would like.

Check out www.freelancer.com, as well. It's a bit more expensive but you can get more targeted Twitter followers.

Software Automation

Twitter is built on open source software, which means that program developers have created hundreds of applications and websites that work well with Twitter's platform.

Some of them, like www.TweetAdder.com and many more like it, do the work of following and unfollowing people for you, to grow your Twitter accounts for you. Most serious Twitter marketers use these tools to get 100,000 Twitter followers in 30 days, or as many as 1 or 2 million Twitter followers within 12 to 18 months.

Note: Twitter only allows you to have up to 10 different Twitter accounts. If it detects that you have more than 10 accounts, or if Twitter users flag you for spamming them with too many promotional affiliate offers, for example, Twitter will close down your accounts. I suggest that you send traffic to your blog, where Twitter users can get the useful, interesting information you will provide them and then also find out about products they can buy, rather than simply sending them directly to an affiliate offer.

How to Make Twitter Easier

As Twitter increased in popularity, more and more websites came along to make the experience for users faster, simpler, and more convenient.

Sending out 140-character updates may sound easy, but the platform can be surprisingly complex.

Many of these sites are useful for laptop entrepreneurs. There are great ways to track statistics, manage your accounts, set a tweet schedule, or learn about the most popular topics on Twitter at any given time. Depending on how you use Twitter, you'll find various websites and applications more successful than others.

My 21 Favorite Twitter Applications and Websites

TweetAdder manages multiple accounts at the same time and grows your list of followers *for* you on autopilot.
- www.tweetadder.com

SocialOomph lets you write a tweet now and schedule a publication time. It also automates certain Twitter functions, like following anyone who follows you or automatically sending welcome messages.
- www.Socialoomph.com

Twellow is a search directory of people sorted by area of expertise, profession, or other attribute listed in personal profiles on Twitter.
- www.twellow.com

TweetSpinner does the whole autofollow thing but allows you to filter by location (so you can, for example, follow all folks tweeting about pregnancy in New York). It also creates dynamic tweets and a few other cool things.
- http://tweetspinner.com

TwitterLocal lets you see recent tweets that were generated from a particular location. Great for meeting people near you or getting a sense of what's happening in a particular location.
- www.twitterlocal.net

TwitrBackgrounds offers a collection of high-quality free Twitter backgrounds, personalized backgrounds, and custom designed backgrounds.
- www.twitrbackgrounds.com

Tweetburner gives you click statistics for the links you post in Twitter, so you can and see how many clicks each receives.
- www.tweetburner.com

TweetBeep is similar to Google Alerts, in that it will send you an alert whenever your preset keyword is mentioned on Twitter or when somebody links to your site. Type in your selected keywords and

TweetBeep will send you an e-mail, either hourly or daily, with tweets that contain them.

- www.tweetbeep.com

Tweetmeme tracks the most retweeted posts on Twitter.

- www.tweetmeme.com

Hellotxt is a service that enables you to update Twitter, a host of other microblogging sites, and social networking sites including Facebook, LinkedIn, hi5, and Twitter with one click, from a single dashboard.

- www.hellotxt.com

TwitPic lets you share photos directly to Twitter from your cell phone.

- www.twitpic.com

Twistori displays in real time all the tweets that start with your choice of "I love," "I hate," "I think," "I believe," "I feel," or "I wish." The effect is like peering into the stream-of-consciousness thoughts of the whole online community.

- www.twistori.com

TweetDeck is your personal browser for staying in touch with what's happening now, connecting you with your contacts across Twitter, Facebook, and other social networking sites.

- www.tweetdeck.com

Twitterfeed offers to automatically tweet posts published on a user's blog using RSS.

- www.twitterfeed.com

Twitaholic provides you with the top 100 Twitter users based on followers.

- http://twitaholic.com

Twtpol allows you to create a poll, engage your followers, and get feedback.

- http://twtpoll.com

CelebrityTweet aggregates the tweets from all of the celebrities on Twitter.

- www.celebritytweet.com

CouponTweet offers a one-stop-shop for the Web's best deals, discounts, and coupons. Users save money with discounts found through Twitter.

- www.coupontweet.com

Twtcard takes the hassle out of greeting cards by letting you send a twtcard instead. Just enter your 140-character message (that's all people really want to read anyway), add your Twitter name, select a

silly face, and create your card. The end result is a cute little card that you can share with anyone, anywhere.
- www.twtcard.com

Twitter Counter gives you an overview and graph of your Twitter stats.
- www.twittercounter.com

Twitdom is a Twitter applications directory with over 2,000 Twitter apps.
- http://twitdom.com

■ ■ ■

Let's move on to some longer case studies on using Twitter. They'll give you insights into how to use Twitter to improve the marketing strategy for your business, promote offers to your followers, and gain additional revenue.

Case Study–Joey Bushnell

"I built a list of 2,000 subscribers in two months thanks to Twitter, started making $2,000 a month, and I quit my job!"

Joey Bushnell worked at an insurance brokerage for a few years, and while the money was good, he hated his job and yearned to break free from the rat race.

After attending one of my seminars, he set up some Twitter accounts and quickly got a few thousand Twitter followers.

Instead of promoting affiliate offers to his followers, he focused on building his mailing list (the money is in the list!) by giving away free information through his opt-in pages (this means people had to type in their name and e-mail address to receive the information).

Within a couple of months he had a mailing list of 2,000 opt-in subscribers thanks to free traffic from Twitter. He started earning $1,500 to $2,000 a month from marketing directly to them via e-mail, and he quit his job!

Case Study–Ali MacKenzie

"I made $1,600 in my first 16 days, thanks to Twitter!"

I first met Ali MacKenzie at my Speed Cash Seminar.

During one of the breaks she came up to me and said:

"Mark, just wait and see. One of these days *I'm* going to be on stage sharing my story with the audience on how I successfully make money online!"

And lo and behold, within a few months she was making $2,900 a month thanks to Facebook and social media sites!

In fact, like Dominica, she also took action straightaway at the end of the seminar's final day!

A short while after the event, she sent me a message informing me that she was already profiting from her new Twitter and Facebook business!

"I made $1,600 in my first 16 days after your Speed Cash seminar, thanks to Twitter!"

How did she do this? She simply modeled the same strategy used by Mili Ponce, Paul O'Mahony, Alexandra, Johny, Corinna, Raoul, David Blair, Dominica Alicia, and many others. She grew her list of Twitter followers and then promoted ClickBank.com affiliate offers to them.

Case Study–Dominica Alicia

"I make $2,000 a month on autopilot thanks to Twitter!"

Dominica Alicia attended half a dozen of my seminars and even volunteered at a couple of these events, as well.

Dominica set up some Twitter accounts as soon as she came home from the Social Media Summit, and quickly built them up to a few thousand followers.

She didn't hang about. She took action immediately!

Dominica sent me an e-mail shortly after the Social Media Summit, informing me that she had started making money online within a week.

"I made my first sale within four days of your seminar, and I now make $2,000 per month on autopilot!" she said.

Dominica has hundreds of thousands of Twitter followers across her various Twitter accounts, and her method is to drive traffic to her blog, rather than send them directly to a sales offer or an affiliate offer.

By the way, she also manages Twitter accounts for other businesses, and makes over $15,000 a month thanks to her Social Media for Businesses company. (Learn more about this strategy in Chapter 8.)

Summary

- Twitter is a free microblogging platform that allows you to post tweets (short messages of 140 characters or less) for your followers on Twitter.
- Twitter currently has 100 million active users logging in at least once a month and 50 million active users who use the site every day.
- There are five primary ways to make money using Twitter:
  1. Promote your business to your followers.
  2. Promote affiliate products to your followers.
  3. The direct response approach.
  4. Sell your tweets to advertisers on sites like SponsoredTweets.com. If your Twitter account has around 20,000 followers, you can expect to get paid approximately $6 to $10 per tweet.
  5. Buy cheap Twitter traffic using websites like Fiverr.com and AdRetweet.com.
- You can grow your list of Twitter followers by having a link to your Twitter account in your e-mail signature and on your website, sending valuable content to your Twitter followers on a regular basis, finding relevant prospects for your business and then following them on Twitter, buying gigs on Fiverr.com, and using software automation tools that build your list of followers *for* you.

- To avoid being seen as a Twitter spammer and having your accounts banned, send Twitter traffic to your blog, and use Twitter to build your mailing list rather than as a way to promote affiliate offers.
- Automate your tweeting (check out socialoomph.com, twuffer.com, feedmytweeterpro.com, and twitterfeed.com).
- Build a niche-specific following (don't try to be all things to all people).
- Outsource! Don't do all the work yourself.
- To find out more about how you can get traffic from Twitter, YouTube, and other social media sites check out The Social Media Millionaires Summit on DVD at www.laptopmillionaire.tv/dvd.

7 Fiverr

Fiverr.com is an online marketplace where people post the jobs (described as "gigs" on the site) they're willing to do for you for just $5. Here are some examples of some of the gigs currently listed on Fiverr.com:

- I will promote and deliver around 10,000 unique views to your YouTube channel for $5.
- I will add 1,000 real followers to your Twitter account for $5.
- I will invite 12,000 of my loyal friends to join your Facebook fan page and send you proof for $5.

In Chapter 8, I'm going to tell you about outsourcing. Outsourcing is the practice of having certain job functions done *outside* your business instead of having an in-house employee handle them. Well, Fiverr.com is a micro-outsourcing or microsourcing marketplace.

When I started using Fiverr.com myself, I spent $340 on buying gigs that offered to promote my Facebook pages. I paid these providers $5 each to promote my Facebook pages to their 5,000 to 50,000-plus friends and fans on Facebook.

Within two months I had a list of over 12,000 Facebook page fans, thanks to these gigs. This means that I was paying less than $0.03 per fan. Where else can you build a list of 12,000 prospects for your business for just $340?

The return on investment was simply spectacular, considering that we generated $22,000 from a single webinar promoted to that list on Facebook, and then went on to average $0.10 per fan per month.

I followed up this experiment recently by spending another $140 on Fiverr.com gigs to promote two new Facebook pages I set up. Within 36 days I had 4,930 new Facebook fans, at a cost of less than $0.03 per fan. They're not particularly targeted but still very profitable.

As I mentioned in Chapter 5, when you have a Facebook fan page, you can post a status update on the wall and it will be seen by your page's fans in their newsfeeds each time they log in to their Facebook account.

This means you get free exposure over and over again, which, in turn, means you can get free traffic over and over again.

Typically, Internet marketers can make $0.05 to $0.25 per fan, per month, by promoting offers three to seven times a week to their Facebook fans. Based on my experience—and that of the dozens of Facebook marketers I have interviewed—I believe you need approximately 50,000 Facebook fans to regularly make $5,000 a month.

When I mentioned these results to the Laptop Millionaire, he told me I needed to think bigger. "The larger entrepreneurial story here," he said, "is that Fiverr.com gets 60 million visitors a month, and it is valued at $450 million dollars. We should be thinking about creating online marketplaces that add value to hundreds of thousands of people, like this one!"

A good mentor always gets you to see the bigger picture and have a bigger vision for what you can achieve.

In the meantime, I was happy to see that my clients were finding one more way to attract traffic and make a full-time living as laptop entrepreneurs.

Three Ways to Make Money on Fiverr.com

There are three main ways to make money using Fiverr.com. You can:

1. Buy gigs to get more traffic or exposure.
2. Buy gigs and then sell them on at a higher price (arbitraging).
3. Sell gigs on Fiverr.com and then upsell other services to your buyers.

Buying Gigs on Fiverr.com

This is my preferred Fiverr strategy. As a marketing test, I bought 68 gigs on Fiverr.com, and I had these gig providers invite their Facebook friends and fans to "like" my Facebook pages, with an incentive message that read: "Mark Anastasi is giving away his special report '21 Millionaire Secrets That Will Change Your Life' at http://tiny.cc/21freegift."

This resulted in adding more than 12,000 Facebook fans across my various Facebook pages in less than 10 days. I then got 881 registrations for my webinar that was promoted exclusively to my Facebook friends and fans, which brought in $22,000 in sales in just 90 minutes (more on webinars in Chapter 11).

Buying these gigs only cost me $340.

Quite a few of my seminar attendees also enjoyed some success from buying gigs on Fiverr.com.

Ben H. told me he spent $25 on Fiverr.com and he got 1,247 visitors to his website (that's just $0.02 per click), and within seven hours he made $497 back—a 2,000 percent return on investment!

Alusine Sesay found a person on Fiverr.com who offered to tweet any-one's message to his 82,000 Twitter followers. When Alusine contacted the seller and asked him what these 82,000 people were interested in, he found out that they were fans of the popular online game Mafia Wars.

Armed with that information, Alusine then went to ClickBank.com, Pay DotCom.com, and various cost-per-action (CPA) networks to find a great affiliate offer relating to the Mafia Wars game. He then bought that gig for $5 and told the provider to send out this message with his affiliate link: 'Dominate Mafia Wars! Get this strategy guide with the latest tips, tricks, strategies, and cheats at http://bit.ly/mafiawars.'

The result? He spent $5 and made $674 back in less than 24 hours (that's a 13,480 percent ROI)!

Another example is Shaqir Hussyin. He spent $5 on Fiverr.com and made a $10,000 sale. Not a bad return on investment! Here's his advice regarding Fiverr.com:

Here bro, I'm going to give away the farm. I bank anywhere between $100 and $500-plus per one to two shots of Facebook message blasts to my Facebook group members. Here are four simple steps to make easy cash:

1. Go to www.Fiverr.com and find people who are willing to market any product or service to their fans, groups, or their Twitter followers. You can find people with 100,000 followers who can get you mass clicks. You will have to pay them five to 10 dollars, and you can market whatever you want to them.

2. Find out what group or audience they have.

3. Then find a relevant ClickBank offer and shorten the affiliate link with www.bit.ly so that you can track how many clicks you got from that gig.

4. Write a killer message and tell them to send it to their followers and fans.

   Last month I had a $10,000-sale come in from Twitter using this method.

By the way, Fiverr.com is not the only website that offers such gigs. Check out these other microsourcing websites as well:

- www.tenbux.com
- www.zeerk.com
- www.gigbucks.com
- www.mturk.com
- www.dealerr.com
- www.sevenstew.com
- www.jobsfor10.com
- www.gighour.com
- www.taskarmy.com

I often get the question, "If it's so simple, why don't these gig providers promote affiliate offers to their lists of Facebook fans or Twitter followers?"

The short answer is that maybe they do that as well, but affiliate promotions can be a bit hit-or-miss, and they prefer the regular income of knowing that they can make an extra $30 a day, every day, from selling some gigs on Fiverr.

Or maybe they have no idea about affiliate marketing, and they've simply built up a large Facebook page or a list of Twitter followers by accident, and then heard they could monetize it by selling gigs on Fiverr. Maybe they don't know any other way to monetize their Facebook page or Twitter account.

Getting the Most from Buying a Fiverr Gig

Fiverr.com has a feedback system, so you can see what buyers say about their experience with a particular buyer. Make sure you buy gigs from sellers that have lots of great feedback.

Fiverr.com gigs can provide huge returns on investment, if you buy with discipline and you do your research beforehand. I recommend spending a couple hundred dollars a month to get extra exposure and traffic for your websites thanks to Fiverr.com.

Make Money from Fiverr Arbitraging

Another way to profit from Fiverr.com is the Fiverr arbitraging strategy. This means you buy a gig for $5 on Fiverr.com and then sell it for $30 to $150 on another website. With this strategy, you profit by simply being the middleman.

Several of my seminar students use this strategy with great results. For example:

Dwayne buys gigs like "I'll be your girlfriend on Facebook for a week" for $5 and then sells it on USFreeAds.com for $150! When I asked him what other types of gigs he sells, and on what sites he resells these gigs, here's what he said:

USFreeAds is the main one, then AdlandPro. The other sites like HubPages and Wetpaint don't really bring in the traffic.

Sean C. said:

For a mere $15 you can go on Fiverr and purchase the following three gigs: "I will create your Fan page for $5," "I will invite 10,000-plus of my Facebook friends to like your Fan page for $5," and "I will get you 1,000-plus likes for your page for $5." You can easily charge $100 for this package on Flippa.com, eBay.com, DigitalPoint.com, or Free lancer.com, making you a quick and hands-free $85 profit.

Following my webinar about Fiverr.com, Paul Wakefield decided to try his hand at Fiverr arbitraging, as well. Here's what he had to say about his experience:

Thanks to Fiverr.com I'll make at least an extra $60,000 this year alone.

I've made thousands of dollars this year thanks to Facebook, and now I've also made $6,000 so far simply using Fiverr.com to offer services to local businesses.

My strategy is simple. I simply find local businesses that require services such as logo design, web design, article writing and so on, and then I find gigs to meet that demand.

For example, I offer a service such as "We will design you a company logo." I charge the customer $150 for the logo. I purchase a gig for $5, and that's $145 clear profit from not even doing the work. I average roughly four clients a week wanting logos and it costs me just $20 and I make $560 a week in clear profit. So by doing only roughly 10 percent of the work and with only four customers a week that's an extra $2,240 a month income.

I also offer three-page web design—you can buy a gig where someone will set up a three-page Wordpress site for just $5—and I offer web design and setup for $750. Again, that's a clear profit of $745 from one customer, and I'm not even doing the work. I expect to make an extra $60,000 this year by getting 10 customers a week.

Kevin Taylor, a young entrepreneur who makes up to $8,000 a month selling gigs on Fiverr.com, has this advice to give about Fiverr arbitraging in his e-book *Same Day Salary*:

One more final quick way that you can make money on Fiverr is to go to places like Elance.com, eBay, WarriorForum.com, DigitalPoint.com, and with gigs in mind that people are offering, see if there's a window of opportunity for you to be the middleman and put two and two together while making a nice profit.

So, for instance, someone could be offering 10 backlinks for $5 on Fiverr, and on DigitalPoint.com people may be willing to pay $20 for 10 backlinks. So contact the user at Fiverr, and say you're looking to get a lot of backlinks so will be sending him a lot of orders soon.

Then post on DigitalPoint.com you are offering 10 backlinks for $20 or whatever you want to charge, get the order from them, forward it to the user at Fiverr.com, and voilà! Subtract $5 from whatever you charge and that's pure profit just from being the middleman. Get 10 orders from that a day making $15 profit per time and you're making $150 profit a day!

Again, at this point I usually get the question, "Why would someone buy something for $150 on this website when they could buy it for just $5 on Fiverr.com?"

The answer is extremely simple: They don't know that they can buy it on Fiverr.com for $5! Heck, they've probably never even heard of Fiverr.com!

Buying and selling microsourcing gigs might sound like a lot of tedious work—and it is—but you could, of course, hire an outsourcer to do this for you on a daily basis (more on Outsourcing in Chapter 8).

Make Money from Selling Gigs on Fiverr.com

There are thousands of people making a part-time income—or even a full-time income as you'll read in a moment—by selling their gigs on Fiverr.com. And there are thousands of different types of gigs you could be selling. In fact, if you are interested in selling gigs on microsourcing websites like Fiverr.com, I recommend you start by browsing through Fiverr.com to see what gigs are popular.

When researching the Internet for information about how my students can profit thanks to Fiverr.com, I came across the story of Vaughn Fry, a movie critic who spends part of his time making money with Fiverr.com to help pay off his student loans. Vaughn sells several different gigs, but his most successful one has been this one: "I will make you a customized Twitter or YouTube background image for $5."

I also came across the website of Kevin Taylor, a young laptop entrepreneur from London. He recently revealed how he's making close to $8,000 a month from selling gigs on Fiverr.com.

Some of the gigs he has listed on Fiverr.com make him 10 sales a day, while some gigs only bring in a few sales a week, but altogether he claims that he averages 70 to 80 sales a day, with $280 to $320 in profit per day. What is great about this is that this business costs him absolutely nothing—posting your gigs on Fiverr.com is free of charge—and he can run his business from anywhere in the world from his laptop.

Kevin recommends offering simple services that don't require much of your personal time to deliver:

I've got up to over $300 pure profit a day with this method from doing just a few hours' work each day on something that I'm good at. In the past four weeks I've made over $8,000 from these methods and principles alone.

Now if you have a gig that you are making just 10 sales a day with, you're making $40 per day net. That's $1,200 a month. Now the more streamlined and efficient you can get this, the more on auto-pilot your income will be. I've had a few gigs that are making 70 to 80 sales a day, which is $280 to $320 pure profit generated in a single day.

Granted that is not all from one gig, but the gigs are free to post so why not post numerous gigs each day? After all, it's free traffic! And $280 a day is $8,400 a month, and $320 is $9,600 a month.

As you can see, a key part of the strategy is selling something that you're good at. You can make money with minimal effort while offering something of quality and substance.

Another profitable strategy is upselling other services to your buyers to increase your profits. For example, if someone has just paid $5 to get 500 Twitter followers, why not contact them after you've delivered the gig and say to them: "Thank you very much for your business. I hope you are satisfied with the results. I would love to help you and your business further. Would you like to get 50,000 Twitter followers for $500?"

Or: "Thank you for purchasing my $5 gig. I hope you are pleased with the 200 fans. Would you like to purchase an additional 10,000 new fans for $500?"

It's best to keep these messages short and pithy and say upfront what you're offering. From there, you both can discuss any particulars. A simple follow-up message like this one can take a small part-time Fiverr-based business that makes $30 a day and turn it into a decent full-time income.

Martin Djoumbe is another young laptop entrepreneur who uses this marketing strategy. Martin is only 20 years old, and yet he makes thousands of dollars per month on Fiverr selling just a single gig over 100 times a day, and this business takes him less than eight hours a week to run. His one and only gig is this:

"I will get you 750 targeted Twitter followers in 48 hours for $5."

This is a great title for a gig, because it's specific, it explains exactly what you get, and it explains the exact time frame you can expect it in.

The most popular gigs on Fiverr.com tend to be focused on getting more Twitter followers, because Twitter followers are a valuable commodity. As you look for services to offer, find things that are in high demand, such as Twitter followers, or services that people want that have minimal competition.

Automating Your Fiverr Strategy

By integrating strategies from other sites such as Twitter and Facebook, you can make your Fiverr experience even easier.

What is interesting about Martin Djoumbe's story is how he promotes his gig to get more buyers. He's got three virtual assistants (outsourcers from the Philippines, each of whom he pays $200 a month), and he has them perform two specific tasks.

First, on each gig page there is a white cross on a red background that allows you to share your gig at the touch of a button through Twitter, Facebook, e-mail, Myspace, Delicious, StumbleUpon, Google Buzz, Technorati, Reddit, Digg, Messenger, Friendster—and 326 more social media and bookmarking websites. His outsourcers make sure the gig is promoted across all these sites.

Second, he gets his outsourcers to use Tweetdeck (www.tweetdeck.com) and TweetAdder software (www.tweetadder.com) to get over 100 orders a day for his Fiverr gigs. How does he do this? He uses the autoreply function in TweetAdder to send message to Twitter users who post relevant tweets, like "I really want more followers on my Twitter account."

Perhaps you remember the Twitter direct response strategy I mentioned in Chapter 6? TweetAdder has an autoreply function that allows you to select keywords in peoples' tweets that would trigger an automated response from your software.

For example, every time someone on Twitter posts a tweet with keywords like "Twitter follower," "Twitter followers," "I want followers," "Follow me," "Follow me please," "Please follow," "Please RT," "Thanks for the follow," "Follow back," or "I follow back," Martin's TweetAdder account automatically sends an autoreply to them with a message like this:

"I saw you tweeted about more Twitter followers, I can help you here (link)." Or: "I can get you 750 targeted followers for only $5 here (link)."

With more than 2 million visitors a day coming to Fiverr.com, it's not difficult to make some decent sales every day, especially if you have interesting gigs to offer.

"Most people have no idea how to sell their gigs on Fiverr.com," says Martin. "So there isn't really that much competition, if you know what you're doing."

Summary

- Fiver.com gets 60 million visitors a month and is valued at $450 million.
- There are three main ways to make money using Fiverr: You can buy gigs to get more traffic to your website, you can buy gigs and then sell them at a higher price point (Fiverr arbitrage), or you can sell gigs.
- Before you buy a gig, find out the target market or audience of a specific gig provider. What are their friends, fans, and followers interested in?
- Make sure you buy gigs from sellers who have lots of great feedback.
- If you're a freelancer and a piece of your service could be performed for $5, then consider Fiverr to market your services.
- When *selling* gigs, only sell gigs that are easy to fulfill and that take you just a few seconds or a minute to do—or, even better, that only take your *outsourcers* a minute to do.
- If you're selling gigs, remember, the smartest thing you can do is upsell your buyers to a higher-priced offer. For example, send them a message saying: "Thank you for purchasing my $5 gig, and I hope you are pleased with the 200 fans I delivered for your fan page. Would you like to purchase 10,000 new fans for $500?"
- Fiverr.com gigs can provide huge returns on investment. I recommend spending at least a couple hundred dollars a month to get extra exposure and traffic for your websites using Fiverr.

8 Outsourcing

It had been 18 months since I'd started testing these social media marketing strategies, and I was now making money using YouTube, Facebook, Twitter, and Fiverr. I was ready to impress the Laptop Millionaire with all this newfound knowledge, and I was looking forward to offering up some vital information that could help him grow his business. It would be cool to repay the favor, I thought to myself.

But before I could do that, I wanted to fix a problem I kept coming up against: Most of the social media strategies I was using were very tedious and repetitive and often tied up my time. I found myself spending hours in front of my computer screen, answering e-mails, sending out tweets, adding friends on Facebook, posting comments on blogs, and so on.

So how could I use more leverage, make more money, *and* free up my time? That's where outsourcing comes in.

Outsourcing is the practice of having certain job functions and tasks done outside a company instead of having an in-house employee handle them, so that you concentrate on what you do best and where you create the maximum value. It can be considerably cheaper to source workers from overseas, especially if you live in a country that has a high cost of living like the United States or the United Kingdom.

For example, you can outsource your daily Internet marketing tasks to English-speaking workers in the Philippines, who will work full-time for you for just $200 to $250 a month.

By performing these tedious and repetitive tasks (working on your blogs, Twitter, Facebook, YouTube, Fiverr, and eBay accounts) they can turn these platforms into automated income streams for your business.

Accelerating Your Income with Outsourcing

"I've Made $125,000 in Two Years Thanks to Outsourcing"

I first came across the concept of outsourcing in 2008 at the Canada Marketing Summit in Vancouver, where I was giving a talk on information marketing. Jeff Mills, a former youth pastor of nine years from Minnesota and now a full-time laptop entrepreneur, was explaining how he'd made $125,000 in two years thanks to outsourcing. Jeff explained that he spends approximately $5,000 a month on outsourcing and gets a 300 percent to 400 percent return every month.

Here is what Jeff said about how outsourcing changed his life:

> I never thought outsourcing would be a part of my business when I first got started as a laptop entrepreneur. As a matter of fact, I really did not know what outsourcing was or even understand it.
>
> But, then I began to study business owners who were more successful than me, and I attended seminars where I got to network with them. I discovered something very important. All these successful business owners had *people*. Employees, virtual assistants overseas, helper teams—staff!
>
> I, on the other hand, did not have any staff, so I did everything myself and barely had any time to grow my business. I decided to devote some time to learning about outsourcing and how to manage outsourcers. I could not have imagined how this would change my life and the incredible results this would produce.
>
> I currently contract with 10 outsourcers, who mostly work full time, at a labor cost of $5,000 per month. What is great about this is that I get a 300 percent to 400 percent monthly ROI. I spend $5,000 but these outsourcers bring in $15,000 to $20,000 a month in revenue.

Imagine having 400 hours per week of labor time being dedicated to your company. This is the output I get with 10 outsourcers!

Here is a list of nine tasks my outsourcers do for me:

1. Build niche Wordpress websites that sell affiliate products.
2. Write and spin articles.
3. Submit articles to hundreds of article directories.
4. Write press releases and submit them to directories.
5. Make videos and submit them to video sites like YouTube.
6. Social media marketing and engagement, using automation tools.
7. Contacting potential joint venture partners for webinar swaps.
8. Doing graphic design and building custom templates for my websites.
9. Answer phones, sell my services, and offer customer support.

Do you see how doing this can give the laptop entrepreneur his time and freedom back? This allows you, the business owner, to get back to the basics of *growing* your business instead of *being* the business and doing all the work yourself. It gives you much more leverage! Like Michael E. Gerber—the author of *The E-Myth*—says, business owners need to be working *on* their business, not *in* them.

How has outsourcing made me money? Well, the first time I did it, it was spectacular. I was selling a high-end travel membership and needed my site to get more traffic. So I hired a company in India to do my search engine optimization (SEO) and it cost me about $300 to get started, with a $75-a-month maintenance fee. Within six months, my sites were all number one in the search engines. This exposure brought me over $800,000 worth of business because I was able to occupy the top spot on Google. Not a bad ROI on a $1,000 budget!

I then created my own SEO company, TrafficMills.com, to handle online marketing and website development for dentists, personal trainers, plumbers, and other service providers in "backyard America." We expanded this service and now offer it all over the world. My job is simply to get the clients. Then my team of outsourcers does all of the work. Since I started my SEO company, it's done over $125,000 in just two years, and I pretty much outsourced everything and run it as an absentee owner. My two favorite places to find overseas outsourcers to do my marketing and run my business are the Philippines and India. I can hire overseas agents there to do my work for just $2.30 to $4.00 an hour.

Outsourcing is not just about delegating labor and work—when done correctly, it's about lifestyle design. When your income is taken care of every month and you don't have to worry about it, you are free to decide how you want to spend your day. "Should I work 9 to 5 today or just 9 A.M. to 11 A.M.?" "Should I work all my life to retire later or take mini-retirements with several months or years off, vacations all through my life, where I work a bit and play a bit?"

"Should I take the family down to the lake or sit in my office and work all day? Oh—my team can do my work, let's go to the lake!"

Too often, that lifestyle of freedom eludes business owners because they end up doing all the work themselves and are likely the first ones to show up at work and the last ones to leave after a grueling 14-hour workday. Outsourcing can allow you to have a life of fulfillment and meaning, beyond just doing the mundane, repetitive tasks of running a business.

Recently there has been a great surge in micro job outsourcers doing small jobs for people on sites like www.sevenstew.com and www.fiverr.com. These sites allow people to find workers anywhere in the world to do tasks for $5 to $49. It also allows people to become outsourcers easily and start making money if they're unemployed or stay-at-home moms, for example. Many people complain about not having jobs or not making money online. But, there is an abundance of jobs they can provide to people on these micro jobs websites and they'll get paid to do them. Each job might take them 2 minutes, or 10 or 30 minutes, but they can make $40 or $50 a day this way—sometimes more.

Since I started outsourcing, it's been a great blessing in my life, allowing me to travel, speak all over the world, meet people and make new friends, and live my days with purpose and freedom.

I would love to show you exactly how I do this, and you can watch my five-day outsourcing video training course at www.outsourcedtv .com. You'll learn tips, systems, and methods to give laptop entrepreneurs and small business owners their time and freedom back.

Watch Jeff Mills's presentation at the Traffic Generation Summit at www .laptopmillionaire.tv/jeffmills.

Growing Your Business with Outsourcing

"My Filipino Workers Earn Me $18,000 to $22,000 per Month and I Play Golf Every Day!"

John Jonas of www.replacemyself.com is another laptop entrepreneur whose life was changed thanks to outsourcing. His story is remarkable in that he was *forced* to use outsourcers when unfortunate personal circumstances meant he couldn't run his business for a while.

John said, "Virtual assistants can become your secret weapon, that is, if you know exactly how to get the best out of their time. Knowing their skills, honing them, and utilizing their best potentials will not only improve your pool of talent, but it will also convert these talents to income—*your* income."

John and his wife were expecting their second child, but due to complications with the pregnancy, his wife was forced to remain bedridden for the rest of her term.

This meant that John had to stay at home to take care of their other child and his wife and could no longer run his business himself by going to his office every day.

That is when he decided to hire some outsourcers.

Here's John explaining how outsourcing impacted his life and the lives of the people he taught his methods to:

When I got started doing outsourcing, the owner of the online clothing store Backcountry.com told me:

> When you're ready to start outsourcing the right way, make sure you go to the Philippines. In India, when you tell someone something and they say, "Yes," that means, "Yes I heard something come out of your mouth." It does not mean, "Yes, I understood what you said." The Philippines is *very* different.

I took the leap and hired my first Filipino worker. Life has never been the same.

Everything in my business is easier because they're capable of doing my work for me. Not just the work I don't want to do, or don't know how to do, but they actually do the work that I'm good at doing. This frees up my time completely.

When someone else in your business is capable of doing the work you're doing in your business, everything changes.

These are the top seven ROI activities that my virtual assistants do for me:

1. Article directory submission
2. Forum posting
3. Blog commenting
4. Video marketing
5. Social networking (Twitter, Facebook, LinkedIn, SocialMarker, Digg, etc.)
6. Blogging
7. Directory submission

These activities grow our traffic sources and therefore grow my online business.

Five years later, I've made more than $5.1 million directly from work my Filipino workers do for me. I play golf every day while things still get done in my business. I have a business that one of my Filipino workers built for me that makes me between $18,000 and $22,000 per month.

I'm the one who manages the business and calls the shots, but I don't do the work of updating the website and getting more traffic to the site.

Hiring full-time people in the Philippines for around $250/month (40 hours per week) will change any entrepreneur's chance of success.

Watch John Jonas explain how to profit from outsourcing live on stage at the Speed Cash Seminar by visiting www.laptopmillionaire.tv/johnjonas.

Hiring Outsourcers and Automating My Business

The first order of the day was to hire a virtual assistant to help me run my Internet business and take care of my overflowing inbox. I was receiving more than 500 e-mails a day!

I went to the Craigslist Manila website (http://manila.en.craigslist.com .ph) and I posted an ad. Within hours, I started receiving CVs and within a week I had found the perfect virtual assistant.

Her job description included:

- Customer service and e-mail management.
- Database management: creating and updating my databases.
- Communications: dealing with the DVD duplication company, printing company, fulfillment house, couriers, copywriter, web designer, and so forth.
- Event management: booking venues, finding crews, logistics and AV, and so on.
- Financial management: preparing monthly sales and expenses reports, paying suppliers via PayPal, and so on.
- Travel arrangements: Booking flights, hotels, taxis, transport, holidays, arranging luxury skiing retreats for me and my high-end clients, and more.
- Marketing: transcriptions of interviews, updating eBay listings, researching potential joint venture partners and affiliates.

At a cost of just $500 a month, my virtual assistant freed up about 70 percent of my time. It felt amazing! Especially since I no longer had to spend hours each day replying to e-mails from clients!

I then hired a second outsourcer to manage my social media and marketing campaigns. His tasks include:

- Managing my Facebook account.
- Managing my YouTube account.
- Managing my LinkedIn accounts.
- Managing my Twitter accounts.
- Updating my blog.
- E-mailing my list of subscribers with updates.
- Updating my membership sites with new content.
- Buying gigs on Fiverr.com.
- Managing my Facebook pages.
- Getting more fans for my Facebook pages.
- Managing my Facebook Ads campaigns.
- Organizing Facebook Events to promote my webinars and seminars.
- Inviting my subscribers to join me on Facebook.
- Using Socialoomph.com and TweetAdder to automate social marketing.

- Using SocialMarker.com to spread our links and videos to 50 of the best social bookmarking sites in under 15 minutes.
- Joining Internet marketing-related groups and pages on Facebook to post comments on their walls and/or to find potential joint venture partners.

And, of course, my third outsourcer was none other than Attila, the web designer from Hungary who had set up all of my websites since the beginning. For $15 an hour, I could get any kind of website or web page set up quickly and efficiently.

With my business running on autopilot, my websites selling my products and 60,000 to 90,000 visitors a month coming to my sites, I was free to focus on the areas that I enjoyed the most and where I could produce the most value: creating new products, writing, and speaking.

"Isn't this Exploitative?"

I'm often asked at seminars why so many laptop entrepreneurs hire out-sourcers and virtual assistants from the Philippines rather than from any other country.

The answer is that the majority of Filipinos speak fluent English (the Philippines was under the sovereignty of the United States between 1898 and 1946), a large percentage of the population has higher education degrees, the cost of living is very low (the average salary is $207 a month), and there is a culture of respect toward employers and an eagerness to achieve *results* and earn their keep. Finally, it is apparently considered to be prestigious in the Philippines if you work for a U.S. or foreign boss.

I'm also often asked whether paying someone from the Philippines $200 a month is exploitative.

Have a look at these statistics on the average monthly wage paid in the Philippines for different professions (source: www.worldsalaries.org/philippines.shtml):

- Hotels and restaurants: $133
- Car mechanic: $144
- Construction work: $147
- Postman: $160

- Education: $186
- Real estate: $189
- Manufacturing: $195
- Accountant: $278
- All sectors: $207

With an estimated population of 94 million people, an unemployment rate of 7.1 percent (there are 2.9 million unemployed people in the Philippines), and an average salary of $207 a month, I don't think there's anything wrong with hiring virtual assistants from the Philippines for $200 to $250 a month.

I think what is wrong is how inflation in the West has robbed us of our purchasing power and pushes our cost of living higher and higher.

Have you tried living in the United Kingdom? Prices of goods and the cost of living are horrendous! It's called "rip-off Britain" for good reason. And things aren't any better in the United States. The value of the U.S. dollar has fallen by more than 90 percent since 1971!

How to Hire an Outsourcer

You can hire outsourcers from all over the world, including the United States, the United Kingdom, Europe, India, the Philippines, and other countries on any of these websites:

- elance.com
- onlinejobs.ph
- oDesk.com
- freelancer.com
- vWorker.com
- Guru.com
- ContentDivas.com
- 123employee.com
- Scriptlance.com
- HireMyMom.com
- PeoplePerHour.com

A lot of the outsourcers on these sites are freelancers that you can hire directly, usually for a very reasonable fee. But a large number of the so-called workers on these sites are actually large business process out-sourcing (BPO) companies that will offer to do the work for you at a rate that is double what a freelancer would charge (these BPOs charge a fee for managing the outsourcers for you).

Personally, I prefer to use Craigslist Manila to find and hire outsourcers directly. Thanks to this site, you can hire hundreds of well-educated workers in the Philippines, who are fluent in English, for just $200 to $300 a month. You can even hire full-time web designers to work for you for as little as $500 a month.

Here's how the process works.

First, go to http://manila.en.craigslist.com.ph and click on "Post to Classifieds."

You will then need to click on "Job Offered" and select a category.

I tend to choose the categories admin/office jobs or writing/editing jobs, or web/HTML jobs, or business/management jobs (there are 32 different categories to choose from).

Once you go through the required steps and submit your job description, you should receive 5 to 10 CVs over the next two to four days from people in the Philippines eager to start working for you. You can always repost your job offer once a week to get more results.

Once you've gone through the CVs and selected a few interesting ones, add these people on Skype and conduct a brief interview with them to check their level of English.

Ask them why they want this job, ask them about previous jobs they've held, ask them about what they want from this job, and so forth.

If you like one of the applicants, give that individual a simple task to complete, for example:

- Create a Facebook page on gardening.
- Create a new Facebook account.
- Contact 20 potential joint venture partners on Facebook.
- Set up a LinkedIn account.

Key Qualities Your Outsourcer Must Have

1. They *must* speak English well.
2. They *must* complete your first task well and on time.

3. They *must* have the right attitude and desire to help you grow your business.

4. They *must* have their own computer and Internet access at home.

Activities Your Outsourcers Can Perform for You

Once you've set up your business and you have a product or service to sell, here is a list of some activities your outsourcers could perform for you to free up your time, get you more traffic, and make you more money:

Customer Service and Administrative Tasks
- Customer service, e-mail management, and answering phone calls.
- Updating your databases of clients and of subscribers.
- Managing projects and coordinating members of your team.
- Event management: booking venue, managing logistics and AV, and so forth.
- Preparing monthly sales and expenses reports, paying suppliers.
- Travel arrangements: booking flights, hotels, taxis, holidays, and more.

Web Design
- Setting up blogs and websites.
- Setting up membership sites.
- Graphic design.

Writing and Content Creation
- Transcribing interviews.
- Writing e-books and courses.
- Updating your membership sites with new content.

Traffic Generation
- Researching and contacting potential joint venture partners for ad swaps.
- Contacting potential joint venture partners for webinar swaps.
- Managing your Facebook account.
- Managing your YouTube account.
- Managing your LinkedIn accounts.
- Managing your Twitter accounts.

- Using Socialoomph.com and TweetAdder to automate social marketing.
- Updating your blog.
- Using SocialMarker.com to spread your links and videos to 50 of the best social bookmarking sites in under 15 minutes.
- Joining groups and pages on Facebook related to your target market to post comments on their walls and to find potential joint venture partners.
- Building niche Wordpress blogs that sell affiliate products.
- Updating your eBay listings.
- Creating Facebook pages.
- Managing your Facebook pages.
- Getting more fans for your Facebook pages.
- Managing your Facebook Ads campaigns.
- Organizing Facebook events to promote your events.
- Inviting your subscribers to join you on Facebook.
- Writing and spinning articles.
- Submitting articles to hundreds of article directories.
- Writing press releases and submitting them to directories.
- Making videos and submitting them to video sites like YouTube.
- Buying gigs on Fiverr.com to get you more traffic.
- Buying gigs on Fiverr.com for $5 and then selling them for $100 to $150.
- E-mailing your list of subscribers with updates.
- Posting comments on online forums relevant to your niche.
- Posting comments on blogs relevant to your niche.
- Posting comments on YouTube videos relevant to your niche.
- Uploading video responses to YouTube videos relevant to your niche.
- Submitting your websites and blogs to online directories.

With your outsourcers busy making you money, *your* role will entail:

1. **Hiring and training outsourcers** (give them clear instructions, show them exactly what they need to do).
2. **Tracking their individual results** (traffic generated, affiliate commissions earned, growth of number of Facebook fans, growth of mailing list, and so forth).

3. **Find relevant offers and affiliate products for them to sell** (and maybe also write the messages for them to use).

You can outsource all of these tasks too, of course, in due course.

How to Manage Your Team of Outsourcers

There are three things that are vital when managing your team of outsourcers. First of all, they must send you a daily update via e-mail. Second, you must track the amount of traffic and sales each outsourcer is generating. And third, you must reward your top-performing outsourcers and get rid of the nonperforming ones.

1. **They absolutely must send you a daily update.**

This is a short e-mail detailing what activities they completed that day, what challenges they encountered, and how they got around them.

2. **Tracking your outsourcers' results.**

Georgina Lany assigns one target market to each outsourcer she hires, and sets up one ClickBank affiliate account for each one. So if she's earned $1,400 this month in her weight loss ClickBank account, for example, she knows that this is thanks to her outsourcer responsible for the weight loss market.

The Laptop Millionaire had as many as 80 outsourcers at one point. He also tracked each one's results by the affiliate commissions generated in each of 80 ClickBank accounts (remember: setting up ClickBank affiliate accounts is free).

Another way to track the traffic they generate: Create shortened links with www.bit.ly, tiny.cc, budurl.com, tinyurl.com, or ow.ly.

3. **Motivating your team—The carrot and stick approach.**

Reward your best-performing outsourcers (e.g., give them a $100 bonus, or a Flip camera as a bonus, etc.), and fire your worst-performing outsourcers every two to three months. The process of rewarding your best outsourcers and firing the nonperforming ones will result in having a solid team of well-trained outsourcers.

"I Make $45,000 a Month on Autopilot!"

More and more of my students are hiring outsourcers in the Philippines. I recently received this update from Dominica Alicia:

> Thank you Mark. Since the last time we spoke I almost tripled my monthly earnings. I am now making $45,000 per month, providing internet marketing services to businesses. I have a team of 12 Filipinos and a project manager here in the UK. My only task is networking! Everything is so well organised that I can almost call it "passive income."

Find out more about Dominica's strategies in Chapter 9.

And Paul Wakefield recently told me how having a team of outsourcers working at generating traffic for him all day long is allowing him to take some time off to travel to the Far East:

> I'm hiring three more outsourcers, to take my team to eight people. This will spread my current work load a bit better and then I'll increase my 2.5 month trip to India to a 6 month trip traveling around the far east, safe in the knowledge that my team would still keep doing what they do best.

■ ■ ■

The case studies for this chapter show how others have used outsourcing strategies to make their lives easier. These case studies offer tips and strategies you can use when you're ready to hire your own outsourcers.

Case Study–Georgina Lany

"I make $11,000 per month thanks to my outsourcers!"

In Chapter 5 we saw how Georgina Lany is making money using Facebook. Her secret weapon, she says, is her team of outsourcers.

Thanks to outsourcing, Georgina got 20,324 new Facebook friends in less than two weeks and made $8,243 in her first month online—while she was on holiday in Crete.

Georgina Lany has 10 full-time outsourcers now. She pays them $180 to $200 each, per month. They work at growing her Facebook accounts, Facebook pages, and groups, and perform other social media tasks daily to get her more traffic every day.

Each outsourcer earns her approximately $600 to $1,000 in profit per month, mainly by promoting affiliate products from ClickBank for her.

Here is Georgina's seven-step strategy, in a nutshell:

Step 1: Hire 1 to 10 outsourcers at http://manila.en.craigslist.com.ph and offer $180 to $200 a month for a virtual assistant who will help you with your Internet marketing tasks.

Step 2: Each outsourcer creates and manages four (or more) Facebook accounts.

Step 3: Each outsourcer focuses on one specific target market (e.g., weight loss).

Step 4: Each outsourcer joins 100 relevant Facebook groups and Facebook pages per Facebook account.

Step 5: Each outsourcer adds 150 to 200 new friends a day from those pages and groups.

Step 6: Each outsourcer creates one new Facebook group and 1 new Facebook Page per Facebook account (i.e., four Facebook groups and four Facebook pages per outsourcer, initially—though this can grow to *hundreds* of pages and groups per outsourcer).

Step 7: Each outsourcer posts four updates a day on the Facebook pages' wall, four posts a day to the Facebook accounts' wall; and sends two messages per week to her Facebook group members.

As a result of all this online activity, Georgina gets at least 2,000 clicks per month per outsourcer, from highly targeted sources of traffic and makes approximately $1,000 in affiliate commissions per out-sourcer per month on average.

This number grows naturally as your outsourcers get better at their jobs and as your Facebook pages grow. In fact, I met up with Georgina recently in New Zealand and she told me she is now making $11,000 to $14,000 a month thanks to this strategy.

Case Study–Mili Ponce

"My outsourcers each earn me $600 to $1,500 a month in profit!"

In Chapter 4, I explained how Mili Ponce started making money thanks to Twitter. I caught up with her recently on Skype, and she told me she now has five full-time outsourcers in the Philippines, earning her over $5,000 a month.

As I mentioned in Chapter 1, every day these outsourcers go to Twitter.com and search for keywords like "I must lose weight," "I want to make money," "I am making no money," "I need a job," and so on.

This allows them to find people who are tweeting about these topics *that day*!

They then contact these people by sending them a direct message within Twitter and share with them information about a product that can solve their problem.

(Remember: There are over 12,000 digital products and hundreds of different categories to choose from at ClickBank.com.)

The cool thing about this strategy is that you can make money even if you don't have a single follower on Twitter!

Each outsourcer can earn $600 to $1,500 a month in profit for Mili, using this strategy.

Case Study–Matt Traverso

"I've already made over $3,000 in my first month with this strategy!"

Matt Traverso, a speaker and trainer, joined my coaching program and implemented the outsourcing strategy straightaway. He hired three outsourcers from the Philippines and made $3,000 in his first month from this strategy alone.

Yes Mark, I'm one of the long-term members of your coaching program (which is truly a fantastic treasure trove of tools and strategies to make money online—*fast*!) and I've just applied the basic Facebook strategy you taught us.

I just put an ad on Craigslist looking for Facebook outsourcers in Manila (just like you suggest) and selected three outsourcers out of all applicants and trained them.

Each one of them is managing four to six accounts, adding approximately 1,400 new friends a week.

I started with this strategy about a month ago and I've already made over $3,000 with this strategy alone!

Matt recently sent me these very, very kind words:

Mark, your work is truly beyond fantastic. Having researched the work and strategies of hundreds of Internet marketing experts, I can say that what sets you miles apart from all the other so-called experts *anywhere* is that you really do care about your customers. You're totally honest, authentic, genuine, sincere, humble—and that's what makes you the best, *bar none*!

You approach Internet marketing with great respect, love, caring, and a huge heart. Your own thinking must be, "Okay, here's something that I do know and that really works, and what I want right now is to show people, as clearly and simply as possible, how easy this stuff is and how they can immediately use it to get results! And I'm committed to making sure they do exactly that!"

Summary

- How could you use more leverage, make more money, *and* free up your time? That's where outsourcing comes in.
- Outsourcing is the practice of having certain job functions and tasks done outside a company instead of having an in-house employee handle them, so that you can concentrate on what you do best and where you create the maximum value. It can be considerably cheaper to source workers from overseas.
- You can hire outsourcers at websites like: Elance.com, oDesk.com, Freelancer.com, vWorker.com, Guru.com, ContentDivas.com, 123Employee.com, Scriptlance.com, HireMyMom.com, PeoplePerHour .com, or Craigslist Manila.
- Key qualities your outsourcer must have include English fluency, being able to complete their tasks well and on time, the right attitude and desire to help you in your business, and they must have their own computer and Internet access at home.
- Track each outsourcer's results by having them send you a daily e-mail update and by checking how much traffic and how many sales they generate for you per month.
- Outsourcers can help free up your time and grow your business by taking care of:
  - Customer service and administrative tasks.
  - Managing projects.
  - Web design and graphic design.
  - Writing, content creation, and product creation.
  - Traffic generation and social media management.

9 Local Business Marketing

Five years into my life as a laptop entrepreneur, I was making more money than ever before, I was getting more *traffic* than ever before, and I had more than 30 different income streams.

And, of course, the best part was that I could run my entire business from my laptop.

I was profiting from e-books, health products, CD home study courses, DVD home study courses, private label rights products, product licensing, affiliate links in free special reports, e-mail marketing and autoresponder e-mails, YouTube videos, Facebook pages, Facebook Ads, Fiverr.com gigs, Twitter, outsourcing, article marketing, blogs, SEO, pay-per-click advertising, eBay, teleseminars, joint ventures, direct mail, buying and selling web businesses, coaching programs, workshop tickets, seminars, and public speaking!

Between 2007 and 2009, a revolution occurred in the way people used the Internet and how they interacted online. People from all over the world were spending more and more time on websites like YouTube, Facebook, and Twitter. I could see that my traffic was increasingly coming from these social media sites, and I couldn't wait to tell the Laptop Millionaire about the strategies I'd uncovered.

We met again. It had been over a year since our last meeting, as he had relocated to his home in Perth, Australia, after a brief stay in Monaco, then Gibraltar, and then Portugal.

I told him that over the past 18 months I'd been looking into social media marketing strategies, and I started explaining how he could benefit from implementing these strategies and get more leverage by hiring some outsourcers, but he interrupted me.

"Way ahead of you, old boy!" he said, with a hearty laugh. "Remember how I set up 6,000 blogs and used SEO to get them ranked on the first page of Google, and then sold the leads to real estate developers?"

"Yes . . ." I replied, wondering where he was going with this.

"Well, I've been making over $100,000 a month by offering social media and SEO services to businesses. I have just 14 clients, by the way, and I employ 35 outsourcers at the moment."

And here I was thinking I'd be teaching him something new! The Laptop Millionaire still had the edge—he was thinking *bigger*.

Instead of messing about with $5 gigs on Fiverr, or making $0.20 per fan on his Facebook page, or being satisfied with just earning $700 a week using Twitter, he was looking at how to leverage social media to present large businesses with a deal they could not refuse.

It turns out that he was charging medium-sized businesses up to $30,000 to set up their websites, their SEO activities, and their social media presence, and then adding a monthly maintenance fee. He had started out by selling this service to real estate companies that he had been selling leads to previously.

The Laptop Millionaire had built a team of 35 outsourcers to manage and update his 6,000 blogs (at one point he had as many as 80, but he pruned down his team to the 35 best-performing ones), and this team was also responsible for delivering $100,000 worth of services a month to his 14 local business marketing clients.

What astounded me the most about the Laptop Millionaire's new business, was that his overhead was only $9,000 a month—the amount he paid his 35 outsourcers in the Philippines and India.

This local business marketing business model sounded extremely interesting, very profitable, and scalable, too. I knew that a lot of people were making decent money as social media managers or even as Facebook managers, but I hadn't realized the scale to which you could build up such a business.

"You're making $100,000 a month from just 14 clients?! Why didn't you tell me about your new venture?" I asked, feeling a bit hurt that he had kept this under wraps until now.

"This is a very recent development. I only started three months ago!" he explained apologetically.

"I first came across this business model during a seminar in Atlanta, where I saw Kevin Wilke share how he makes over $1 million dollars a year doing Internet marketing for local businesses.

His presentation was titled "The Local Business Money Machine," and he kicked it off by saying that great wealth is made in times of change and in times of depression in the economy."

I had heard good things about Kevin Wilke, but I hadn't come across this information before.

"If you want to make a lot of money, do simple online marketing for local businesses. They've been hit hard by the recession. What used to work for them (e.g., Yellow Pages, newspaper advertising, leaflets) no longer works, and those things are extremely expensive, anyway," the Laptop Millionaire continued.

The big opportunity, he explained, was that there are more than 1 billion local searches a month (for example, "Chicago plumber" or "Bethesda hair salons") and this number is growing by 50 percent a year.

As I took out my journal to take notes, he continued: "Do simple online marketing for them and get paid $1,000 to $5,000 a month from each client. Then outsource the work to your virtual assistants in the Philippines for $300 a month. That's an 80 percent to 90 percent profit margin right there. With 20 clients at $5,000 a month, you are making a seven-figure income."

"Great, but what exactly are you offering these clients?" I asked, wondering what kind of offer would entice a business to the point of paying so much a year for a business service.

The Laptop Millionaire opened up his own journal and started reading out the marketing tasks his team performed for his clients. Things you can do for your local business marketing clients include:

- Get links in local directories.
- Get them Google local placements.
- Set up their Facebook pages.
- Set up their Twitter accounts.
- Set up their LinkedIn accounts.
- Set up their YouTube accounts.
- Set up their blogs.
- Set up their opt-in page.
- Upload YouTube videos.
- Article marketing.

- Social bookmarking (e.g., SocialMarker.com).
- Online press releases (e.g., WebPR.com).
- Search engine optimization.
- Build their mailing lists.
- Manage their social media accounts (Facebook, Twitter, YouTube, and so on).
- Local pay-per-click advertising (e.g., for "Atlanta plumber" keyword).
- Identify your client's ideal customers and what keywords they search for.
- Arrange joint ventures for them.
- Get them ranked in the local business directories.
- Send them a report each month, highlighting their online presence.
- Online reputation management.
- SMS marketing (text messages).
- Website redesign.
- Mobile website design.
- Create a Facebook App.
- Create a mobile phone App.
- Rent out highly optimized websites to them, or rent advertising space on websites for them.

Every month you can get them ranked for more and more keywords, he explained, and every month you could simply add one new traffic method. By doing some of these activities for your clients, they can get ranked in the top 10 results on Google for their main keywords in as little as 7 to 30 days, and you can turn your client into the number one authority online for its local market. That is extremely valuable for any business.

The Keys to Local Business Marketing

I was starting to understand better why companies would be willing to spend so much money on these types of marketing contracts. But I still had a couple of questions.

"What kind of clients should you target? Small, local businesses that don't have an online presence? Medium-sized businesses? Fortune 500 companies?" I asked.

"Good question. I believe the best type of customer is one that has high 'customer value' (each new customer you help them get is worth a lot of money to them), and high search volume.

"For example, community and house-related professions (builders, carpenters, real estate agents), or cosmetic surgeons and the 20 or so subniches there are very interesting, since they can break even at just one or two new customers.

"If you help them get 5 to 20 new customers a month, you have radically changed their lives! Conversely, you might want to stay away from hairdressing salons or restaurants, as these businesses typically have low transactional value."

"I see," I said. "And what exactly do you say when you're approaching these businesses? Do you say, 'Give me $30,000 because you're clueless about how to use SEO and social media and if you don't your competition is going to crush you'?"

"Ha ha! Yes! Well, sort of! When selling your service to potential prospects, your elevator pitch should be simple and to the point: 'I work with local businesses to do their online marketing for them, so that they show up at the top of the search engines.'

"Make sure you position yourself in the right way, as an expert. Remember that what you have to give them is extremely valuable, and they need you desperately!"

Acquiring Customers

The Laptop Millionaire suggested using this pitch: "I am currently looking for two clients that have the ability to *double* their sales. What would happen if you doubled your sales in 90 days?"

He also advised me to never offer one-time sales deals to clients. Always insist on signing long-term contracts for it to be worth your time.

Before he left, he told me to listen to an interview by Jon Keel, one of the first local business marketing entrepreneurs out there. He was making millions of dollars a year from his business, and he was Kevin Wilke's mentor.

From that interview, I would find out that Jon Keel's primary target market comprised business owners of $2-million to $50-million privately owned companies.

He says that the fact that Yellow Pages, direct mail, and TV advertising are no longer as effective as before is a massive challenge for small and medium-sized businesses. As he puts it, new media is replacing old media, and business owners' biggest challenge right now is that they desperately need more customers.

Like I always say to my own customers: No matter what business you are in, you are in the business of acquiring customers!

Jon explains that with this business model, the annual value of his average client is $10,000 to $15,000, and his lifetime customer value (LCV) is $75,000 to $100,000. He also says that his business relies a lot on word-of-mouth referrals.

He also states that you should, "Focus on overdelivery. Underpromise and overdeliver. We always do something more than we said we would do. For example, if we've told them we'll get them ranked in Google for 10 to 20 keywords, we'll throw in an extra 60 keywords that they are now also ranking for. This is why we get so many clients now from referrals. I often ask my clients, 'You understand that 90 percent of my business comes from referrals, right?'"

Jon Keel explained in that interview that he has worked in 85 different niches and markets, and he says he prefers to work with businesses that have high-end customers, high-paying clients, such as attorneys, physicians, personal injury attorneys, divorce attorneys, dentists, periodontists, orthodontists, cosmetic surgeons (and subniches), high-end home remodelers, and others of that type.

When speaking to a prospect, he advises using a consultative selling approach—ask them questions, let them *tell* you what they want...and then sell *that* to them!

And when it comes to finding new customers, one of his strategies includes using local Yellow Pages directories to see who is paying the most for advertising, and then contacting them directly to tell them they're *schmucks* for using the Yellow Pages to promote their businesses! (Well, maybe he doesn't quite use the word "schmucks," but you get the idea!)

Another idea that I liked for picking up new clients comes from one of Kevin's students. He uses postcard marketing to get clients to his brand-new local business marketing service: "In one month, I sent out 125 postcards to local businesses. I got 23 leads and four clients at $2,000 a month—*each*!"

I met up with the Laptop Millionaire again a few days later, at the Busaba Eathai restaurant in London's Soho district, before going out to watch some stand-up comedy at our favorite joint, the Comedy Store in Piccadilly Circus.

"I listened to that interview with Jon Keel, the other day. Fascinating stuff. I love how scalable this business model is. So, do you think I should start a local business marketing company myself?" I asked.

"Definitely not," was his deadpan reply.

His answer took me aback. This was the first time he had advised me against going for a business model that clearly worked.

"What do you mean?!" I blurted out.

"You love creating products and sharing exciting ideas and inspiring people with stories. You love speaking at seminars. Focus on that. It's what you're good at and it's what makes you happy. This corporate services stuff would make you money but you wouldn't be happy doing it."

He had a point. I felt the happiest when I was on stage, sharing interesting new ideas with my clients. And whenever I spent too long away from the stage, I would find myself delivering seminars to . . . my furniture and to the pebbles on the beach. It's a serious condition and I'm seeking professional help.

Well, I did not start a local business marketing company.

But my girlfriend did.

From Zero to $3,000 a Month in Just Seven Weeks

That's right. I told her about my conversation with the Laptop Millionaire and three weeks later she set up www.oneworld-marketing.com.

Just four weeks after that she had a car rental company, a luxury holiday property rental company, and a Caribbean investment property company as clients, and she was earning an extra $3,000 a month from helping them with their SEO and social media management.

She got these first three clients simply by speaking to them when she was using their services and telling them, "I offer SEO and social media management for businesses. I can help you get more clients for free, thanks to the Internet."

The demand for this type of service was stratospheric. I remember one day I was heading out for a Mastermind meeting with other business owners. I went for a haircut first, and when the hair salon owner asked me what I do, and I told her Internet marketing, she asked me if I could do their SEO for them. I then drove to the town where the meeting was being held, stopping to pick up some sushi for the meeting. The owner of this sushi place asked me where I'm from—on account of my peculiar accent—and what I do, and again, I replied: Internet marketing. He then asked if he could hire me to promote his restaurant online and told me that he wanted to sell sex toys online in Cyprus! I took the sushi, and made my way to the wine bar where the meeting was taking place. And yes, you guessed it, the owner of that wine bar asked me for online marketing services to help him sell his imported wines across the island.

Like I said, the demand for Internet marketing services, SEO, and social media management is huge. According to Sam Bakker, the 22-year old founder of local business marketing consultancy LikeLifeMarketing, there are over one million medium-sized businesses around the world, with average revenues of $3.6 million dollars a year, and their average marketing budget is $24,000 a month. What do they all need? More clients!

The Most In-Demand Job in the World

Well-known marketing expert Ryan Deiss says that the demand for this kind of expertise is such that there are currently 10,000 jobs available for each social media manager applicant. He calls it "the most in-demand job in the world."

When his friend Kate Buck started managing the Facebook presence of some local businesses (www.kbjonline.com), he described this as "The odd-ball 'job' my friend Kate stumbled upon that makes her a cool $10,000 a month income part-time! It's great fun and it's so easy a 10-year-old can do it."

Well, I don't know about 10-year-olds, but dozens of my students—including a 14-year-old—started their own local business marketing company in 2010, after attending my Social Media Summit in London and learning about this business model. With 1,300 attendees at this event, it was one of our most successful seminars to date. Here are some of the success stories to come out of this event.

"I Make $4,000 a Month Thanks to Local Business Marketing!"

Entrepreneur Danny Quigley attended my workshop and a couple of my seminars, then set up his business (www.socialmediasolutionsexpert.com) providing Internet marketing services for local businesses. He said:

Hi Mark, I'm making $4,000 a month from social media consulting and social media management for businesses. I set up and brand their

Twitter, Facebook, YouTube, and LinkedIn accounts, as well as their blogs. I also train them in the correct strategies to engage with their customers. I'm now being asked to do workshops after a few people heard me speak at small social media presentations. And I'm getting 140 new subscribers on my mailing list a week thanks to my Facebook page!

"I Agreed to a $3,000 Deal to Do Facebook Marketing for a Company within Four Weeks of Studying Your Course!"

Martin Welch (www.martin-welch.com) is one of my joint venture partners and a fellow Internet marketer from the United Kingdom. He recently posted this message on Facebook:

> Hi Mark. Today I agreed to a $3,000 deal to manage Facebook marketing for a company, within four weeks of studying your Facebook course. My input is only about 20 minutes a day. Thanks for adding the value, Mark.

"We Made $2,871.40 with Facebook Management in Three Weeks without Leaving the House!"

Jelle Kaldenbach is a 15-year-old student from the Netherlands. Together with his mother, they made $2,871.40 in their first three weeks, thanks to Facebook management for businesses.

After implementing what he learned, Jelle and his mother set up www.bedrijfinsocialmedia.nl and found a local business that happily paid them $1,200 for a Facebook fan page and $1,500 for a Facebook application to get traffic. They also arranged a special deal where they are now getting paid $0.60 for every fan who joins their clients' Facebook pages.

Listen to my interview with Jelle Kaldenbach at www.laptopmillionaire .tv/jelle.

"I Made $34,000 This Month from Securing an Offline Internet Marketing Consulting Client!"

Sanjib Mukherjee is a personal development coach specializing in teaching meditation and yoga. He attended many of my seminars, and he e-mailed me recently to let me know that he had secured his first Internet marketing consulting client.

Just wanted to share some news with you. Last week I secured my first offline consulting client (to help with their Internet marketing strategies)! This is an initial $34,000 project, which will rise further upon completion! So much of the knowledge I have learned has come from your seminars, so I wanted to share my joy with you! Looking forward to your seminar this week, as always, I know it will be fantastic!

"I Make $3,400 a Month from Selling Marketing Services Online!"

Matt Duggan attended my Social Media Summit and the Facebook Seminar, and he sent me this update:

"I'm currently making around $3,400 per month, mostly via selling services online (doing weekly webinars and training videos for various business owners). It's great as a start but I want to go so much higher.

One of my goals is to work with you and maybe appear on stage at an event through the list-building I'm doing on Facebook (using the methods I learned at your Ultimate Facebook Seminar earlier in the year). You are one of my very first big inspirations in the world of Internet marketing and for that, I will always be truly grateful.

"I Make $2,500 a Month Thanks to Local Business Marketing!"

James Tudsbury is from South Africa originally, and he currently resides in the UK. He attended my Traffic Generation Summit and other events. He now makes approximately $2,500 a month providing Internet marketing services for his clients from his website www.MonsterDigitalMarketing .com, as well as testing various online strategies.

Hi Mark, I make a full-time living ($2,500 per month) providing Internet marketing services for offline and local businesses. I like to take on clients that pay me a monthly residual income, which makes this a very sustainable business model and a business that can be sold one day. I am preparing a series of seminars for local businesses in London, which will result in having many more clients, I also build up my passive income revenue from selling information products and by doing my own private internet marketing, including affiliate marketing, CPA marketing, social media and mobile marketing. I've been coming to your seminars for a while, and I'm always putting things into action. I am experimenting with mobile marketing strategies at the moment, because I believe that it provides the biggest opportunity for online and offline/local-business marketers, right now and in the foreseeable future.

"We Have Clients In 7 Countries now as well as Subsidiaries in India and Lithuania!"

Mark Donnan is a serial entrepreneur. His background includes the launches of Haagen Dazs, Tropicana, Mars Ice Cream, and Tesco.com in the United Kingdom. He attended the Social Media Summit, where he discovered the potential of social media and social media management for business.

His new business, Froggo Marketing, charges $5,000 to $15,000 up-front for setting up the marketing campaigns (graphics, building sites, setting up social media accounts, and so on), and from a few hundred to $9,000 a month for the maintenance fees, SEO, and to run paid advertising campaigns.

Thank you Mark for organizing The Social Media Summit. You opened my eyes to the endless possibilities of applying my marketing knowledge to the Online world, and as a direct result, I set up the digital marketing agency, www.froggomarketing.co.uk a year ago. Froggo has simply exploded since we last met. We have clients now in 7 countries as well as subsidiaries in India and Lithuania. We're hitting the business market with an agency-type approach, with the aim of providing top level service through a highly trained team of relationship managers, where our success is based on the success of our clients. All after you showed me how at my first ever Summit. I can't thank you enough, Mark!

"I'm Making $30,000 a Month Thanks to Facebook Marketing for Local Businesses!"

Sam Bakker is a 22-year-old Internet marketer from Wellington, New Zealand. He spoke recently at my workshop in Auckland, where he revealed that he makes $30,000 a month thanks to Facebook marketing for local businesses.

He creates Facebook pages, Facebook applications, and Facebook ad campaigns for his clients (mostly New Zealand, Australian, and U.S. businesses), and he charges as much as $120,000 per client for a one-year contract.

Listen to my interview with Sam at www.laptopmillionaire.tv/sambakker.

How to Make Money Thanks to Local Business Marketing

Step 1: Create Your Offer and Set Up Your Website

Let's go back to the example of the local business I helped set up. When we were setting up www.oneworld-marketing.com we simply looked at other websites in this field and crafted three main offers: the Social Media Domination Package, the Search Engine Domination Package, and the Total Internet Domination Package.

We could have also offered web design and graphic design services, as well as other packages, but we wanted to keep things simple to start with.

Since you are offering services that help companies have an effective presence online, you must make sure that your website looks professional.

To create our offers and our website we looked at some other local business marketing and SEO businesses. I recommend you have a look at the following websites:

- www.seopartner.com
- www.kbjonline.com
- www.froggomarketing.co.uk
- www.improved-results.com
- www.wealthbusinessexperience.com
- www.socialmediafrontiers.com
- www.ibrandboost.com
- www.josephbushnell.com/Site/socialmediamanagementpackages.html
- www.bedrijfinsocialmedia.nl
- www.connectify.co.uk
- www.socialmediasolutionsexpert.com

Our web designer then created our own site. You can find thousands of freelance web designers on sites like Elance.com and vWorker.com.

Remember, there are dozens of different services you can offer your clients, including:

- Search engine optimization.
- Local pay-per-click advertising.
- Lead generation.
- Get links in local directories.
- Get them a Google local placement.
- Set up their Facebook page.
- Set up their Twitter account.
- Set up their LinkedIn account.
- Set up their YouTube account.
- Set up their blog.
- Set up their opt-in page.
- Upload YouTube videos.
- Article marketing.
- Social bookmarking.
- Online press releases.
- Build their mailing list.
- Online reputation management.
- Manage their social media accounts (Facebook, Twitter, YouTube, etc.).
- Identify your client's ideal customers and what keywords they search for.
- Arrange joint ventures for them.
- Get them ranked in the local business directories.

We didn't know yet how we were going to deliver all the elements in each package, but that did not worry us because we knew where we could *find* people who *did* know! (Check out Step 3 further on.)

Step 2: Get Clients

You've put together some offers and your website is online? Great! You're ready to start marketing your services and bring in some money!

But first, have a think about what your 15-second elevator pitch is going to be. Some suggestions:

"I offer SEO and social media management for businesses. I can help you get more clients for free, thanks to the Internet."

"I can help you dominate the top five positions in Google for your main
keywords and crush your local competition."

"I am currently looking for two clients that have the ability to *double*
their sales. What would happen if you doubled your sales in 90 days?"

"I help business owners triple their sale thanks to effective direct
response advertising."

You get the idea. Work at crafting an irresistible pitch that gets your
prospective clients chomping at the bit to work with you.

Here are 10 ideas to help you get more clients and grow your local
business marketing company.

1. Call Up Yellow Pages Advertisers

Check out your local Yellow Pages
and see who has the largest display ads in there. Call them up and ask them
how their advertising is working for them lately and whether they would be
interested in doubling their sales using SEO and social media traffic tactics.

And, of course, you can find advertisers in magazines, newspapers, local
newspapers, trade magazines, newsletters, direct mail sent, classified ads,
posters and banners, and so on.

Remember to use the consultative selling approach—ask your prospects
questions, let them *tell* you what they want and then sell *that* to them!

2. Find Facebook Pages That Have Very Few Fans

Sam Bakker recom-
mends the following simple strategy: Find businesses that have Facebook
pages but that have very few fans. Then contact them and explain that you
can help them get their social media and Internet marketing campaign back
on track, generating thousands of fans and leads for their business.

The fact that they have a presence on Facebook demonstrates that they
are interested in doing social media, and the fact that they don't have many
fans demonstrates that they don't really know what they're doing and they
need your help.

Check out the website www.socialbakers.com/facebook-pages, which
shows you how 1.5 million Facebook fan pages are performing, in 200 different countries! This is a great tool for identifying underperforming fan
pages in a specific country.

3. Network! Go Meet Businesspeople and Tell Them What You Do

This
is probably the fastest and most effective way to get clients when you are

getting started. Attend business and networking events, join LinkedIn, spend time at places where businesspeople hang out, and when they ask you, "So what do *you* do?" casually mention that you specialize in helping businesses double their sales within 90 days using SEO and social media marketing.

As I mentioned earlier, simply renting a car, renting a luxury holiday property, getting a haircut, buying some wine, or getting some sushi can provide you with an opportunity to get a new client!

Marketing expert, copywriter, and author Dan Kennedy tells the story of being on a flight to Europe, sitting in first class surrounded by business-people. When the gentleman sitting next to him asked him what he did, Dan quipped quite loudly, "I help business owners triple their sales thanks to effective direct response advertising." A line of businesspeople formed behind him waiting to speak to him and hire his services!

4. Postcards   As I mentioned earlier, an idea that I liked for picking up new clients comes from one of Kevin Wilke's students. He uses postcard marketing to attract clients to his new local business marketing service. He creates a list of local businesses in his area and then sends out a simple promotional postcard with his elevator pitch on the card. Here's what he told me:

"In one month I sent out 125 postcards to local businesses. I got 23 leads, and four clients at $2,000 a month each!"

If you are interested in doing postcard marketing check out www.mypostcardprinting.com (U.S.) or thepostcardcompany.com (U.K.).

5. Sell Gigs on Fiverr.com, and Then Upsell!   As mentioned in Chapter 7, Fiverr.com gets 60 million visitors a month, most of whom are business owners looking for more traffic and exposure for their businesses.

You could task one of your outsourcers to sell your $5 gigs on Fiverr.com (e.g., "I will send five tweets to my 60,000 Twitter followers for you for $5"), and then upsell your Social Media Domination package, for example, or an "I will get you 100,000 Twitter followers for your business for $1,000" type of package.

6. Create a Database of Businesses and Send Them a Free Report   This is something we started doing after picking up a car rental company as a client. I wrote a special report titled "Seven Ways to Double Your Car Rental

Business Thanks to Internet Marketing," including our website and contact details at the end of the report ("Here's what you can do, but let us do it for you!" was our final message), and then one of my outsourcers created a database of car rental companies for him to send this report to via e-mail and through the post.

Once you've created a special report, you can, of course, adapt it to any number of different businesses (car mechanics, plumbers, accountants, financial planners, dentists, orthodontists, chiropractors, massage therapists, cosmetic surgeons, decorators, builders, and so on) and create a database of any one of these specific types of business by finding them on Google or in the Yellow Pages.

7. Give Talks   Many of my students are picking up new clients by giving talks at networking events, evening seminars, property meetings, or even by organizing their own seminars and events.

Become a public speaker and present the benefits of doing SEO and social media marketing, and you will have more clients than you know what to do with.

8. Use LinkedIn   Create an account on LinkedIn.com and start networking online with millions of other business owners.

There are currently more than 141 million LinkedIn users in 200 countries around the world—and a large proportion of them are businesspeople.

9. Do Webinars   Webinars (or web seminars) are usually 90 minutes long, and this technology allows you to have up to 1,000 of your prospects from around the world watch your screen and listen to you in real time. They can even interact with you and ask you questions by typing them into the webinar interface.

This is probably the single most powerful and leveraged way for getting 10 or more clients at a time, without even having to leave your house.

The first time I ran a webinar I got 200 new clients and generated an extra $200,000 in sales in 90 minutes. Find out more about webinars in Chapter 11.

10. Get Referrals   "Why do you want referrals? Because more wealth is created—or lost—through word of mouth than any other single business action known. Yet few businesses have formalized, systematic, and proven referral-generating methods in place," says marketing consultant Jay Abraham (check out Jay Abraham's 93 Extraordinary Referral Systems CD course at http://tiny.cc/jay93).

Remember to always ask for a referral after getting your client some phenomenal results, using a request like this:

"I'm glad you're delighted with the results so far. Is there any other business owner that you know who might be interested in our services? Could you please put us in touch with them?"

To watch 12 of the world's leading experts explain their marketing strategies live on stage at the Local Business Marketing Summit go to www.laptopmillionaire.tv/lbms.

Step 3: Deliver the Service

In order to fulfill our orders and deliver the services we had sold, we built a team of three experienced outsourcers who could do the SEO, web design, and social media work we required. It cost us $1,200 a month but with clients paying us $3,000 a month, and then ramping this up to $11,000 a month very quickly, it was a small investment to make.

We could have, of course, outsourced the entire service, like my friends Suraj Sodha and Ben H. have done. For example, Suraj resells the packages on offer at www.seopartner.com for $1,000 to $1,500 a month, and pockets $600 to $800 profit per month on each contract. And Ben resells a web design service for $1,500 and gets $1,000 profit per client! Neither Suraj nor Ben do any of the work other than selling and communicating with the clients.

A third option is for you to become an SEO and social media expert, and then do all of the work yourself. But this is not a good idea because if you are selling your time you will be limited in how many clients you can take on, and, therefore, you will not be able to grow your business beyond a certain point. Find good people who can deliver the service for your clients!

To track your progress, be sure to have each of your outsourcers prepare a monthly report, highlighting the progress made with regards to their rankings in Google and the other major search engines, how many leads have been generated, how many fans or followers they have, and so forth.

Case Study–Cher Pearce

"I'm managing the mobile marketing side of their marketing campaigns!"

Cher Pearce attended a few of my Internet seminars, including the Listbuilding Masterclass, ClickBank Summit, and the Millionaire Bootcamp for Women.

She has been making a full-time living online for the past two years, and she recently told me that she is doing local business marketing.

I've just had a phone call today confirming that a large entertainment company is very interested in having a contract for me to manage the mobile marketing side of their marketing campaigns, and has invited me in for a meeting with the CEO on Monday to go over the finer details and see how I can help them make even more money.

They have 10 bowling alleys and entertainment sites, we'll probably test text marketing for 1 site first, but then if I can get them to roll it out to the other 9, this could be huge!

If you take into account that this site turns over $125,868 per month—and that's not even their biggest site—it could be a huge deal.

And that's just one deal.

This is only the second business that I have approached regarding text marketing. The first was a restaurant that I had a meeting with yesterday and I'm starting work for them next week!

Case Study–Laura Wilson

"I make $12,000 a month working just eight hours a week, thanks to local business marketing!"

Laura Wilson is an Internet entrepreneur. Laura attended my workshop and quite a few of my Internet marketing seminars, and at the

Ultimate Facebook Marketing Seminar I invited Laura to present her business strategies to our clients.

> Hi Mark, I have now set up my own business—www.ibrand-boost.com—doing Facebook management and social media management for other businesses.
>
> I offer six different packages now: YouTube Brand Boost Package ($153), Twitter Brand Boost Package ($153), Facebook Brand Boost Package ($310), Local Brand Boost Package (local business listing in Google for $153), High Exposure Promo Package ($467 per month), Total Business Brand Boost Package ($2,355 per month).
>
> I also give away a free "Alkaline Diet Recipes" e-book at www.alkaline-diet-health-tips.com, and then sell a $97 health home study course for people who want to lose weight and be healthy.
>
> My Internet businesses are bringing in $3,000 to $5,000 a month and the potential for growth is very exciting!

Case Study—Joey and Christina Bushnell
"We quit our jobs and now make a full-time living thanks to social media!"

We saw in Chapter 6 how Joey Bushnell built his list of 2,000 subscribers using Twitter and was able to quit his job as a result. Check out how he now makes money thanks to social media management:

> Hi Mark, about two years ago I worked full-time at an insurance brokerage. The money was good but I hated my job. I had no feelings or passion for it; it simply paid the bills. I quit my job just over a year ago and formed my own social media marketing company (josephbushnell.com).

Three months ago my wife was able to quit her job and work for me full time to help us grow our business even quicker.

Today we completely run and manage social media marketing campaigns for U.K. small and medium-sized enterprises.

Our clients are so varied; they range from manufacturers of envelopes, bean bags, and edible gifts, to graphic design, sales trainers, churches, private detectives, tax consultants, network marketers, SEO firms, a golf course, an Italian restaurant, web programmers, and more!

We are enjoying our work and also the benefits that it brings for our family. Thank you!

Case Study–Dominica Alicia

"I make $45,000 a month on autopilot thanks to social media management!"

Dominica Alicia is from Poland originally, and she started making money using Twitter after attending the Social Media Summit. She makes $2,000 a month in passive income thanks to Twitter, but recently she also set up a local business marketing company (www.wealthbusinessexperience .com), and within a few weeks started earning a very good income online. Her business offers the following services: web design, Facebook advertising, Internet marketing campaigns, local marketing, SEO, social media management, video marketing, consulting, and workshops.

Thank you, Mark. I've learned a lot thanks to your seminars. I made my first sale within four days of your seminar, and I now make $2,000 per month thanks to Twitter on autopilot.

I now focus primarily on working with local businesses, providing with many different services, such as: website design, website hire, social media management, SEO, video marketing, local search marketing, email marketing, PPC (Google Adwards and Facebook Ads).

I always charge more than $1,500 per client per month, and I make sure I deliver a *lot* more value than that!

Another service that I offer is that I create websites for keywords like "Kensington plumber," for example. I get them ranked number one in Google thanks to SEO, and then I rent out these well-optimized sites to the highest bidder! This produces a nice passive income stream for me every month.

I also provide consulting services for companies which advertise on Groupon, in order to help them leverage this great opportunity. Most of the companies have no plan whatsoever. They are getting lots of one-off sales, but they haven't got any sales funnel, no upsells or downsells in place. And that's where I come in with my advice. My team simply contacts the companies that they see advertise on Groupon! Simple!

Early last year I started attending professional networking meetings (in some cases you need to pay around $800 a year for membership). Now I speak regularly at business events and for organisations like BNI (Business Network International), my local Chamber of Commerce in London, The Athena Network, and 4Networking. Thanks to networking I am getting clients who can afford to pay my $750 per hour fee. In fact I recently got two "high-ticket" clients paying me $10,000 per month for SEO and social media services.

I was also promoting my workshops and online classes on Groupon over the summer, and I had almost 850 sales. The most important thing is that these were targeted leads… contact details of business owners and decision makers from London and surrounding areas. I built a list of 800 people, who know me right now and trust me. Some of them have already invested in my services and consultancy.

Now I don't need to market my services much, because I get a lot of referrals.

Since the time we spoke last time I almost tripled my monthly earnings.

I am now making $45,000 a month, providing these internet marketing services to businesses.

I have a team of 12 Filipinos and a project manager here in the UK. My only task is networking! Everything is so well organised that I can almost call it "passive income".

Local marketing allowed me to create the lifestyle I want, but this is just the beginning! I am growing this business to six figures a month.

Case Study–Adrian Clark

"I started six months ago and I generate close to $7,000 a month, working from home!"

I set up my local business marketing company six months ago and I generate close to $7,000 a month, working from home. I have six large clients each paying $9,000 per year as well as smaller clients who are paying on a month-by-month basis, depending on how their budget runs.

The work that I have undertaken for them varies. Some clients had a social media presence, however, they didn't fully know how to move it forward and utilize it correctly. I handle Twitter, Facebook, and LinkedIn for some clients, getting them targeted followers and fans.

To get new clients, I simply contacted the businesses directly by joining my local Chamber of Commerce as well as going to breakfast meetings sponsored by the Federation of Small Businesses. The first few events were a bit scary, however, I used them to pick up on feedback that others had for me, concerning business cards, fliers, and so on.

I am now contacting big corporate companies and I use the line, "Hi, my name is Adrian and I am a social media manager for a small business. I was wondering how you do your social media marketing?" The response on that has been great.

My advice to anyone wanting to start in this business would be to have a look in your area. You might be surprised at how many large companies on your doorstep are willing to talk to you about helping them if you ask.

Case Study–Runè Johansen

"I have 20 clients in Norway, Sweden, and Germany paying me $1,700 to $10,000 a month!"

Norwegian entrepreneur Runè Johansen is the CEO and founder of the Internet marketing agency www.2beSeen.no, with clients in Norway, Sweden, and Germany. Runè has attended many of my seminars to keep up with what's going on in the online marketing industry, and at a recent event he shared from the stage how generates more than $500,000 a year by offering social media management and online marketing campaign consulting services.

Internet marketing consists of so many tools that companies can't keep up with them. They don't know where to begin, they don't understand it, but they want a piece of the action. If you become a valued advisor and consultant to a business, helping them get great results and caring about achieving that outcome, you could have a client for life.

The beauty of offering this type of services is that all companies must focus on sales and marketing, otherwise they're out of business. No sales, no business. It's that simple.

I now have 20 clients, paying me $1,700 to $10,000 a month.

Summary

- If you want to make a lot of money, do simple online marketing for local businesses. They've been hit hard by the recession. What used to work for them (e.g., Yellow Pages, newspaper advertising, leaflets) no longer works and those things are extremely expensive, anyway. They know the Internet is the future, but they have no time to learn or implement these new marketing techniques.

- Make sure you position yourself in the right way, as an expert. Create an elevator pitch such as "I offer SEO and social media management for businesses. I can help you get more clients for free, thanks to the Internet," or "I can help you dominate the top five positions on Google for your main keywords," or "I help business owners triple their sales thanks to effective direct response advertising."

- The best type of customer is one that has high customer value (each new customer you help them get is worth a lot of money to them) and high search volume—for example, builders, carpenters, real estate agents, or cosmetic surgeons. These companies and service providers often don't have in-house marketing teams and look for freelancers to help.

- Focus on overdelivery. Underpromise and overdeliver.

- When speaking to a prospect, use the consultative selling approach—ask them questions, let them tell you what they want, and then sell that back to them!

- Get clients by calling up advertisers in the Yellow Pages; find Facebook pages with few fans; network and speak to business owners; give talks to gatherings of business owners; send out postcards to local business owners; sell gigs on Fiverr.com and then upsell your services; create a database of businesses and send them a free report that highlights how you can help them; set up a LinkedIn account and grow your connections online; offer webinars; and always ask for referrals!

- To find out more about how you can profit from helping Local Businesses get an Internet presence check out The Local Business Marketing Summit on DVD at www.laptopmillionaire.tv/dvd.

10 Membership Sites

"**I**'ve been a laptop entrepreneur for a few years now, and I'm ready to take things to the next level. If I shouldn't start a local business marketing company, then what do you recommend I do to take my business forward?" I asked the Laptop Millionaire.

"Two things," he replied. "Membership sites and webinars."

"Membership sites and webinars?" I asked, perplexed. "What do you mean, 'membership sites and webinars'?"

The Laptop Millionaire had just shared with me a fantastic business model, one that was simple, scalable, profitable, in demand—local business marketing—and just as quickly he moved on to something else.

And now he was telling me to use membership sites and webinars.

"Let me explain," the Laptop Millionaire continued. "I recently got interested in membership sites when I saw how many of our fellow laptop entrepreneurs were profiting from their own members' sites.

"Dan Bradbury has 300 members paying him $37 to $497 a month. Lee McIntyre has 1,000 members paying him $97 a month. Dean Holland has 600 members at $97 a month. Neil Asher has 70 members at $597 a month. Chris Farrell has over 4,000 members at $37 a month. They're generating $42,000 to $150,000 a month simply by providing fresh information to their members every month.

"Membership programs or continuity programs are nothing new. Magazines subscriptions, print newsletters, book-of-the-month or CD-of-the-month clubs, satellite or cable television services, and so on are all membership programs. The Internet has simply provided a new distribution vehicle. Online membership sites are simply websites with password-protected areas for paying members. The fee to access specialized content is typically in the $27 to $147 a month range.

"The main advantage for customers is that they receive unique, high-value, up-to-date information regularly. They benefit from the fact that you are aggregating the purchasing power of hundreds of subscribers to pay for your top-notch, up-to-date research on a monthly basis. And the fact that they are drip-fed this information can help them learn better, rather than being overwhelmed by a huge amount of information all at once.

"The main advantage for the site owner is that you're getting paid monthly for your content, and you have a steady source of recurring income, as opposed to the peaks and troughs of product launches."

I started taking notes. The Laptop Millionaire hadn't steered me wrong so far, so I wasn't about to dismiss his advice to me. But I didn't quite understand how this new business model applied to me.

"I sell e-books and DVDs, mostly. And I do some coaching. What do membership sites have to do with my business?" I asked.

"According to marketing expert Ryan Deiss," he continued, "laptop entre-preneurs need to shift from selling products to selling subscriptions. You can make a lot *more* money from a lot *fewer* customers, thanks to continuity programs."

The Laptop Millionaire gave me this example. To make $5,000 a month you simply need:

500 people to give you $10/month
250 people to give you $20/month
167 people to give you $30/month
125 people to give you $40/month
100 people to give you $50/month
50 people to give you $100/month

If you wanted to make $60,000 a year from selling e-books, he explained, you might need to get 1,500 new clients a year. But with a membership program, you might just need 50 to 100 clients paying you $97 a month! That's 20 times *fewer* customers, to make the same amount of money . . . he had my attention.

"Also, like I said earlier, you really enjoy researching new information and sharing it with people. Having a membership site would allow you to charge your clients for a monthly newsletter that would contain your new research, for example. Imagine having 200 members paying you $97 a month to learn one new marketing strategy a month from you. That's $20,000 a month in revenue, from work you already do anyway. Or what if you get 200 members paying you $97 a month to be part of a DVD-of-the-month club, where you send them one DVD from your seminars per month?"

I was beginning to see the potential. I had 24,000 subscribers on my mailing list at the time. I was sure that at least 500 of them would be interested in being part of my $97-a-month membership program if I created one.

"The key thing here is leverage," he continued. "You get to leverage your information, your knowledge, and your research. You get to leverage your current content, for example, the video content of your seminars. You get to leverage your relationships with other laptop entrepreneurs by interviewing them to find out their strategies, and making them available in your membership site. And, you get to sell all that content over and over again to 100 members, or 500 members, or 1,000 members. Now that's leverage."

The Laptop Millionaire had just shared with me a new six-figure-a-month business model. He was right. I already had content, and I created new content every month simply from my regular research into new marketing techniques and business strategies.

"Let me share with you the seven different types of membership sites that you could create," he continued.

Seven Types of Membership Programs

As the Laptop Millionaire explained how I could profit from different types of continuity programs, I took lots of notes and refrained from asking him the dozens of questions that already were circling around in my head.

Here are the seven types of membership programs he outlined for me.

1. Content-based Membership Sites

With a simple content-based membership site you can provide new content to your members every month that could include any of the following elements:

- A new "Special Report" created every month
- Video tutorials (Camtasia screen capture videos, for example)
- Expert interviews
- An Ask-the-Expert page
- Recommended resources
- Articles

You can charge $37 to $297 a month (or more) for this content.

Examples of content-based subscription sites are restaurantowner.com, rockstarfitnessmarketing.com, or insidermusicbusiness.com.

The profit margins can be huge, because by keeping the content online there are no fulfillment costs. Kavit Haria makes $80,000 a month from his membership sites selling how-to-make-money-from-your-music type information to musicians from all over the world with an 83 percent profit margin.

Remember that you don't need to be the expert yourself. You can simply be the publisher of the information and pay an expert to provide the content every month. And you don't need any special skills or technology.

Finally, content-based membership sites are extremely easy to set up and update (more on this later).

2. Monthly Newsletters

I subscribe to various newsletters myself to keep abreast of topics I am interested in, including StansberryResearch.com's investment newsletter, the "Sovereign Man Confidential" newsletter on how to protect your assets, and Expansions.com's newsletter on conspiracy theories (don't ask!). Prices vary from $17 a month to $397 a year, and you get a monthly newsletter sent to your inbox with all the latest information.

Nick Laight has thousands of members at www.whatreallymakesmoney .com, and he charges $150 a year for his business opportunity review newsletter.

To watch Nick Laight explain how to profit from your own newsletter, live at the Internet Millionaire Bootcamp, go to www.laptopmillionaire.tv/ nicklaight.

3. Online Software-as-a-Service and Internet Services

Software, hosting, autoresponders, webinar services, shopping cart tools, and so on can be amongst the most lucrative residual income streams you can have online, because they can become an integral part of someone's business and these people might stay on as paying members for years.

Examples include GoToWebinar.com (webinar service provider), GetResponse.com (autoresponders), HostGator.com (hosting), and 1ShoppingCart.com (shopping cart tools).

Why not license some software or have some created for you by a web programmer? I recently licensed a YouTube-related software tool for $2,000, and then had a software programmer from www.vWorker.com create another tool for $1,500. I gave access to these two software tools to my clients for only $37 a month, and at one point I had 1,187 paying members on this continuity program.

4. CD/DVD of the Month

This has a very high perceived value (higher than a paper newsletter, for example) and is incredibly easy to set up.

For example, Kunaki.com or Disk.com can get a CD sent out for only $5 to $6. You simply upload your content to their site (for example, an MP3 file or an MP4 file), and then simply upload an Excel spreadsheet with your list of customers every month, and they duplicate your disks and send them out to that list.

DoubleYourDating.com provides interviews every month with dating experts through a CD-of-the-month program (they charge $30 a month; it's a massive eight-figure business! And a competitor sends out a DVD each month for $79 a month!).

Another real-world example of this was the now-defunct Columbia House Record Club offer of five CDs for just pennies. It attracted millions of subscribers a year with that irresistible front-end offer (the back end was a $40 a month recurring membership). By the end of 1955, the Columbia House Record Club boasted 128,000 members who purchased 700,000 records. In 1975, it surpassed the 3-million-member mark. The company shipped its one-billionth record in 1990 and membership exceeded 10 million by the end of 1991.

"If I was starting all over again I would go for a DVD-of-the-month club!" says membership site expert Lee McIntyre.

To watch Lee McIntyre explain how to get up to 1,000 members for your continuity program go to www.laptopmillionaire.tv/leemcintyre.

5. Free Community Sites

These sites are good for lead generation (building your list). They have the potential to become viral and give you credibility in your marketplace. The challenge is that most free community sites don't go viral and never build up the critical mass necessary to make them viable and profitable. This model can be a bit hit-or-miss.

Examples of free community sites include:

- HearandPlay.com: with 80,000 musicians, founder Jermaine Griggs generates up to $1,000,000 a year selling products to his members.
- PsychCentral.com: an independent mental health network featuring original peer-reviewed editorial content, news, research briefs, and more. It gets more than 1.1 million visitors a month.
- FitDay.com: more than 2.2 million members worldwide.

6. Done-for-Them Services

Examples of done-for-them monthly continuity programs include:

- Private label rights sites (PLR)—you get a new PLR product and website each month.
- Trading signal services—for example, my friend Guy Cohen offers his incredible OVI stock market indicator to traders for $97 a month (www.oviindex.com).
- Access to databases—for example, real estate auctions lists, or car auctions lists, bank property foreclosure lists (www.bankforeclosure list.com, for example, gives you access for free for seven days, and then it costs $97 a month).

One of my all-time favorite business success stories is that of a monthly done-for-them newsletter subscription service created by the late John Gommes.

He hired one woman for $1,400 a month to research and list every week all the free competitions people could enter to win free stuff. Among those she identified were competitions like "Win a free car by entering the Wal-Mart supermarket draw!" and "Win a free holiday to the Caribbean by entering the Thomas Cook draw!" and "Win a year's supply of wine," or "Win a free toaster!"

He promoted this newsletter service through direct mail in the United Kingdom, and he signed up more than 50,000 paying members and made millions of dollars a year from it.

7. Fixed-term Membership

With fixed-term memberships, content is delivered for a specified term (e.g., a six-month tutorial with weekly lessons sent via autoresponder e-mails). Content is created just once and is then sold over and over again.

This is very easy to set up and run. It is the same as the content-based subscription site, but people know how long they're going to stay on as members.

With content-based membership programs, members *could* stay on for months and months (sometimes years) but the average member only stays on for four months. It is common to lose 10 percent to 15 percent of your members every month, but as long as you grow by 20 percent a month or more your membership base should keep expanding.

Having a fixed-term membership can increase the stick rate from the average of four months to six months because the members know and expect to pay for the duration of the six-month program, but you lose the 10 percent of members who would have kept paying you for over a year in an open-ended content-based program.

Choosing a Topic for Your Membership Site

"Can a membership site be about anything at all?" I asked the Laptop Millionaire.

"Not exactly. There needs to be demand for this information—same as when you are creating e-books or online courses. Ask yourself, are people willing to pay for this information? Are they buying this information somehow right now? Remember what I taught you right at the beginning, about how to choose the right target market. Do you remember the criteria?"

I thought about it for a moment, smiled, and said: "Yes. I actually always refer back to those criteria when gauging a business venture: There must be a lot of demand for the information; a pain in that market that you can resolve; it needs to be a large enough target market; and there needs to be good back-end potential."

The Laptop Millionaire responded, "Exactly! Well remembered! By the way, the well-known laptop entrepreneur Matt Bacak has made millions of dollars thanks to continuity programs, and he says that his top five money-making niches online are:

1. Real estate investing
2. Weight loss
3. Network marketing
4. Wealth building
5. Internet marketing

"Ah yes. I remember reading somewhere that you can never be too rich, too thin, or too beautiful," I added.

"By the way, when choosing a topic for your membership site, there needs to also be a justification as to why someone would need to pay monthly as opposed to paying a one-off fee," the Laptop Millionaire continued. "Are there new innovations and new marketing strategies coming out every month? Are updates to databases, updates to software, or server maintenance fees needed every month? Are people paying for you to maintain and moderate an online forum? Are they paying to be coached by you and to have their new questions answered every month?"

How to Set Up Your Membership Site

"Once I've chosen my target market, and I've created the content for them, how do I actually set up my membership site?" I asked the Laptop Millionaire.

I had lots of content and I could create tons more simply by calling some experts through Skype and recording the call with the CallBurner application. Content was not a problem. But I had no idea about the technical aspect of setting up a members-only password-protected website.

He said, "You don't need to worry about this, because your web designer will know how to do this. There are many membership management programs out there, including WishList, InfusionWP, MemberGate, aMember, and lots more. Personally, I recommend using aMember.com, with ClickBank.com or 2CheckOut.com as your payment processor," he explained.

The aMember program creates the password login system to access your membership site program, and manages the relationship between your website and your payment system. This means that if someone stops paying their monthly membership, the aMember software disables their login details.

I ended up using aMember for my first membership site, but it's so complex that you won't be able to make any changes or updates to your membership site yourself—you would need to keep paying your web designer every time you needed to make even the smallest change.

Instead, why not use the Wordpress blog plugin called WishList (http://member.wishlistproducts.com). It's very simple to use. Watch the excellent video by Ryan Deiss on how to set up a membership program in 12 minutes or less, at www.continuityblueprint.com/12minute.html.

For processing monthly recurring payments, you will also need ClickBank.com or 2CheckOut.com, or alternatively your own merchant account and payment gateway. The Laptop Millionaire did *not* recommend using PayPal.

"Last year I went to www.vWorker.com and hired a web programmer for $4,000 to create an autoblogging software tool for me, as I needed it for my outsourcers to update my 6,000 blogs on autopilot," he explained. "I then decided to start selling this tool, and by doing webinars for my own mailing list as well as doing five joint venture webinars, I got 600 members paying me $97 a month for access to this software. That was a $60,000-a-month income stream for my business . . . and then PayPal froze my account, with more than $120,000 in it! What was 10 times worse than that was that those 600 monthly payments were cancelled in PayPal! That $60,000-a-month income stream . . . poof! Gone! Overnight!"

The Seven-Step System for Building Profitable Membership Sites in 72 Hours or Less

Lee McIntyre is a former teacher who quit his job, decided to join the growing ranks of laptop entrepreneurs, and went from zero to having over 1,000 paying members for his www.getmoremomentum.com content-based membership site in just six months. He is considered to be one of the leading experts in the world on how to set up and profit from membership sites. Following is an outline of his seven-step system for building profitable membership sites.

Step 1: Decide on the Continuity Model You Will Use

How do you want to deliver content? Some examples include a newsletter, DVD-of-the-month club, software, coaching program, and so on.

Step 2: Decide What Your Front-End Offer Will Be

It's harder to sell a continuity program than a one-off information product, because people want instant results. A continuity program implies that your customers need to learn something over a period of a few months, so conversions tend to be lower.

The easy way to sell a membership program is to make an irresistible $1 offer that includes a 14-day trial membership. Check out www.getmoremomentum .com/platinum to see how this is done.

In the video sales letter at www.getmoremomentum.com/platinum notice how the $1 offer is made: "This is risk-free to you: simply pay $1 now. And you can cancel this easily! *Plus* you get to keep the four bonuses worth $788 just for giving us a chance!"

Typically 4 to 8 percent of the visitors to the site take up the $1 offer, and 60 percent of them get billed in the first month (in other words, 40 percent cancel before the 14-day trial expires). With these statistics, to get 30 new members joining every day you would only need 350 to 700 visitors per day (that's 10,000 to 20,000 visitors per month to get 900 new members joining your continuity program).

Step 3: Create Three Months' Worth of Content

You don't need to create 12 months' worth of content before you start profiting from your membership site. Simply create the first three months' worth of content (for example, three special reports, three screen capture videos, and three interviews with experts).

Check out Chapter 1 for 12 ideas and suggestions on how you can create content.

Step 4: Create Your Bonus Products

Create at least four bonus products worth $97 each, that you will give away for just $1 as an incentive for people to try your membership program.

Think about problems that people in your market have that your bonus products can provide solutions for.

For example, I recently paid $1,500 for an investment newsletter titled "Matt Badiali's S&A Junior Resource Trader." Why? Because I wanted the free special reports that came with the 14-day trial membership, such as:

- How to Make 4,000% or More Gains with Tiny Gold Stocks
- This Tiny Silver Miner Is Set to Become One of Latin America's Biggest Players
- The #1 Gold Stock to Own Now
- The Secret to Safely and Reliably Making 1,000% Returns in Commodities
- The World's Most Valuable Asset in a Time of Crisis

Do you see how a few free bonus reports can make a membership offer sound irresistible? I was straight in there with my credit card!

By the way, what is the world's most valuable asset in a time of crisis? The answer is farmland; $1,500 well spent.

Step 5: Set Up Your Selling System

This is when you would need to create a video sales letter, where you explain your offer.

For a complete course on how to set up video sales letters, go to www .laptopmillionaire.tv/videosalesletters.

Step 6: Implement Evergreen Lead Generation Methods

Now that you have your members site set up and a video sales letter that funnels people into your membership program, you need to start driving traffic to your website.

This can mean creating YouTube videos, setting up an affiliate program and getting affiliates on board, running pay-per-click campaigns (more on this in Chapter 12), or running webinars with joint venture partners and having the webinar replays continue to draw in new members.

Step 7: Create Your Back End

The secret to making a lot of money from your continuity programs is to have multiple high-end products and offers (worth $500, $1,000, or $3,000) to sell to your customers *after* they have become members.

These are referred to as your back-end offers or upsells.

Some marketers use web scripts that rotate different back-end offers every time a member logs in! Cheeky!

If you have 100 members paying you $97 a month, that represents approximately $10,000 a month in income.

If 10 of your 100 members buy a $1,000 offer from you every month, this represents an *extra* $10,000 a month, for a total of $20,000.

Even if you only have 20 members paying you $97 a month and 2 of them buy a $1,000 offer each month, that's a nice $4,000 a month—*just* from having 20 members on your continuity program!

My First Ever Membership Site

Armed with all this great knowledge, a couple of months later I decided to launch my first membership site. It was called The 5K Mastermind, and every month I would write a special report on a specific strategy for making $5,000 a month as a laptop entrepreneur.

My members would also get a new interview with a successful laptop entrepreneur and access to the videos of my seminars like the Social Media Summit, the Speed Cash Seminar, and the Traffic Generation Summit.

I put together three months' worth of content. I had my web designer create a graphic for the program and set up the members' area (he used the aMember service and 2CheckOut.com for processing payments), and now I just needed to get people in. My goal was to get 200 members at $97 a month.

I asked the Laptop Millionaire what would be the fastest way for me to do this, and he replied that he got 600 new members in his continuity program by running six webinars. He explained to me how to run a webinar (more on this in the next chapter) and how to make an offer at the end of the webinar.

I decided to run a webinar for my subscribers in which I would teach them five marketing strategies, and then present my new 5K Mastermind offer.

I created four special report bonuses that members would get for free just for joining the 30-day trial membership for $1:

1. How to Make $250 a Day Thanks to YouTube
2. How to Make $3,000 a Week Thanks to Facebook

3. How I Turned $952 into $30,000 in 7 Days
4. 7 Ways to Get 5,000 Subscribers in 30 Days or Less

After the first webinar, I had 100 new members on board! I was ecstatic! I repeated the webinar another two times and was up to 220 members in the program. This was after just three weeks. In the fourth week, I created three short videos, each one talking about how you could get one of the bonus reports for $1 simply for trying out the membership. So the first video was about YouTube marketing, the second one was about Facebook marketing, and the third one was about list-building. Each of these three front-end offers would funnel people into the membership program.

I promoted the 5K Mastermind program for six weeks and then never promoted it again, because I was busy with other projects.

Twelve months later I saw that we had had 485 clients sign up for the membership and that it had added $100,000 in net profit to my bottom line, without me having to do any extra work. And this was after promoting it only six times to my own mailing list.

"Bloody hell," I thought to myself. "I could have made $500,000 extra this year if I'd continued promoting my membership site!"

The case studies for this chapter give examples of how others started making steady incomes through online membership sites. There are a variety of strategies to offer people content and instruction, and these are some of those ideas in action.

■ ■ ■

Case Study–Mark Lyford

"I made $320,000 in my first year thanks to my membership sites!"

Mark Lyford attended a few of my Internet marketing seminars, as he was planning to launch a membership-type business. Thanks to his membership sites like www.internetmarketingpass.com he made an impressive $320,000 in his first year online.

What makes this story all the more incredible is that he had *zero* money when he got started—in fact, he had to *borrow* $20 from a friend so that he could upload and sell his first e-book on the Internet!

He made $1,000 in his first month online, $5,000 in his fourth month online, and $15,000 in his sixth month online. Fast forward 12 months, and he now has 320 paying members in his various online membership sites, earning him $20,000 a month in recurring income.

Case Study–Lucy Johnson

"I have 261 personal trainers as members, paying $197 a month!"

Lucy Johnson is a former fitness and aerobics instructor from the United Kingdom. After attending a few Internet marketing seminars and trying different strategies, she came across the idea of doing webinars.

She implemented this strategy and ran a webinar for personal trainers who wanted to learn new marketing tactics. By selling her coaching program during her first few webinars, she made $26,000 in 21 days!

She then decided to create a membership site where she would teach one new marketing strategy a month to personal trainers and fitness instructors: www.rockstarfitnessmarketing.com.

How does she get people to join as members? She ran a webinar and made a $1 trial membership offer at the end of the webinar. Apparently a massive 48 percent of the personal trainers and fitness instructors who watch the webinar replay sign up for the $1 offer!

Lucy charges $197 a month for her membership program, and she currently has 261 members. This means a whopping $40,000 a month in recurring income!

Case Study–Matt Watson

"I make $50,000 a month thanks to my horse betting membership site!"

Matt Watson is a blind musician from the United Kingdom, and he attended two of my Internet marketing workshops a few years ago.

He developed a horse race betting system called "The Favorites Phenomenon," which proved to give betting enthusiasts very good odds for predicting horse races.

He set up the membership site at www.fpsystem.co.uk, and he charges $147 a month for access to his program. He now makes over $50,000 a month from his membership program.

Case Study–Dwayne Kerr

"I make $15,000 a month thanks to my Law of Attraction expert interviews membership site!"

Dwayne Kerr attended a few of my early seminars.

He interviewed 24 experts on the law of attraction and put these MP3 recordings in a membership site. Customers can access these interviews for $27 a month, and every month Dwayne does a new interview.

He currently has 500 members, earning him $15,000 a month in recurring income.

Case Study–Kavit Haria

"I make $80,000 a month thanks to my continuity programs and membership-based courses!"

Kavit's niche market is musicians. Specifically, he helps musicians get gigs and make money from their music.

He has 80,000 subscribers on his mailing list from all over the world, including some pretty well-known artists!

He decided to convert his www.insidermusicbusiness.com business and products into memberships and continuity programs.

He told me that he makes over $80,000 a month in recurring income from his membership programs, with an 80 percent profit margin! That's over $1 million a year, working from home!

Summary

- If you wanted to make $60,000 a year from selling e-books you might need to get 2,000 new clients a year. But with a membership program, you might just need 100 clients paying you $97 a month. That's 20 times fewer customers, to make the same amount of money.
- With a membership program you get to leverage your information, your knowledge, and your research. And, you get to sell all that content over and over again to 100 members, or 500 members, or 1,000 members. This business model is very scalable. With your membership program you can make a nice part-time income, or seven figures or even eight figures a year.
- Membership programs are nothing new. Online membership sites are simply websites with password-protected areas for paying members.
- The main advantage for customers is that they get to benefit from the purchasing power of hundreds of subscribers to pay for your latest research on a monthly basis. And the fact that they are drip-fed this information can help them learn better, rather than being overwhelmed by a huge amount of information all at once.
- There are seven types of membership programs: content-based membership sites, monthly newsletters, online software-as-a-service and Internet services, CD/DVD of the month, free community sites, done-for-them services, and fixed-term memberships.
- To set up a membership program you need a content management system, such as aMember or WishList, integrated with your website and with a payment gateway such as ClickBank.com or 2CheckOut.com.

- The easy way to sell a membership program is to make an irresistible $1 offer that includes a 14-day or 30-day trial membership.
- Video sales letters and webinars are the easiest and most powerful ways to get lots of members to join your continuity program.
- The secret to making a lot of money from your continuity programs is to have multiple high-end offers to sell to your members.
- To find out more about how you can profit from membership sites and discover "21 Ways To Make Money While You Sleep" check out The Passive Income Summit on DVD at www.laptopmillionaire.tv/dvd.

11

Webinars

"If you liked what I just told you about membership sites, you're going to love this!" the Laptop Millionaire said with a smile.

"There is exciting new web conferencing technology that laptop entrepreneurs are now using that until recently was only available to large corporations at a cost of more than $100,000 a year. Thanks to the advent of high-speed broadband Internet, multinational companies could have their executives videoconference in real time with other executives thousands of miles away, rather than spend millions of dollars a year flying them around for meetings.

"Well, the price of videoconferencing technology has kept coming down, and laptop entrepreneurs can now do live video presentations (also known as web seminars or webinars) for up to 1,000 people at the same time for just $99 a month!

"Here is why this is so exciting: You can use webinars to sell your products or services to large numbers of your prospects and make a lot of money fast—without ever leaving your house! Laptop entrepreneurs are making $20,000 to $200,000 or more in 90 minutes from home!"

The Laptop Millionaire was right. Many of my fellow laptop entrepreneurs made a fortune thanks to webinars:

- Adeel Chowdry made $250,000 in 90 minutes.
- Alex Goad made $330,000 in 90 minutes.

- Oli Tee made $2 million thanks to webinars.
- Jeff Mills made $1.5 million in three months thanks to joint venture webinars.
- Sam Bakker generated $100,000 a month thanks to joint venture webinars.
- Brian K. and Mike W. made over $4 million last year thanks to joint venture webinars.
- Tom X. made $2.5 million in four months thanks to joint venture webinars.
- Nathan Jurewicz made $5 million in his first year online thanks to webinars.
- Greg T. did $10 million in sales in his first year online thanks to joint venture webinars.

I hadn't heard the Laptop Millionaire so excited in a long time. "Imagine having 1,000 of your clients watching your presentation on your computer screen, listening to you, and even interacting with you, in real time!" he continued.

"At the end of a webinar, after you've spent 60 minutes sharing great content with the participants, you can make an *offer* to them. For example: 'If you enjoyed this webinar and would like our help with implementing this strategy, join our coaching program at XYZ.com.'

"I started using webinars in my business, and I got 600 paying members and a $60,000-a-month income stream from doing just six webinars," he said.

What is truly incredible is that webinars typically have a conversion rate of 10 to 20 percent as opposed to online sales letters that convert at 1 to 2 percent, on average. Imagine outselling your best-written sales letters on your websites 10 times over! And webinars allow you to sell high-ticket offers priced at $1,000 to $4,000, whereas it is usually difficult to sell products that cost more than $200 directly from a website. With a conversion rate that is 10 times better, selling offers that are priced 10 times higher, some laptop entrepreneurs are experiencing a 10-fold increase in their sales thanks to webinars!

"And the best thing of all," the Laptop Millionaire concluded, "is that you can run a webinar from anywhere in the world!"

10 IMPORTANT REASONS WHY YOU MUST DO WEBINARS

1. You can make a *lot* of money easily and *fast*, while educating, informing, and adding value to your prospects!
2. Webinars convert much better than websites or online sales letters. It is typical to close 10 percent of your attendees at a $1,000 price point (as long as you have a good offer). In other words, having 100 targeted prospects on your webinar can bring in $10,000 in sales from a single 90-minute webinar.
3. They cost next to nothing to run (no hosting, no website necessary, just a $99/month gotowebinar.com subscription).
4. Webinars give you massive leverage! You can talk to hundreds of prospects at the same time.
5. You can do webinars from home, or from anywhere in the world, from your laptop.
6. You don't even need a website, a product, or even a mailing list to make money with webinars. (Check out the joint venture webinar business model.)
7. They help you build your relationship with your clients and prospects.
8. They work in any market.
9. If you've built a mailing list of prospects and clients, promoting a webinar to them can be a *very* lucrative way of monetizing your list of subscribers or your social media lists of followers and fans. In fact, doing webinars is a great way to *build* your mailing list!
10. You can earn *passive* income from your webinar replays (recordings of your webinars that play over and over again forever, generating sales!)

How to Set Up a Webinar

Before I share with you eight ways to make money using webinars and six ways to promote webinars, let me explain how you can set up a webinar in

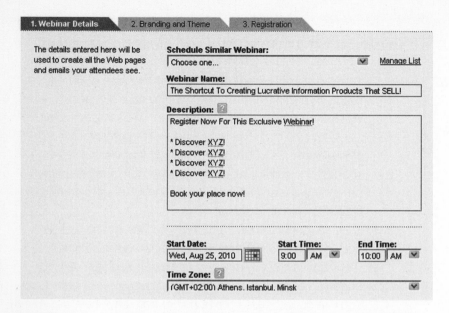

FIGURE 11.1 Setting Up a Webinar Only Takes a Few Minutes

less than three minutes—yes, setting up a webinar is *that* easy. To start, simply register an account at www.gotowebinar.com/s/TAF (you'll get a 45-day free trial), and when you log in, click on Schedule a Webinar. You will then see this screen (Figure 11.1).

First, you will need to give your webinar a title. Try to make this something that will arouse curiosity and compel your subscribers to want to sign up. Appeal to their self-interest. For example, try something like: "How to Make $5,000 a Month Thanks to XYZ" or "How to Lose 30 Pounds in 60 Days Thanks to Alkalizing and Energizing!"

Next, you need to add a description. Once again make this engaging and enticing to compel people to sign up. Once you have given your webinar a title, a description, and you have set the time and date, scroll to the bottom of the page and you will see the Specify Panelists option.

A panelist is someone who will be taking part in the webinar with you; for example, a guest expert that you are interviewing or who is delivering a PowerPoint presentation on the webinar. Simply add their full name in the box to the right and their e-mail address in the corresponding box.

You can have as many panelists as you like, although typically you will be the only panelist, when you deliver your presentation to your webinar attendees. The second most common webinar model involves joint venturing with an expert, where they deliver a 90-minute PowerPoint presentation, then make an offer, and you split the sales 50–50. In that scenario, you would type in yourself and your joint venture partner as the panelists in that section.

This is the page where you can brand your webinar registration page with your own logos and pictures. Personally, I simply upload my logo.

After you press "Save and Continue" at the bottom of this page, the final step involves setting up the registration form. On this page you can specify what information you require your attendees to provide before they will get access to your webinar. I recommend you simply ask for first name, last name, and e-mail address.

You could also ask your registrants to type in their number one question regarding the topic. This lets you know what they really want to learn and could prove invaluable in converting them to a sale or creating a best-selling course.

Click on "Save," and your webinar registration page is ready. An e-mail will automatically be sent to the panelists you selected, informing them of how to sign in to the webinar. Congratulations—your webinar set up is now complete and ready to go live.

The next step will be to promote your webinar and prepare your presentation.

On the day of your webinar, launch it 10 minutes before its scheduled time by pressing the "Start Broadcast" button in your GoToWebinar account.

This control panel (Figure 11.2) will appear on your screen, allowing you to manage the webinar and interact with the attendees.

I only use a few of the control options. For example, when it is time to start the webinar, I click on "Show My Screen." This allows all the participants to see my screen and hear my voice.

If I am doing a joint venture webinar, and I want to hand over the controls to my partner so that the audience can see his or her screen, I click on "Change Presenter."

If I want to interact with the webinar attendees and see the questions they are typing in, I click on "Questions."

Also, I highly recommend you click on "Start Recording" to record your webinar. This video can then be used to broadcast a replay or you can sell this video recording as a product or add it to your membership site as additional content.

During Your Meeting

For You

As the meeting organizer you can share either your whole screen or choose to just show a specific application. Record your meeting sessions – including all phone and microphone audio – for future review and reuse. Interact on the screen using the pen, highlighter, arrow and spotlight tools. ◼◂

- **Audio conferencing via phone and computer** ◼◂
- **Full desktop sharing**
- **Specific application sharing***
- **Recording*** ◼◂
- **Invite others on the fly**
- **Instantly change presenters**
- **Transfer keyboard and mouse control**
- **Drawing tools***
- **Multiple monitor support***
- **Mac and PC support**
- **Chat**

For Attendees

Attendees see what you show them. You can work together by sharing keyboard and mouse control or see each other's work by changing presenters.

- **Audio via phone and computer**
- **Cooperatively edit documents on screen**
- **Mac and PC support**
- **View meetings on an Apple® iPad™** Read more ◼◂
- **Chat**

FIGURE 11.2 The GoToWebinar Control Panel

Eight Ways to Make Money Thanks to Webinars

I have found eight ways to profit from webinars, though this technology is so versatile I wouldn't be surprised if I come across a few more webinar-based business models.

Thanks to webinars you can make money by:

1. Promoting your own webinar and selling your offer during the webinar.
2. Running a joint venture webinar with someone else (they do the presentation, they sell their offer, and you split the sales 50–50).

3. Uploading your webinar replays on your website (generate passive income from people watching the replays and buying the product).
4. Creating products by recording your webinars and selling them.
5. Running webinars for businesses and getting paid for it.
6. Being a webinar joint venture broker (bring a webinar presenter and a marketer together for them to make money, and you get a cut).
7. Running day-long webinar marathons and webTV shows.
8. Selling a six-week webinar coaching series (group coaching via webinars).

Let's explore these eight business models in a bit more detail.

1. Promote Your Webinar, Deliver Your Presentation, and Make an Offer

You can use a webinar to deliver a PowerPoint presentation to anywhere from 10 to 1,000 of your prospects or mailing list subscribers.

For example, you could deliver a PowerPoint presentation titled "How to Use YouTube to Build Your Mailing List and Grow Your Business for Free," or "Seven Hypnobirthing Tips for Pregnant Women," or "The Skinny Bitch Secrets to Weight Loss," "How to Build Your MLM Downline," or "Three Steps to Reversing the Symptoms of Arthritis Naturally."

At the end of a webinar, after you've spent 60 to 90 minutes giving great content to your webinar participants, you can make an *offer* to them. For example: "If you enjoyed this webinar and would like our help with implementing this strategy, join our coaching program at youtubemarketingexperts .com."

What I find astonishing about webinars is how complete beginners are making very good money from their first few webinars.

"We've Made $3,000 in 48 Hours Thanks to Our First-Ever Webinar!" Eileen Bowley and Suzanne Barnett of "Keep IT Simple Software Training" help businesses increase their productivity and their sales by using software applications and Internet technology. They recently made $3,000 in 48 hours, thanks to their first-ever webinar!

"We were so excited—it was like winning the lottery!" they wrote. "Or better even, as we knew we had taken the necessary action, came out of our comfort zone, and put the effort into it. We know we will make more sales. Our advice to people: *just do it*!"

"I Made $10,100 in Four Weeks Thanks to My First-Ever Webinars!" Gary McGeown is a seminar promoter in Ireland, and we got to spend some time together at my Internet Marketers Skiing Retreat. When Gary started doing webinars, he made an extra $10,100 in four weeks!

As he puts it, "Webinars really are going to be like having your own infomercial program delivering your content and offer to your target market."

"I Made $26,000 in 21 Days Thanks to My First-Ever Webinars!" Lucy Johnson is a former fitness and aerobics instructor from the United Kingdom. After attending a few of my seminars and trying different strategies, she found out about webinars. She implemented this strategy and ran a webinar for personal trainers who wanted to learn new marketing tactics. By selling her coaching program during her first few webinars, she made $26,000 in 21 days!

She then set up a $147-a-month membership site and ran a webinar to promote it. The webinar *replay* converts at 48 percent and recently got her 261 paying members and $40,000 a month in revenue!

How to Deliver a Profitable Webinar Presentation For delivering an effective webinar presentation that makes you money, create a PowerPoint presentation that contains the following four parts:

1. At the beginning, tell your story and establish your credibility (why people should listen to you).
2. Then, in the middle bit, deliver great content (for example, three strategies for getting traffic using YouTube).
3. After approximately 60 minutes, identify the problem they need to solve. (For example: "You really need to grow your mailing list but you don't want to spend a fortune on advertising to drive more traffic to your site.")
4. Finally, provide the solution by offering your product or service.

There are many things you can do to ensure you sell well during your webinar:

- Have an irresistible offer! Make sure your product or service is simply amazing, offered at a reasonable price, and add some fantastic bonuses to the offer that are worth a lot more than what you are charging for your product. Also, offer a money-back guarantee so that buying becomes a zero-risk proposition for your prospects.

- Offer proof that your product or service is great—have testimonials, case studies, screenshots of results, and so on.
- Make sure you explain everything in your offer very well.
- Be enthusiastic about your offer.

The objective of your sales webinar is to overcome your audiences' buying resistance while persuading them to take action. Buying resistance shows up in comments such as: "You don't understand my problem." "How do I know you're qualified?" "I don't believe you." "I don't need it right now." "It won't work for me." "What happens if I don't like it?" "I can't afford it."

Take their concerns away by addressing these objections during your webinar.

By telling your story and establishing your credibility at the beginning of the webinar, and by delivering great content, you are taking care of the "You don't understand my problem," and "How do I know you're qualified?" objections.

By reminding them of the problem they're experiencing, what they are missing out on, and what it will cost them if they don't take action right now, you are addressing the "I don't need it right now" objection.

By showing proof that this works, through testimonials, case studies, and demos you are addressing the "I don't believe you" and "It won't work for me objections.

By offering a payment plan (for example, "pay in three installments") you might be overcoming the "I can't afford it" objection.

And finally, by having a money-back guarantee you address the "What happens if I don't like it" objection.

2. Do a Joint Venture Webinar with an Expert, and Have Your Partner Sell during the Webinar

A joint venture (JV) is a collaboration between two businesses for the purpose of making money. It is usually set for a short period of time, and allows companies to profit from opportunities they might not be able to individually.

Some examples of JVs in the corporate world:

- BP and Esso joint venture on oil exploration projects.
- IHOP restaurants and Disneyland did reciprocal voucher promotions.
- CompUSA stores sell computers and hardware. It set up a computer training division, with the service delivered by another company.
- The *USA Today* newspaper promotes some toll-free numbers, and they split the profits with the company that owns and operates these services.

When I first started out in the seminar business I called up the Laptop Millionaire and I asked him what would be the best way to promote my seminars. Should I buy a lot of advertising space in newspapers? Should I invest in public relations? Should I distribute flyers or do direct marketing?

The Laptop Millionaire had run a seminar business and made $5 million in two years in the early 2000s, but he ended up with large offices and 50 staff members. "It was like a zoo. Like running a kindergarten. I hated it," he said. So he shut down his seminar business and found more leveraged ways to make money, just using his laptop.

He said, "To promote your seminars, simply do joint ventures."

I typically had 80 to 100 people attending my small personal development workshops when I started out. Then I got 20 joint venture partners e-mailing their mailing lists for me and I got 1,000 attendees at my next seminar! They e-mailed their lists for free, by the way, in exchange for me reciprocating at a later date, by mailing my list on their behalf.

Other examples of joint ventures:

A marketer once approached me with an idea. He had a mailing list of 6,000 clients who would be interested in my latest DVD home study course. He offered to cover the cost of the direct mail mailing. I would fulfill on shipping the DVDs to the new customers, and we'd split the profits.

Three weeks later we had made 150 sales at $597 each and generated close to $90,000. The cost of the direct mail campaign was only $4,000, and we each walked away with $40,000 in profits!

Another time, Jonathan Jay told me the story of how he wanted to promote his $3,000 How to Become a Life Coach course, but he didn't have any money to pay for advertising. Luckily, his friend had a personal development newsletter that went out to 32,000 subscribers every month.

Jonathan convinced him to include his promotional flyer in the newsletter. Thanks to this JV he got 20 new clients straightaway and banked $60,000 in three days!

When it comes to Internet marketing, the term "joint venture" or "JV" usually means: "I'll e-mail my list for you, if you e-mail your list for me."

This practice is generally referred to as a JV or an ad swap, but you might also see it described as partnership marketing, fusion marketing, or even host beneficiary agreements.

If you want to find some great joint venture partners, ask yourself these brainstorming questions:

- "Who can buy or sell a *ton* of my stuff?"
- "Who else has my *ideal* clients?"
- "What else do my clients *want*?"
- "What else do my clients *buy*?"

Combining the concept of joint ventures with the technology of webinars is a powerful mix. You can truly make a fortune in a very short period of time thanks to joint venture webinars.

Why would you want to do joint venture webinars? Well, if you are the one *promoting* the webinar, this means that you don't have to create a PowerPoint presentation, you don't have to have a product to sell, and you don't have to deal with the customer service and delivery of what was sold (your joint venture partner will do all that and give you 50 percent of the money). This is also a great way to monetize your mailing list and your social media presence.

If you are the one *delivering* the presentation during the webinar, you get to benefit from mass leverage because your joint venture partner has just spent three to four days marketing your webinar to their list. You just need to show up and deliver a 90-minute presentation. Heck, you don't even need to leave your house.

Now, imagine having 20 or 100 or even 500 joint venture partners promoting your webinar for you? When you have a good webinar presentation that converts well, it is not surprising to have 20 joint venture webinars lined up in a single week. In other words, you would get 20 joint venture partners promoting your webinar to their respective mailing lists, and you deliver that presentation 20 times in a week, on these 20 different webinars.

Is this a powerful, highly leveraged business model? Well, look at these results from the past year:

- Oli Tee made $2 million thanks to webinars.
- Jeff Mills made $1.5 million in three months thanks to JV webinars.
- Sam Bakker generated $100,000 a month thanks to JV webinars.
- Brian K. and Mike W. made over $4 million last year thanks to JV webinars.
- Tom X. made $2.5 million in four months thanks to JV webinars.
- Greg T. did close to $10 million in sales, in his first year online, thanks to JV webinars.

How I Made $200,000 in Sales in 90 Minutes Thanks to a Webinar   Thanks to the Laptop Millionaire's advice and guidance, I have generated hundreds of thousands of dollars in sales using webinars. A few weeks after our conversation, I decided to run my first-ever joint venture webinar. Basically, another expert was going to make the presentation and sell his $1,000 offer. All I needed to do was *promote* the webinar, and we'd split the sales 50–50.

Five days before the webinar, I started telling my subscribers about it and I got approximately 1,000 people to register for the event, which meant I could expect approximately 300 to 380 of them to show up for the actual event.

I wanted to get more people onto the webinar, as a webinar can hold up to 1,000 participants at the same time.

With time running out, I offered $1,000 to two joint venture partners of mine for them to promote the webinar to *their* mailing lists as well. (I was offering to pay them for a solo ad.) It would take them just five minutes' work to send out an e-mail, and they would each pocket $1,000 pure profit. Not a bad deal for them.

What *I* would get in return would be exposure to over 500,000 subscribers on their combined mailing lists.

My $2,000 investment paid off. Thanks to this additional last-minute exposure we got an extra 1,200 people registered for the webinar, with 2,240 registrations in total.

More than 700 people from around the world watched the webinar live (and hundreds more watched the webinar replay the next day), and my joint venture partner presented his offer and did a massive $200,000 in sales in 90 minutes!

How Tom Made $2.5 Million in Four Months Thanks to Joint Venture Webinars   Tom is a young entrepreneur from Australia in his mid-20s. He attended my Speed Cash Seminar and started making money online pretty quickly.

A few months later, I introduced him to a friend of mine who is a software developer, because I didn't have time to help promote his social media software. Tom ended up licensing the software from this programmer, packaging it, and selling it for $2,000. Once a day, he would run a webinar with a different joint venture partner (someone who would promote the webinar to their mailing list). By marketing this powerful social media automation software tool, Tom did $2.5 million in sales in just four months, thanks to joint venture webinars.

3. How to Generate Passive Income from Webinar Replays

A very smart way to leverage your webinars and earn multiple streams of passive income from them is to record them and upload them onto your website.

Personally, I use the Webinar Replay System at www.strategicsystems products.com, which is bringing us thousands of dollars a month in extra income. This service costs $199 a month and allows you to have as many as 50 different webinar replays delivered every day. Imagine the power of having *50* 90-minute-long infomercials that sell your products and offers every day.

Other services include StealthWebinar.com, LiveWebinarReplay.com, and Evergreenbusinesssystem.com.

Webinar replays are a great way to *double* the sales from your live webinar. If 500 people register for your webinar and 30 percent of them actually watch it live (150 people), that leaves 350 people who could watch the replay of the webinar over the next few days or weeks.

For example, 27-year-old former TV producer Corinna X did her first webinar recently and made $16,000 in sales in 90 minutes (this was just four months after she started her Internet business! She says it would have taken her two and half years to earn that much money in her job). Her webinar was titled How to Get 100,000 Twitter Followers in 30 Days, and she offered a $997 coaching program at the end.

What has been interesting is that she has been making another $4,000 a month from the webinar replay. People download her free report about

Twitter; they read it and find her e-mail address in there; they e-mail her asking her for more information; she sends them to the webinar replay, and they sign up for her coaching program!

4. Make Money by Creating Products from Your Webinar Recordings

Here is an interesting idea for profiting from webinars: Why not have three to four experts on a webinar and record it as a product?

Or, what if you do six webinars on a specific topic and bundle them together as a product that you sell from your website?

You could do these six webinars yourself, or perhaps have six presentations from six different experts, record them, and sell that as a bundled product.

"I Made $9,000 in Five Weeks Thanks to My First-ever Webinars and I'm Turning My Webinar Recordings into New Products!"   David Lee is a property investor, and he runs workshops on property investing. Thanks to his first few webinars he made $9,000 in five weeks. Better still, he is now turning his webinar recordings into new products that he can sell from his website.

Also, you could use your webinar registration page as a flycatcher page to find out what people want, and create a product that answers all of their questions.

A really cool feature on GoToWebinar is that when you set up a webinar registration page (Figure 11.3), you can ask registrants a question. For example, "What is your number one question about making money with Twitter?"

We got over 300 questions submitted in 24 hours, including:

- How can I increase my number of Twitter followers?
- How can I convert my Twitter followers into buyers?
- How soon can you expect to have a return on the investment?
- What should I say in my tweets?

This market research is invaluable in helping us create an e-book, a course, or an information product. Based on what our target market is asking us, some of the products, courses, or features we could include in this product might be:

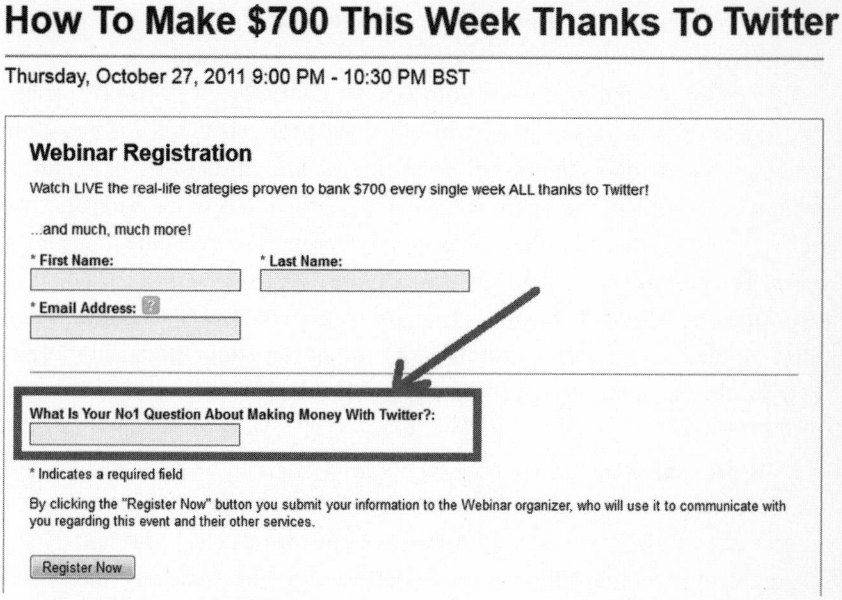

How To Make $700 This Week Thanks To Twitter

Thursday, October 27, 2011 9:00 PM - 10:30 PM BST

Webinar Registration

Watch LIVE the real-life strategies proven to bank $700 every single week ALL thanks to Twitter!

...and much, much more!

* First Name:

* Last Name:

* Email Address:

What Is Your No1 Question About Making Money With Twitter?:

* Indicates a required field

By clicking the "Register Now" button you submit your information to the Webinar organizer, who will use it to communicate with you regarding this event and their other services.

Register Now

FIGURE 11.3   GoToWebinar Registration Page Can Also Act as a Powerful Market Research Tool

- How to Get 100,000 Twitter Followers in 30 Days!
- How to Convert Your Twitter Followers into Buyers!
- How Many Tweets to Send per Day, and How to Write Your Tweets!

5. Make Money by Running Webinars for Businesses

Most business owners have no idea about how to run a webinar or how profitable they can be for their business. You can make a fortune by helping them promote their products and services to their database of clients using webinars.

Two of my favorite webinar success stories are how Australian marketer Steven Essa became a laptop entrepreneur and made $18,000 in his first webinar, and how U.S. joint venture broker Oli Tee made $2 million last year running webinars for another business.

How to Profit from Running Webinars for Businesses   In this specific type of joint venture, what you will bring to the table is your webinar organizing skills (you will see, it's very simple). What the business owner will bring to the table is a product to sell and a mailing list of prospects to promote the webinar to. Here's how it works in a nutshell:

1. Join GoToWebinar at www.gotowebinar.com/s/TAF (45-day free trial).

2. Find business owners or experts who have products to sell and a mailing list of prospects and clients. (Note: You can find thousands of business owners by looking at the Yellow Pages and classified ads in newspapers, and you can find thousands of experts at RTIR.com, Amazon.com, Facebook pages, Technorati.com, or simply by googling "XYZ expert.")

Contact at least 100 business owners or experts (via Facebook, letter, phone, e-mail, or a combination thereof) and offer to help them sell more of their products. A simple template for you to adapt:

Dear Mr. Jones,

My name is John Smith and I recently came across your website. I believe I can help you sell a lot more of your products. I specialize in organizing webinars for successful business owners/experts such as yourself.

Webinars can *generate tens of thousands of dollars in sales in just 90 minutes*, at no cost to your business. Furthermore, webinars are a great way for you to connect with your audience and increase your sales, your authority, and your recognition in your marketplace.

My team can set everything up for you. We do not charge any money for this service, but instead propose a profit-share arrangement. We make you a lot of money, or we don't get paid a cent.

If you would like to discuss this in more detail, please feel free to contact me on 123–456-7890.

Warm regards,

John Smith

3. You set up the webinar for a certain time and date (for example, 8 P.M. to 9.30 P.M. EST on Wednesday, April 14). GoToWebinar gives you the link to the webinar registration page. With your help, the expert or business owner promotes the webinar to his list (via e-mail or direct mail).

4. The business owner delivers a presentation and makes a special offer to the webinar participants. You process the sales and split the money 50–50.

"I Made $20,000 in 90 Minutes Thanks to My First-ever JV Webinar!" Chris N. has attended many of my seminars and told me that he made $20,000 from his first webinar.

He didn't have his own product to sell, so instead he used the webinar joint venture strategy. He found an expert who had an offer and a mailing list, and he approached him with the idea of running a live webinar with him.

Chris would set up the webinar in GoToWebinar.com and would promote the webinar using social media websites like Facebook, Twitter, Social-Marker.com, as well as Fiverr.com and a bit of pay-per-click advertising.

The expert had to prepare his PowerPoint presentation and put together a fantastic offer for the webinar participants. He also had to promote the webinar to his mailing list.

In the end, they did $40,000 in sales from this 90-minute webinar, and they split the sales 50–50!

6. Make Money as a Webinar Joint Venture Broker

After I ran my first joint venture webinar, I was amazed to see that we had generated $200,000 in sales. And more sales were coming in every day from the webinar replay.

I sent a message to my 140 joint venture partners, telling them that they should promote this webinar, too, as it converted very well and it would make them money.

The presenter of that webinar thanked me for doing this, and offered me a 5 percent cut from all these joint venture webinars I had arranged for him. I thanked him and told him this was not necessary. But I still banked the $20,000 commission check that brokering these joint ventures had generated.

I realized that one could make money from being a webinar JV broker. Instead of finding someone who has a product to sell *and* a mailing list of prospects, why not find someone with a list, then find someone else with a relevant product to sell to that list, and organize a joint venture webinar for them? You can organize the webinar and interview the presenter during the webinar, while the list owner promotes the webinar to his mailing list.

7. Make Money from Multispeaker Webinar Seminars

Some variations of these webinar-based business models include running a day-long webinar like a live one-day multispeaker seminar, where six or so webinar presenters alternate during the day. The first presenter starts at 10 A.M., the next presenter follows at 11 A.M., the third presenter starts at 1 P.M., and so on.

The webinar host and the six webinar presenters all promote this live one-day webinar event, and they all benefit from the exposure.

The webinar host, it is interesting to note, makes 50 percent of the sales from each presenter. That's 50 percent of the sales from the first presenter, 50 percent of the sales from the second presenter, and so on. This can be quite lucrative if it's well done and there are thousands of people registered for the event.

As a side note, I used Ustream.tv recently to broadcast my live four-day, London-based seminar to our clients and students all around the world. This technology opens up very interesting new possibilities for speakers, experts, seminar promoters, authors, therapists, and others.

Another possibility that has been opened up thanks to online video and broadband Internet, is the idea of WebTV shows or video podcasts. Andrew Lock gets 108,000 viewers a month to watch his WebTV show titled *Help! My Business Sucks!* and generates millions of dollars a year from selling his offers during his shows. Check out my webinar with Andrew Lock in which he explains this strategy at www.laptopmillionaire. tv/andrewlock.

8. Make Money from Selling a Weekly Webinar Coaching Series

A final way to profit from webinars is to simply *charge* for them.

Andrew Bridgewater recently offered a six-week webinar series in which he coached live participants to weight loss success. His clients paid $400 each to get access to six live weekly webinars where they could interact with Andrew, ask him questions, and get coached by him (this is group coaching delivered by webinar as opposed to one-on-one coaching).

"I Make $200,000 a Month Thanks to Telesales and Group Coaching Webinars!"   One of my joint venture partners explained to me how he makes $200,000 a month selling his weekly group coaching program that he delivers via webinar:

We're selling a group coaching program where users get 52 weeks of training and weekly group Q&A webinars with me personally.

We have a two-step process where we call and set an appointment and then sell on this call. Our best guy converts one in six calls, which pretty much means about four sales a week for between $3,000 and $5,000 for each sale.

It's actually a pretty simple setup. We just have four phone guys, one appointment setter, and a sales manager who looks after everything. And, of course, there are no affiliate commissions to pay so it all has extremely high margins.

Six Ways to Promote Your Webinar

1. Promote to Your Own Mailing List

Promoting your webinar to your mailing list of subscribers is of course the best and fastest way to get people registered for your webinar (see Chapter 2 on how to build your list). It doesn't cost anything to send e-mails to your list, and because they already know you, like you, and trust you (hopefully) they are much more likely to register for a webinar you promote. (See Figure 11.4.)

2. Joint Ventures and Ad Swaps

You can arrange joint ventures or ad swap deals with other marketers in your field. This means they will e-mail their list to promote your webinar in exchange for you reciprocating the favor at a later date (check out http://safe-swaps.com). What's great about having someone e-mail their list for you is that it represents mass leverage (you gain exposure to possibly tens of thousands or hundreds of thousands of your idea prospects), and you benefit from that person's endorsement—he is recommending you to people that know him, like him, and trust him.

3. Solo Ads

Alternatively, you can buy solo ads to promote your webinar. This means paying mailing list owners to e-mail their lists for you (see list of solo ad providers at www.laptopmillionaire.tv/soloads). This can be a bit hit-or-miss, as most solo ad providers' lists are no longer very responsive.

 Adeel Chowdhry *NEW* Last Thursday's Webinar stats: 3 emails sent, 658 registered, 252 turned up, 90 mins later ==> $48K in sales! Anyone with a good list want to do a Webinar soon?

about an hour ago · Comment · Like

FIGURE 11.4 Internet Marketer Adeel Chowdhry's Post on Facebook!

If you'll recall, I paid two of my joint venture partners $1,000 each for them to promote my first webinar, and this resulted in 1,200 more registrations and at least an extra $100,000 in sales. I knew their lists were good, and I wanted to make sure they would send out that promotional e-mail for me. Instead of trying to arrange an ad swap, I just *encouraged* them with some cash to make the deal happen faster.

4. Promote Your Event on Facebook and Twitter

You can also promote your webinar to your Facebook friends and your Facebook fans (create a Facebook event), and to your Twitter followers, too.

5. Pay-Per-Click Advertising

You could, of course, use Facebook Ads, Google AdWords, or Yahoo! Search Marketing to pay to send traffic to your webinar registration page (pay-per-click advertising), but this can be expensive.

6. Buy Fiverr.com Gigs

A great way of promoting your event is by finding 20 people on Fiverr.com willing to promote your webinar to their Facebook fans or Twitter followers. At $5 per Fiverr gig, that $100 could potentially give you exposure to 100,000 people. Depending on the topic of your webinar, this could possibly get you enough registrations for your event to make it very profitable, though it might be that you need to buy 100 gigs (cost: $500) to get that critical mass of registrations.

How I Used Fiverr and Facebook to Make $22,246 in 90 Minutes   Social media websites like Facebook are *great* for promoting webinars.

I had spent $340 on Fiverr.com to buy gigs like "I will invite my Facebook friends to like your page or join your group." This investment resulted in having more than 12,000 new fans and members on Facebook.

I then did a small marketing test. I wanted to test the effectiveness of Facebook for promoting live webinars, so I ran a five-day marketing campaign using Facebook *exclusively*. The goal was to get as many registrations as possible for my How to Make $3,000 a Month Thanks to Facebook webinar.

I promoted this webinar just through Facebook by letting my 5,000 Facebook friends, 9,100 Facebook group members, and my 1,280 Facebook fans know about the event. Within 5 days, 881 people had registered for the webinar, 300 of them watched the webinar live, and this generated $22,246 in sales! This webinar cost nothing to put on, and best of all I ran it from my bungalow while on holiday on a Greek island in the Mediterranean!

JVwebinars.com—The Webinar Marketplace

I received an e-mail from a student of mine who asked, "Where can I find good webinars to promote?" That same week, I received an e-mail from a joint venture partner asking me if I knew any webinars that were converting well that he could promote to his list. Finally, in the same week, I received a third e-mail from a student of mine who was asked, "Where can I find joint venture partners and affiliates who can promote my webinar?"

This inspired me to launch JVwebinars.com—the online marketplace for webinar presenters and webinar promoters (affiliates) to arrange joint ventures and earn affiliate commissions from promoting webinars. This site also gives stats and information about which are the best-converting webinars.

The Laptop Millionaire had told me to think bigger and to look at creating online marketplaces like Fiverr.com. Well, check out www.jvwebinars.com and let me know what you think.

■ ■ ■

Case Study–Steven Essa

"I made $18,000 in 90 minutes, without a website, a list, or a product, thanks to a joint venture webinar!"

Steven Essa of www.X10effect.com is the world's number one expert on how to run webinars successfully, and he is my webinar mentor. We've become good friends over the years, and he has spoken at quite a few of my live seminars.

Let me share with you the story of Steven's first webinar joint venture deal, in his own words. I like to call this story, *How to Make $18,000 in Sales in 90 Minutes, without a Web Site, a List, or a Product!*

A little while after attending my first-ever Internet marketing seminar and learning about how webinars worked, a friend of mine put me in touch with a lady she knew who could use my help.

I got in touch with her and it turned out she was a barrister, and that she had a law-related product she wanted to sell to her database of 1,000 people.

I found out that she had never e-mailed her list before nor sold anything to them. Instead, her plan was to travel around Australia to deliver seminars and sell her offer.

I strongly advised *against* doing seminars because I knew that the costs, time, and logistics involved in running seminars were horrendous.

Instead I suggested she do a webinar.

I explained to her that with a webinar:

- There was no cost to her.
- It would only take one to two hours of her time.
- She could reach a *global* audience with her offer.

I had a GoToWebinar account, so I knew how to set up a webinar.

So here is what I proposed to her:

- She would create a $3,000 offer for her audience.
- I would set up the webinar through GoToWebinar.
- I would write the copy for the webinar registration page.
- I would write and send out the e-mails to her list.
- I would interview her during the webinar.
- I would arrange to collect the money (we would share proceeds 50–50).

She agreed to this joint venture.

The result: out of 1,000 people on her list, 60 people attended the webinar and we generated $18,000 in sales in one hour.

Watch Steven Essa live on stage at my recent seminar, explaining how *anybody* can make a fantastic income thanks to webinars: go to www.laptopmillionaire.tv/stevenessa.

Case Study–Oli Tee

"I made $2,000,000 (two million dollars!) in 12 months thanks to 50–50 joint venture webinars!"

Oli Tee is a joint venture broker.

He took a company from doing $1.8 million in sales per year to $6 million a year simply by adding two webinars a month to its marketing mix!

For added value, apart from setting up and running the webinars for this company, he also handled the customer service requirements from those sales, and helped with developing new offers for the company to see via webinars. They were selling software tools for $97 each, but he convinced them to bundle these tools together in a special offer, with extra bonuses and coaching included, for $997.

And the best part is he negotiated a 50–50 deal on the webinars. That means he made close to $2 million from running a few webinars every month!

Case Study–Minesh Bhindi

"I make $8,000 a month in passive income thanks to automated webinar replays!"

Minesh Bhindi came to one of my workshops when he was just 17 years old. He set up his own Internet-based business and now earns over $40,000 a month from his information marketing business. His area of specialization is helping people make money in the stock market and by *renting out* gold and silver (the covered calls strategy).

He recently revealed to me that he is *making $8,000 a month in passive income thanks to automated webinar replays.*

That's right—every webinar you do can be recorded and replayed over and over again, generating sales for you *on autopilot.* You can have as many as 50 different automated webinars playing every day.

Case Study–Dave Sheahan

"I made $3,000 in 30 days thanks to my first few webinars, and I will do close to a million dollars this year thanks to webinars!"

I met Dave Sheahan at a seminar in Dublin, Ireland, after my talk there. He attended my workshop shortly thereafter, and he immediately implemented the webinar strategy.

Within 30 days he had made $3,000 online. His business now does six figures a year and is growing fast to seven figures.

Dave wrote 6 *Weeks to a Cover Model Body*, and he coaches people interested in fitness and weight loss.

Here's what he says about webinars:

I run webinars and live streams on a regular basis. I have had huge success with webinars, and I regularly make over $3,000 *per webinar* now.

On the majority of my webinars I make sales at between 10 percent and 70 percent conversion. I also do loads of JV webinars with people around the world.

Facebook is my favorite tool for marketing and has been the source of the majority of my business!

Case Study–Nathan Jurewicz

Nathan Jurewicz is a 29-year-old entrepreneur whose niche is real estate short sales. He made $5 million in his first year online thanks to webinars.

He explains how he marketed 300 webinars to his list, many with joint venture partners, in the past two years and created eight different real estate products in that time frame.

He says that once he knew that his webinar presentation had a good conversion rate, he started contacting potential joint venture partners with this highly tempting proposal: "E-mail your list for this webinar, and I'll pay you $8 per opt in!"

This message got joint venture partners flocking to do webinars with him, and he then had them call their friends in the real estate info-marketing niche to recommend doing joint venture webinars with him.

Listen to an exclusive interview with Nathan Jurewicz at www .laptopmillionaire.tv/nathanj.

Case Study–Wim Belt

"I made $11,000 in 90 minutes thanks to my first-ever webinar!"

Wim Belt is a member of my coaching program, and he runs financial training seminars in the Netherlands.

After hearing of my successful webinar promoted on Facebook, he implemented that exact same strategy and made $11,000 in 90 minutes, thanks to his first-ever webinar!

Hello Mark, I'm glad to tell you about my first results.

We set up our business fan page and invited fans and people in our database to my first webinar.

Nearly 400 people signed up for the webinar and 25 people enrolled for the training.

So, we made $11,000. I'm quite sure this amount will grow the coming weeks. Thanks for your valuable information.

Summary

- Thanks to webinars you can make a lot of money fast, while educating, informing, and adding value to your prospects. Webinars help you build your relationship with your clients and prospects.
- Webinars convert much better than online sales letters. It is typical to close 10 percent of your audience at a $1,000 price point (as long as you have a good offer). In other words, having 100 targeted prospects on your webinar can bring in $10,000 in sales from a single 90-minute webinar.
- Webinars give you massive leverage (you can talk to hundreds of prospects at the same time). You can run webinars from home or from anywhere in the world from your laptop.
- You can promote your webinar by sending e-mails to your list, arranging ad swaps, posting messages on Facebook or tweets on Twitter, buying solo ads, buying gigs on Fiverr.com, or buying pay-per-click advertising.
- If you've built a mailing list of prospects and clients, promoting a webinar to them can be a very lucrative way of monetizing your list. In fact, doing webinars is a great way to *build* your mailing list.
- You can earn *passive* income from your webinar replays (recordings of your webinars that do the selling *for* you).
- You can make a fortune from joint venture webinars.
- Most business owners have no idea about the power of webinar technology. Why not help them run webinars? With this strategy, you don't need a website, a product, or even a mailing list to make money using webinars. You just need a GoToWebinar account.
- Webinars are a great way to get a lot of paying members into your membership program fast.
- To find out more about how you can profit thanks to webinars check out this video of Steven Essa live on stage: www.laptopmillionaire.tv/stevenessa.

12 Online Advertising

It had been a year since I'd last seen the Laptop Millionaire. A lot had changed. He was now living in the South of France with his wife and their newborn baby, and he'd decided to start an entirely new business venture.

His SEO business had generated $6 million the previous year, selling leads and doing SEO for real estate companies, and he had told me tantalizingly that this *new* business could become much bigger and more profitable than anything else he'd ever done.

Naturally, eager to learn from my mentor, I was on the next plane to France. I flew in to the airport of Nice, and drove up to the little village of Coaraze overlooking the Côte d'Azur.

Since we hadn't been to any comedy clubs for a while, I brought him a stack of Louis C.K., Russell Peters, and Michael McIntyre stand-up comedy DVDs. "That'll cheer me up," he said as I greeted him and handed him his present.

"What's up?" I asked. In the eight years I'd known him, I had never seen him be anything other than jovial, excited, and high energy.

"This new strategy I've been working on . . . I've only made one million dollars in profit from it this year," he finally said.

When I congratulated him he replied, "You don't understand . . . half a dozen of my friends are doing *1 million dollars a month*! I feel totally useless!"

Now I *really* had to find out more. What kind of venture could be making him one million dollars a year in profit, with no staff, no offices, no overhead, just him and his laptop—*and have him feel like a failure?!*

We sat at a little café in the town square, not far from where he lived, enjoying a breakfast of croissants and fresh orange juice. Life in the South of France had a certain charm to it that appealed to me. Although my mother is French, I'd only lived in France for a year, when I was 19 years old, in the town of La Rochelle on the Atlantic coast. "Maybe I'll move here one day," I thought to myself.

The Laptop Millionaire started explaining what he'd been up to.

"Let me tell you how *serious* money is being made on the Internet.

"Internet marketing comes down to this simple equation: Traffic = Money. So what do you do if you want to get an *avalanche* of traffic—and fast? What if you wanted to get *millions of visitors* to your website this month? That's where media buying comes in—and by that I mean the practice of buying advertising space (advertising banners) on thousands of highly trafficked websites.

"You see, who controls the majority of the traffic on the Internet? Is it Google? Or Facebook? YouTube or Yahoo!? No. The majority of the traffic is controlled by thousands of affiliate marketers that own millions of websites between them. And a lot of them have joined forces to create these new online advertising networks.

"For example, you can approach these media buying agencies and offer $100,000 to buy 4 million visitors to your site this month. They would then place your advertising banners across thousands of the websites that comprise their advertising network, and you would get millions of visitors for just 2.5 cents per click.

"By agreeing to such large traffic contracts you get to buy huge amounts of traffic at a significant discount. Well, in the past year, working from home, just sitting at my laptop, I spent $600,000 on buying online advertising and I made $1.6 million in affiliate commissions from the products I sold. I was left with $1 million in pure profit, thanks to banner advertising on the Internet."

"That's amazing!" I blurted out. "So, how did you do this exactly? Did you spend $600,000 first, and then started receiving all this traffic?"

"No, no. I started off with only a couple hundred dollars, buying advertising space on a handful of websites. This work involves testing different banners, CPA [cost-per-action] offers, ads, websites, advertising networks, and when I find a profitable combination I ramp up the campaign to get millions of visitors seeing my ads. It's boring as hell, sitting at your laptop buying advertising space and then testing different ads, but it can make you a fortune."

The Keys to Online Advertising

I actually knew a handful of people who were profiting from media buying, but I'd never looked into it myself. I was always focused on getting free traffic and was loath to spend money buying traffic.

"I Spend $400,000 a Month on Media Buying, and I Am on Track to Make $16 Million This Year!"

My first exposure to the world of media buying had come a year prior, when I attended a secret Mastermind meeting of Internet marketers at an exclusive golf resort in Cyprus.

One of the participants was an entrepreneur from Israel by the name of Roy, who revealed to us that he was spending $400,000 a month buying banner advertising and driving that traffic to the best-converting ClickBank affiliate offers.

He was making approximately $1.3 million a month in affiliate commissions, selling over 1,000 products a day on ClickBank. He told us he was on track to make over $16 million in sales that year, thanks to these massive traffic contracts he was buying.

When I told him I preferred to get *free* traffic to my websites, because free traffic equals free *money*, he simply replied: "You know, if you keep your fist closed, no money can come out. But no money can come in, either."

"We Went from Zero to Making $2 Million a Month in Less than Six Months!"

A few years ago, Carlos and Lupe Garcia spoke at Yanik Silver's underground seminar, and they revealed their strategy for securing huge traffic deals, where they buy a lot of traffic at a considerable discount.

Carlos had saved up $10,000, which he placed in a bank account. He then got a credit rating agency to verify that this amount had been blocked in the account, as a guarantee. He then contacted 100 different media buying companies, asking to buy $10,000 worth of traffic on credit.

Using this strategy, Carlos and Lupe were able to get $1,000,000 worth of traffic on *credit*, driving the traffic to high-converting CPA offers. They went from zero to making $2 million a month in less than six months and then scaled the business up to $5 million a month!

To watch Carlos and Lupe's live presentation at the Ultimate Traffic Generation Summit go to www.laptopmillionaire.tv/carlosandlupe.

Seven Steps to Get Started in Media Buying

I told the Laptop Millionaire about Roy and Carlos and Lupe Garcia, and he replied that he knew of them as well, though he had never met them.

He then explained to me how to get started with this strategy.

Step 1. Join some CPA networks and look at the different offers you could promote. Some of the offers the Laptop Millionaire promoted included the FlexBelt (device to tone abdominal muscles—it costs $199, and they pay you $52 per lead) and Bellaplex wrinkle reduction cream (they pay you $32 per lead). He suggested I join the MaxBounty, Hydra, COPEAC, and Never-BlueAds CPA networks (there are hundreds of them out there).

"When applying to the CPA networks, tell them you're going to do media buys and that you plan to set up presell pages. If you drive traffic to your presell page where you review the product, for example, rather than sending the traffic directly to the seller's website through your affiliate link, your conversion rates can be 10 to 20 times higher."

The Laptop Millionaire explained that he prefers promoting CPA offers because they typically have a much higher conversion rate than affiliate offers. "You have a 168 percent higher chance of succeeding with CPA marketing rather than standard affiliate marketing," he said. "With traditional affiliate marketing you get paid when you make a sale. With CPA marketing, you get paid simply for getting people to type in their e-mail addresses. It's much easier."

You can also contact your CPA network manager and ask what offers are selling best.

Step 2. Choose a website with a good affiliate program that you want to promote and type it into the Google Keyword Tool (www.googlekey

wordtool.com). This will give you keywords that are relevant to that website. For example, if you type in www.weightwatchers.com you will find that relevant keywords include "lose weight online," "online weight loss tools," and so on.

You can also type the URL of the product you are promoting and paste it into Googleadplanner.com. You're going to see an affinity score—it tells you what other sites these visitors are going to.

Step 3. Type these keywords into Google, and make a list of the websites that come up on page one of Google. Since these websites contain similar keywords to the site you want to promote, this means they get similar visitors and are therefore potential locations for your campaign's banner advertising.

Step 4. Type in each of these websites into Quantcast.com—this will tell you how many visitors it gets and whether it accepts advertising.

Step 5. Create some advertising banners (you can get this done for $20 at www.20dollarbanners.com).

Step 6. Now that you've chosen a product to promote, and you've found a website that is relevant and that is getting a lot of traffic, contact that site and offer to buy advertising space for your banners. Never accept the first price they offer you. Negotiate hard to get the price down.

Generally you can expect to pay $20 per 1,000 impressions of your ad, but the Laptop Millionaire showed me how he negotiated with one site to pay $125 to have his banner on the site for 30 days, and got 17,000 views in that month ($7 per 1,000 impressions).

"If you pay $7 per 1,000 views (impressions) of your ad, and you get just 1 person out of 1,000 to buy your offer, you might be making $20 to $30 for every $7 you spend. Of course, if your ad doesn't convert, or the traffic doesn't convert, or the offer doesn't convert, then maybe you'll lose your entire investment. This is why it is so vital to start with a small amount, test what combination works, tweak your ads or change which sites you advertise on, and then ramp up quickly your most profitable campaigns," the Laptop Millionaire concluded.

As an alternative to contacting each site individually (direct media buying), you can go to advertising networks and ask to advertise across hundreds or thousands of relevant websites (these are media buying agencies). One of the best to get started with is adBrite, I'm told. You can start with just $50 to $100. You will be able to log in to your adBrite account to see how many clicks your ads recieved, and you will need to login to your CPA network account or your ClickBank account to see how much commission you've earned.

Step 7. Now that your banners are driving traffic to that affiliate offer, make sure to measure and track your results, and jettison the ads that are not converting or that are not profitable.

Finally, as we were finishing our breakfast, the Laptop Millionaire recommended advertising on at least five different websites at the same time. He said that in his experience, three will break even and two might make you money. He then ditches the three that don't make him money and ramps up the advertising on the sites that made him money, then chooses three new websites to advertise on.

That slow, gradual process resulted in him eventually having a couple hundred or so highly lucrative ads running on a few thousand websites every day, funneling profits to his bank account. On an advertising budget of approximately $1,600 a day, he had been generating $4,380 a day in affiliate commissions, or approximately $2,700 a day in profit for the past 12 months.

"Spending money on online advertising means getting a lot of leverage in your business. After all, do you want to get rich slow . . . or FAST?"

Meeting the "100-Million-Dollar-Man"

Following my visit with the Laptop Millionaire, I decided to hold the Traffic Generation Summit for my clients and bring in traffic generation experts from all over the world. This is when I first heard of Scott Rewick.

Scott Rewick is often called the "100-Million-Dollar-Man," on account of the amount of money he has spent on online advertising. In the past decade, he built *two* 100-million-dollar companies thanks to online advertising, each in less than two years and made a fortune in the process.

After spending 10 years in Silicon Valley setting up start-ups and floating them on the stock market, he decided that rather than talking to investors all day long it would make him considerably happier to become a speaker and help people turn their lives around financially. "If I can simply help someone make his first $100 online, thanks to what I've learned about leveraging online advertising, that makes me happy. I know this will change people's lives!" he says. A man after my own heart!

We chatted on Skype and he shared with me some of his students' successes.

Kevin was a young entrepreneur in his mid-20s. He started out with only $100, placing his advertising banners on a site—and promptly losing that money.

He then tweaked his banner and tried a different website, spent another $100 and made $60 back (which meant he lost $40 on that investment). By the end of the week he broke even—he would spend $100 in advertising and make $100 back. The following week he made a $60 profit.

He kept testing and tweaking and tracking and then ramping up his profitable campaigns.

And this is where the story becomes unbelievable.

He recently spent $500,000 in a single day buying a traffic contract for millions of visitors from an online advertising network . . . and made $250,000 in profit, *in a single day!* In fact, I'm told he's made a whopping $18 million in profit in the past two years.

But that's not the only success story Scott's students have had.

Patrick is a former engineer at Yahoo!. By learning how to buy advertising on blogs, he made over $5 million in profit in just three months!

Simon was selling e-books on ClickBank with little success. But by learning about media buying his fortunes changed, and he now makes over 2,000 sales a day!

"I have a dozen more stories like these," says Scott.

Shaqir Hussyin learned some media buying strategies from Scott Rewick, and, as a result, he made an *extra* $57,000 in a month, he tells me. "Regarding media buying and online advertising, I'm totally killing it with what I'm doing man—I can send 5,000 to 13,000 clicks at a time!"

And I recently received this message from one of my seminar attendees, Jono K.:

Hey Mark, you don't know me yet, but I went to your Ultimate Traffic Generation Summit where I signed up for Scott Rewick's Media Mentors course. This month I'm going to do at least $20,000 in revenue and by the time you hold your next seminar I will have gone past the $100,000 mark. I'll get on stage and tell people about it and hopefully motivate them to do it too!

To watch Scott Rewick's live presentation at the Ultimate Traffic Generation Summit go to www.laptopmillionaire.tv/scottrewick.

Six Ways to Make Money Thanks to Online Advertising

Let me share with you six ways you can use to make money thanks to online advertising.

1. Buy Traffic for Your Website

The simple, straightforward way to profit from online advertising is to pay for banner advertising or pay-per-click advertising on websites relevant to your own product or service.

The key with any direct response marketing is to track your results to make sure that you are earning more than you are spending. You might find that you are only breaking even on your advertising on the front end, but it allows you to quickly build up a large mailing list of buyers and you profit significantly with your back-end sales (upsells).

This is how I like to use online advertising, especially to promote my live seminars. This sort of leverage in your business can be very powerful. Imagine having to call each of your prospects one by one, and communicate with them one by one. And now imagine having your ad displayed on hundreds of websites around the world every day—you are, in effect, communicating to thousands or even tens of thousands of people a day, even while you sleep! Now that's *power!*

2. Media Buying and Affiliate Promotions

This is the strategy that the Laptop Millionaire, Scott Rewick, and Carlos and Lupe Garcia use. They buy online advertising space, send that traffic to CPA offers, and pocket the affiliate commissions.

This practice of buying traffic cheaply on website X to send it to affiliate offers that convert well is also described as traffic arbitraging.

3. Buying Leads

You can pay $2 to $5 (or more) per lead through the cost-per-action networks such as NeverBlueAds.com.

Just as the Laptop Millionaire makes money by generating leads for the clients of the CPA networks (for example, FlexBelt or Bellaplex), you can do the reverse. You can *buy* leads and make money by selling products to them.

I recently attended another Mastermind meeting of Internet entrepreneurs at the Talladega NASCAR race track, in Alabama. My friend Matt Bacak had organized this gathering, and he revealed that he gets up to 10,000 new subscribers a day through the CPA networks at a cost of $2 per subscriber.

While paying $2 per new subscriber can seem high, he knows that he'll make $2 back within the first month, and he can pay for his leads 60 days later.

Very important note: The key when you buy traffic from media buying agencies or CPA networks, is that you must *really* know your metrics. You must know your conversion rates, you must have a highly efficient upselling system, and you must have great back-end offers that people want to buy. Otherwise you will end up losing a lot of money fast!

4. Pay-Per-Click Advertising

You can also buy traffic through pay-per-click (PPC) advertising sites like Google AdWords, Yahoo Search Marketing, or Microsoft Advertising adCenter. You can find a list of 170 pay-per-click advertising networks at www.laptopmillionaire.tv/ppc.

During one of my trips to the United States, I got to spend some time with Keith W., a young, highly successful Internet marketer from Atlanta. He told me he spends $1,200 a day on banner advertising on the Google Display Network (www.google.com/ads/displaynetwork), and thanks to the resulting traffic (more than 10,000 clicks a day) he gets 4,000 new subscribers a day!

A couple of years ago, Ciaran Doyle started buying traffic from Google AdWords and built a 4,500-person mailing list at a cost of approximately $0.72 per lead. He spent approximately $3,200 to build that list and started making $2,000 a month from selling affiliate products to them. He also told me that at one point he was spending $4,500 a month, driving traffic directly to ClickBank affiliate offers and making a profit of $6,000 a month!

When Google AdWords kicked out a lot of its smaller advertisers, he decided to focus on SEO (see Chapter 3).

5. Facebook Ads

As I mentioned in Chapter 5, I've dipped my toe in the media buying arena, by paying for Facebook Ads. I spent $952 on Facebook Ads to promote a friend's seminar, and within seven days we got a return of over $30,000 in sales!

The ad for the seminar got 11,500,000 impressions in seven days (it was seen 11.5 million times by the 279,000 Facebook users on the tiny island of Cyprus), and this resulted in 5,170 clicks (each click cost $0.18), 192 registrations for the event, and 66 people attending the live event.

Recently I found out that the well-known marketer Frank Kern was spending $90,000 a month on Facebook Ads and making back $250,000 a month as a result.

6. Selling Advertising on Your Websites

Finally, a sixth way to make money thanks to online advertising, is to simply *sell* advertising on your websites, blogs, or online newsletters.

We saw in Chapter 3 how the Laptop Millionaire had 6,500 sites earning him, on average, $0.22 per site per day in Google AdSense revenue (that's $1,430 a day in passive income) before he converted them into lead-generation sites, and how Sotiris Bassarakopoulos makes $3,000 a month from his 450 AdSense sites.

So having Google AdSense ads on your website can be one way to monetize the traffic your site is getting (the Google AdSense program allows you to earn money from displaying Google advertisements on your websites; you get up to 68 percent of the revenue generated for every click on an ad on your sites).

Sometimes you end up getting a lot of traffic to your site by sheer luck, and this creates an opportunity to sell advertising. A young Turkish entrepreneur from the northern part of Cyprus told me that the local lottery did not have a website where they could announce the winning lottery numbers (they only announced them once per week on television, and the next day in the papers). Tens of thousands of people were looking for the results online. So he set up a website where he simply displayed the winning lottery numbers every week.

The site quickly started getting traffic, and he went around to businesses to sell his site's advertising space to local businesses.

He made close to $65,000 in the past year, and the local government offered to buy the site from him for $300,000! Another approach to making money from selling advertising involves setting up online review sites.

For example, U.K. entrepreneur Simon Coulson, a former engineer at British Telecoms, set up the business opportunity review website www.business-opportunity-review.co.uk. By allowing users to write reviews about hundreds of different business opportunities, he quickly got dozens of his pages ranked in Google and built up a mailing list of over 70,000 subscribers in just two years and profited from selling advertising space on his site.

He now runs a highly successful seven-figure-a-year business.

Another example of this is Stacy Kellams' www.realestatecoursereviews .com site, where people post comments about real estate home study courses. The site generates up to $100,000 a month in revenue.

A third example of a review site is Internet Brands, a network of 100 websites in eight different niche markets (gardening, cooking, etc.). Within 12 months of launching, thanks to free traffic from the search engines, this Los Angeles-based business was getting a staggering 72 million visitors a month! Its revenue model was based on selling advertising space on its thousands of web pages.

The key to the business's success, I am told, is that the 100 blogs get a lot of user-generated content. This means that readers post comments and reviews about the products and topics discussed on the blogs, and the content is always fresh. This is one of the main criteria Google looks for in a site—and it got these 100 blogs to the top of the search engines for thousands of keywords.

The business was recently sold for $640 million to a private equity firm.

Another strategy for selling advertising involves blogging. By updating your blog regularly, you can attract a large following of people interested in what you have to say.

Successful bloggers derive a large part of their income from selling advertising on their sites. For example, 18-year-old entrepreneur Carl Ocab, from the Philippines, got his blog www.carlocab.com on page one of Google for the highly competitive keywords "make money online" and has since then made over $10,000 a month by selling advertising on his site. Or Yaro Starak, who makes $10,000 to $35,000 a month thanks to his blog (see his upcoming case study).

The case studies in this chapter illustrate how advertising in different venues and formats can bring in extra revenue.

■ ■ ■

Case Study–Anthony Mink

"I make $750 to $1,200 a day thanks to Facebook Ads!"

Anthony Mink is another young American entrepreneur who enjoys the Laptop Entrepreneur lifestyle. He moved from LA to a beautiful place in Costa Rica, and we recently held a webinar together where he revealed how he makes $750 to $1,200 a day in profit thanks to Facebook Ads! (His advertising budget: $5,000 a month.)

His strategy involves setting up a Facebook ad page, for example, for a popular American football team—then advertising it using Facebook Ads to get thousands of people to "Like" his page (they then become fans of the page). Then on this Facebook page he promotes a "Win a FREE American Football Jersey" CPA offer that pays him $1.64 per lead.

Anthony Mink

Hey Guys...Check this out! Here is a good example of FBTC! Yesterday I posted a pic of me making like $1300 just yesterday. That was almost completely off my lists of FB Page all through backend monetization! I spent $324 on Ads yesterday and received 7347 clicks. That got me about 6500 new fans. I made $307 on the front end...so it cost me about $16 for 6500 new fans! Are you starting to see the power in this? I hope so!!! If you have questions...ask!

S¹ Monday at 6:24am · Like · Comment · Subscribe

FIGURE 12.1   Anthony's Facebook Ad

In the example shown in Figure 12.1, Anthony spent $324 on Facebook Ads in one day and got 7,347 clicks ($0.04/click), which resulted in 6,500 fans and $307 in commissions that day!

Anthony paid to get approximately 120,000 fans on his page, but because of the viral growth of this page, he now has over 400,000 fans on his page that he can communicate with at will, *for free*!

Case Study–Yaro Starak

"I make $10,000 to $35,000 a month thanks to my blog!"

Yaro Starak is an Internet entrepreneur from Australia.

He started his blog, www.Entrepreneurs-Journey.com, in 2005, and today, working less than two hours a day he consistently makes $10,000 to $35,000 per month from his blog—he gets over 25,000 daily readers!

He monetizes all that traffic by selling advertising space on his blog, as well as promoting his own products and affiliate products.

Yaro operates his business from his home or on a Mac Air laptop while traveling, he says, and thanks to free traffic from the search engines he generates up to half a million dollars a year with no full-time staff.

> When I first started back in November 2004, I was an absolute beginner.
>
> I quickly discovered that blogging was not only easy to do but also heaps of fun, and I started to build a loyal, responsive readership.
>
> My blog visitor numbers kept growing day-by-day until one day I realized "Wow! I can actually make money with this!" so I threw myself into experimenting with different techniques, including advertising and affiliate programs, to generate income.

Case Study–Krisztina Szekeres

"I make $3,000 to $5,000 a month thanks to media buying!"

Krisztina Szekeres is a 20-year-old Internet marketer from Budapest in Hungary. I met her when she attended the Ultimate Traffic

Generation Summit. Thanks to media buying, she now makes $3,000 to $5,000 a month.

Her story is fascinating. When she was 14, her dad asked if she was interested in learning about Internet marketing and making money online. He was an electrical engineer and knew nothing about marketing, but he had seen an ad online about this.

Krisztina said yes, and he bought her an e-book on affiliate marketing and gave a speech about it in front of her family. Krisztina barely spoke any English, but she was determined to make this work.

She started out with Google AdWords, but the campaigns weren't profitable. She quickly realized that she needed a mentor who could point her in the right direction. That's when she found Carlos and Lupe Garcia, and signed up for their mentoring program. The program cost $10,000, which was a huge amount to Krisztina's family, as the average wage in Hungary was only $500 a month.

She had to borrow that money from her dad, but vowed to make it back.

Learning these strategies was more difficult for her than for most of our seminar attendees. She says, "I remember the first seminar I attended, I was 16, and I could barely understand it. But I took notes, went home, and I translated it! So it took me like two years to learn the language and the expressions like EPC (earnings-per-click), CPM (cost-per-thousand) and so on. There's no Hungarian translation for these words!"

Finally, she had a breakthrough in her fledgling Internet business: "I started out with media buys, like buying banner traffic from websites, cutting Insertion orders. But I wasn't comfortable with that, as I still didn't speak English very well. So I ended up doing PPV [pay-per-view] marketing, which is my favorite traffic source. Tons of cheap traffic! That's where I started to turn profitable."

Krisztina drives traffic to CPA offers, and she often uses Traffic-Vance.com and MediaTraffic.com to buy pay-per-view traffic.

When I asked her what her dad thinks about all this, she replied: "My dad is a great guy. He helped me to find a way for freedom. I decided to give him 50 percent of my profit. He's proud of me . . . but he still doesn't understand what I'm doing!"

Case Study–Tom Limb

"I spent $700 and built a mailing list of 8,000 subscribers in five weeks!"

Tom Limb attended the Ultimate Traffic Generation Summit and started buying traffic on the Google Display Network. He spent $700 and built a list of 8,400 opt-in subscribers in the weight-loss niche in five weeks!

Hey Mark! I first became interested in the Google Display Network after seeing Armand Morin speak at the Ultimate Traffic Generation Summit, great event, by the way. Since then, I have been experimenting with the GDN and promoting ClickBank products in the weight-loss niche.

Since May 25, I have over 8,400 subscribers, and this list is growing by at least 200 per day.

I have also turned over more than $1,600 in sales, and the next stage really is to refine my sales funnel and then scale up, set up new niches, and so on.

I spent around $700 to build the list to 8,000.

You can watch Armand Morin's presentation on how to profit from Google AdWords at www.laptopmillionaire.tv/armandmorin.

Case Study–John Pownall

"I made $1,600 in my first month online!"

John Pownall retired a few years ago and decided he wanted a new challenge. After attending my seminars he tried his hand at pay-per-click traffic arbitraging, and by driving traffic to affiliate websites, he made money practically straightaway.

I attended your workshop and the Traffic Generation Summit weekend in London. We purchased Armand Morin's course, and I have been working through the course materials. I have been on an incredibly steep learning curve!

But the good news is that using Armand's tutorial videos I am now running AdWord campaigns that regularly bring me in a daily income. Obviously the amount varies since I am testing niche products, ads, bids, budgets—you name it. But I have learned how to do it and made $1,600 in my first month online.

I have attached a screenshot of my ClickBank account. I can now take it on from here and start to make more money. I am proof that if you stick with it you can make money on the Internet, no matter what your age is!

Summary

- Imagine having your ad displayed on hundreds of websites around the world every day—you are, in effect, communicating to thousands or even tens of thousands of people a day, even while you sleep. Now that's *power!*
- Buying online advertising means using a lot more *leverage* in your business. After all, do you want to get rich slow . . . or *fast*?
- Free traffic = free money, but paid traffic = the key to your fortune. This quote sums up the idea well: *"If you keep your fist closed, no money can come out. But no money can come in, either."*
- Start with a small investment, test your ads, your conversion rate, and your EPC (earnings-per-click), and try different websites to advertise on. Find out what combination works, tweak your ads, or change the sites you advertise on, and then ramp up quickly your most profitable campaigns.
- CPA offers typically have a much higher conversion rate than affiliate offers.
- Advertise on at least five different websites at the same time. Ditch the campaigns that don't make you money and ramp up the advertising on

the sites that do make you money, then choose three new websites to advertise on.

- There are many ways to profit from online advertising. You can:
  - Buy traffic for your website.
  - Build your mailing list fast and promote offers to your subscribers.
  - Buy traffic contracts (media buying) to promote affiliate offers.
  - Buy leads from CPA networks.
  - Use pay-per-click advertising.
  - Use Facebook Ads.
  - Sell advertising on your websites.
  - Set up a blog and build a following.
  - Set up review sites and get ranked in Google.
  - To find out more about how you can profit from media buying and traffic generation check out The Traffic Generation Summit I & II on DVD at www.laptopmillionaire.tv/dvd.

Final Thoughts

Get a Job or Create Your Own Economy?

I hope that by now you realize there are *dozens* of ways to make a full-time living from home and create your own "economy," thanks to the Internet.

And think about *this* for a minute. If you have a *job*, you can only increase your earnings by getting a raise, working longer hours, or getting another job. If you are a *laptop entrepreneur* on the other hand, you can make more money by:

- Getting more affiliates!
- Creating an UPSELL offer (or creating 50 other UPSELL offers)!
- Getting Joint Venture partners!
- Creating a new ClickBank product (or 50 new ClickBank products)!
- Using autoresponder messages to increase sales!
- Building your list! (Each new subscriber can mean $1 extra per month.)
- Recording your e-book and turning it into a CD course!
- Adding coaching to your offer!
- Adding a 'done-for-you' offer!
- Doing a product launch!
- Interviewing some experts and creating another product!
- Selling your leads!
- Improving your website's conversion rate!
- Adding testimonials to improve conversion rate!
- Licensing your product!
- Buying product licenses to add value to your offer!
- Doing a webinar for your clients and subscribers!
- Organizing a seminar for your clients and subscribers!
- Getting more traffic thanks to pay-per-click advertising!

- Getting more traffic thanks to YouTube!
- Getting more traffic thanks to Facebook!
- Getting more traffic thanks to banner advertising!
- Getting more traffic thanks to solo ads!
- Getting more traffic thanks to blogs!
- Getting more traffic thanks to SEO!
- Getting more traffic thanks to affiliate marketing and JVs!
- Getting more traffic thanks to CPA networks!
- . . . and infinite more options still!

Don't Let Them Steal Your Dreams

The Laptop Millionaire often railed against the educational system, and how it brainwashed people into being stuck in jobs that they hated.

When I came across the ad in a newspaper, for that Welcome to Freedom seminar in London, I asked my former flatmate Henry (he also worked as a security guard) if he wanted to split the costs with me, so that we could both benefit from this.

Henry said no, because he didn't believe that someone might share their real money-making strategies. He thought it was a scam. He was skeptical, he said. The truth was that he was afraid of trying something new, where he might fail at first.

I was skeptical too, but I thought to myself: It's worth taking a chance! I saved up some money and I attended that seminar.

At first I was a bit confused, but soon enough it all made sense, and now, there are days where I make $100,000 in a single day, whilst I'm on the beach. I make money while I sleep. I get to enjoy life.

Unfortunately the same thing can't be said about Henry. He decided that the beers, the cigarettes, and watching TV all day long were worth more to him than a life of freedom, fun, and significance.

As a result of that decision, Henry is still working as a security guard, eight years later, and I'm concerned about him, because apart from being very unhappy, he's morbidly obese, and he still doesn't want to invest in a course!

All I can say is I'm sure glad I decided to attend that event, because it set me on a different path.

"Cynical people are gutless," I once heard The Laptop Millionaire say.

"Don't let them steal your dreams."

Next Steps

I hope you enjoyed reading this book. As the Laptop Millionaire and myself seek out and test exciting new strategies that can help grow your Internet business, look out for the other books coming out in this series, including: *21 Ways To Make Money While You Sleep*, *SpeedCash*, and *The Laptop Millionaire's Guide to Making Money from Your Blog!*

If you would like to join my mailing list to receive my weekly newsletter, watch my seminars on DVD, or find out more about our "Laptop Millionaire" live seminars, please visit www.laptopmillionaire.tv.

You can also apply to join the Laptop Millionaire Coaching Program at www.laptopmillionaire.tv/coaching.

I would love to meet you in person at one of our live events, and I would *love* to hear about your laptop entrepreneur success story! Visit the site and drop us a line.

I believe that anyone with a genuine desire to succeed and add value can become the next *Laptop Millionaire*.

The laptop entrepreneur revolution has just started.

I hope you will join us.

About the Author

Mark Anastasi is an Internet entrepreneur and founder of the Inspired Marketing Group. Organizing events such as The Traffic Generation Summit, The Millionaire Bootcamp for Women, and The Passive Income Summit, he has trained over 12,000 entrepreneurs around the world since 2005. In 2004, he was a broke, unemployed, and homeless former security guard. Thanks to a chance encounter at a seminar, he would set up his first Internet business, going from zero to making $10,000 a month in just 28 days. His mission now is to empower people to take control of their financial future, experience the Laptop Entrepreneur lifestyle, and live life to the fullest.